**Manufacturing Discontent**

# Manufacturing Discontent

## The Trap of Individualism in Corporate Society

Michael Perelman

Pluto Press

LONDON • ANN ARBOR, MI

First published in English 2005 by Pluto Press
345 Archway Road, London N6 5AA
and 839 Greene Street, Ann Arbor, MI 48106

www.plutobooks.com

British Library Cataloguing in Publication Data
A catalogue record for this book is available from the British Library

ISBN   0 7453 2407 X hardback
ISBN   0 7453 2406 1 paperback

Library of Congress Cataloging in Publication Data
Perelman, Michael.
Manufacturing discontent : the trap of individualism in corporate society
  / Michael Perelman.
     p. cm.
ISBN 0–7453–2407–X (hardback) — ISBN 0–7453–2406–1 (pbk.)
  1. Social responsibility of business—United States. 2. Corporations—Social
aspects—United States. 3. Individualism—United States. 4. Consumption
(Economics)—United States. I. Title.

  HD60.5.U5P39 2005
  306.3'4—dc22

                                                                    2005001626

10   9   8   7   6   5   4   3   2   1

Designed and produced for Pluto Press by
Chase Publishing Services Ltd, Fortescue, Sidmouth, EX10 9QG, England
Typeset from disk by Stanford DTP Services, Northampton, England
Printed and bound in Canada by Transcontinental Printing

306.34
P

# Contents

# Acknowledgments

I want to thank Wendy Diamond, Kuau Garrson, Bob Cottrell, Richard Ponorul, Aldo Matteucci, and especially Joanna Bujes for their excellent help. Most of all, I am indebted to Blanche Perelman, without whom this would not have been possible.

# Introduction

This book is about power—raw power—the raw power of corporations alongside the powerlessness of individualism. Never before in the history of the world have corporate powers been as strong as they are today. Corporations brazenly are using their strength to accumulate even more power.

This corporate power is corrosive. Corporations continue to use their power in ways that harm people as consumers, workers, and citizens. I will describe a number of these threats to human and environmental health, education, and even democratic processes, as well as a host of other destructive consequences of corporate power, including the trampling of the individual rights that corporate society claims to hold dear. Corporate power makes idiots of us all—in the original Greek sense the word, which referred to people concerned only with their own individual affairs and not those of the larger community.

The continuing growth of corporate power will be irreversible without concerted political activity. A political movement capable of standing up to corporate power will require that people shed those aspects of individualism that inhibit them from identifying as members of society rather than as isolated individuals.

This book describes how the distorted ideological perception of society within the United States has facilitated the construction of a corporate society in which corporate power grows at the expense of individual. The leaders of corporate society want us to see ourselves as a multitude of individuals satisfying our needs through the alchemy of the market, a market that we rule through the exercise of individual choice. The market's even-handed anarchy is supposed to be our modern wheel of fortune, impassively turning poor workers into kings.

This corporate society represents a twofold threat to the rest of the world. Most directly, the inordinate military power of the corporate-driven United States is capable of laying waste to any part of the world that it so chooses. More subtly, the institutional changes that have infected the United States are spreading throughout the world—partly through the enormous political and military influence of the U.S.

government, and partly through cultural sway. Mostly, however, competitive pressures have been responsible for this ongoing capitulation to the U.S. model.

For those of you outside of the United States, let this book serve as a warning: unless people around the world put up strong political resistance, what has happened in the United States is liable to repeat itself wherever you may be. Even ostensibly social democratic leaders are rapidly dismantling social democracies. Within this environment, pensions, labor market institutions, and environmental regulations all must give way to the logic of the corporate juggernaut. All the while, an evolving international trade regime is giving giant corporations virtually unrestricted freedom to roam the world unencumbered by national regulations. In considering the disaster presently befalling the United States, I am reminded of Karl Marx's citation of the Roman poet, Horace, in his introduction to *Capital*: 'De te fabula narratur!'—it is of you that the story is told.

This book leads to an unmistakable conclusion. Although individualism might seem to be antagonistic to corporate power, it actually reinforces corporate power. Only by joining together larger social groups—social groups that can tap into the potential of their members' individual strengths—will people be able to successfully challenge corporate power. I will explain why, if people allow themselves to become deluded in believing that their strength lies exclusively in their individuality, corporate power will almost inevitably increase relative to that of the rest of society. In short, individualism represents a dead end.

## ATTACKING THE MYTH OF INDIVIDUALISM

The book begins by describing the myth of individualism and the power that this myth has over us. The first chapter offers a brief introduction to corporate society, emphasizing the many ways that corporate rights trump individual rights. This chapter describes how corporations cause problems that make corporate-friendly policies appear to be the only solution, leading to a never-ending spiral of corporate power.

It describes how conservative interests act to blunt the impact of growing protests against the primacy of business interests by actively promoting the false ideology of individualism, expressed by the myth of consumer sovereignty. As the pop artist Andy Warhol has said, 'Buying is much more American than thinking' (Warhol 1975: 228).

According to this warped ideology, individuals are constituted by the choices they make as consumers. No matter that they toil away at mindless tasks day after day. No matter that they are turned into dispensable and interchangeable corporate pawns. When they come home, they can celebrate their freedom and unique identity by freely choosing whether to drink Coke or Pepsi.

This ideological vision of individualism is a warped individualism that allows individuals to make some limited choices, while many of the most important choices lie beyond them. When we come to believe this myth and to define our identity through shopping, not only have we lost the means by which we could act together to create our world, we no longer even see the need for such association. After all, the corporation is our friend and aims to satisfy our every need. In every sense, the myth of individualism is an absolute dead end.

Chapter 2 looks at the negative social consequences of the framing of people as consumers. Consumerism, with its grotesque striving for excess, is antisocial from the start. The attempt of people to distinguish themselves through consumption is self-defeating for all concerned, except for the corporate interests. Besides profiting from consumer excesses, consumerism prevents the sort of social cohesion needed as a counterweight to corporate power.

Consumptionism by definition is never fulfilling. Envy and the desire to distinguish oneself at the expense of others are what drive consumptionism. Within this mindset, nobody can ever have enough. A society that focuses on consumerism leads to what the economist Tibor Scitovsky called, "the Joyless Economy" (Scitovsky 1976).

The chapter explains why disappointment is endemic to a consumer society: Each act of consumption tends to bring about a sense of disappointment in its wake. No purchase, no choice is final; planned obsolescence and a barrage of advertisements make each purchase seem wanting within a short period of time.

Over time, consumerism will prove to be destructive, even for the corporations themselves. In order to maximize profits, corporations try to rein in labor costs needing people to purchase an ever-increasing output. Corporations can only meet these twin objectives when people borrow in order to consume. Eventually, this debt burden becomes more than people can bear, ultimately leading to depressions, which destroy many corporations and can even bring down the entire economic system upon which corporate power depends.

Next, in Chapter 3, I examine what corporate society does to the individual as producer, as worker. While we are formally free to choose our professions, few of us actually get the opportunity to find employment in fulfilling work. The odds are fairly high that a working-class person will find herself or himself with little choice but to take a mind-numbing job. Corporate employers attempt to push workers to the limit, while keeping them fearful of losing their jobs. Increasingly, even professional work, such as that of doctors, is losing the type of independent control that makes such occupations attractive.

Boredom and alienation are only part of what workers must endure. Between 1980 and 1998, approximately 109,000 civilian workers died from work-related injuries. Deaths from occupation related diseases run about three times as high. Unemployment is also dangerous, causing great numbers of deaths from heart attacks and strokes, while contributing to rising rates of homicides and other crimes, as well as taking a serious toll on family life.

We do not hold corporations accountable for the consequences of their relentless drive for profits. Corporations have won all the rights of individuals, but with few of the responsibilities. Chapter 4 describes some of the ruses that corporations use to avoid responsibility. Looking at the subject of corporate crime and punishment, I detail the shockingly lenient treatment of corporate crime, as well as the belief of some federal judges that corporations even have an obligation to commit crimes if this contributes to the bottom line. The lack of corporate accountability sharply contrasts with the harsh treatment of individuals for even petty crime. It raises the question as to whether the unemployed youth who is shut away is not the tragic scapegoat of an inchoate anger that is powerless to find the real culprit.

Chapter 5 describes some of the techniques that corporations use to avoid responsibility, while calling for increased accountability from every other sector of society. More often than not, the call for accountability is part of a larger objective of promoting corporate control of those few parts of society that have partially eluded corporate control, such as public education.

In the next chapter, I look at the techniques that corporations use to increase that anger. This anger helps them to avoid responsibility, while calling for increased accountability from every other sector of society. More often than not, the call for accountability is part of a larger objective of promoting corporate control of those few parts of society that have partially eluded corporate control, such as public education and prisons.

Some have argued that the corporation deserves its privileges and profits as a reward for the risks it takes. In chapter 6, I examine how that economic theory plays out in practice. It is important to note, for example, that not all risk-takers are created equal. As it turns out, the risks (and injuries) that workers face every day are not deemed worthy of any special reward, except perhaps the reward of the job itself. Equally, the reward to society at large for the risks it faces in giving corporations free rein is limited to the jobs that the corporation bestows. Needless to say, in protecting itself against risk, the corporation has the government squarely on its side. When it comes to meeting its obligation to protect workers, consumers, and the environment from hazards that corporations create, the government seems not nearly as eager.

The corporate sector has also been enormously successful in using pseudoscience to distort the nature of the risks that corporations impose on society. Chapter 7 explains how such tactics are destroying what is left of the already-frayed regulatory system. The distortion of risk assessment is particularly clear when comparing the regulations imposed to protect people from terrorism with the regulations used to protect us from corporate-imposed risk, which has taken many, many times more lives than terrorism. The corporate sector has succeeded in hobbling the consumer's right to know about the dangers posed by pollution or by unsafe products, such as a large part of the food supply. If the consumer is king, he is a beggarly sort of king. I close this discussion by considering the precautionary principle as an antidote to the corporate attack on regulation.

The book concludes by looking at our ability as individual citizens to check the growing power of corporations. What can the individual do against a corporate media and a rigged electoral system in which money substitutes for votes? As separate individuals, we can't do much. In creating the corporation, the state recognized that vast projects require vast forces and a scale of investment that far exceeds the capacity of the individual entrepreneur. In fighting the corporation, we must realize equally that no one individual can do much. We must instead work together in powerful blocks to create a sufficient force to defeat the immortal person of the corporation.

In this way we can define our individuality in a different way, as free actors rather than passive choosers.

## THERE IS NO ALTERNATIVE

Key to the rise of corporate power was legal changes that granted corporations the same rights as people, a sad history that I will describe in Chapter 4. Ten years after the state finally bestowed personhood on the corporation, Bram Stoker, the Irish novelist, introduced the world to another immortal individual—Dracula. Loosely based on folk legend, the modern Dracula roamed the globe ensuring his immortality by feeding on the blood of the living. He is the very anti-matter to humanity: solitary when others are social, awake when others sleep, thriving when others sicken and die—much like a corporation. Yet the original intent of the corporation was to provide a human benefit, not to perpetuate itself at the expense of humanity. Its real nature today can only be seen by the light of the needs of real human beings. This book attempts to cast that light so that we can all see and so that we can all act.

The former British Prime Minister, Margaret Thatcher once said, "There is no alternative," meaning that the corporate-driven market is the only possible method for organizing society. Since then, world leaders have almost universally heeded her call in a rush to create a global new liberal society. This book takes issue with Thatcher, showing that corporate society is inefficient, destructive, and inhuman. So, let's get started showing the Thatchers of the world that we are prepared to build a better society.

I had completed this book before the U.S. presidential election of 2004, an election which represented a resounding victory for corporate power. Both candidates largely agreed about supporting the corporate agenda. The deciding factors in the election were largely symbolic issues that had little impact on people's real lives. Perhaps, those who are pushing the corporate agenda will finally overreach themselves, finally forcing people to confront the real issues that affect their lives.

# I

# The Individual Subsumed
# in the Corporate Economy

## THE MYTH OF INDIVIDUALISM

Although the United States is a massively corporate culture, individualism remains such a core value in the United States that it has become a force in itself. Many Americans still pride themselves on their rugged individualism. Indeed, the myth of individualism is pervasive. Popular culture derides conformity. The public flocks to Hollywood movies that tell stories of improbable individuals who surmount impossible odds. Politicians cloak their policies in the rhetoric of individualism—perhaps none more vehemently than Margaret Thatcher, the former British Prime Minister, who inspired much conservative activism in the United States. Thatcher declared: "There is no such thing as society: there are individual men and women, and there are families" (Thatcher 1987). You might think that Thatcher's words would ring hollow, but a surprising number of people still buy into the dream of rugged individualism—what Adam Smith once called "the system of natural liberty" (Smith 1776, IV.ix.51: 687).

Thatcher and her ilk would have us believe that individuals in a market society enjoy an unprecedented degree of freedom because private individuals are in control of their own destinies—which for them is the freedom to get rich. Many people accept this view, leading to wildly unrealistic expectations. For example, in January 2003, while the economy languished and the job market sagged, a Gallup poll found that 31 per cent of Americans expected to get rich at some time in their lives. Rich, in this interview meant an annual income of about $120,000 or financial assets of about $1 million. For people between the ages of 18 and 29, a surprising 51 per cent expected to be rich (Moore 2003). Reality is, of course, completely different. Unless the economy changes radically, the majority of these people will be sadly disappointed.

In terms of consumption, people are also free to choose what commodities to buy within the constraints of their budgets. Many writers have gone so far as to characterize this freedom—which they call consumer sovereignty—as the central principle of market society (for a sampling see Dawson 2003: 8–9).

Supposedly, the whole market system must adapt itself to the individual choices that consumers make. Since "free choices" of individual consumers both define and regulate the market, the mythical consumer is "king." For example, Bob McTeer, president of the Dallas branch of the Federal Reserve Board, published a Free Enterprise Primer on the internet. According to this primer:

> In a free market system, the government doesn't organize, direct and control economic activity. If the government doesn't, who does? Who decides what is to be produced, and how, and in what quantities and quality, and who gets the fruits of production? The answer is that you and I decide these important questions by the way we spend our money. The market system features consumer sovereignty, meaning that the consumer is king. We decide what will be produced by casting dollar votes for the things we want and by not spending on the things we don't want. [http://www.dallasfed.org/htm/dallas/primer.html]

In this spirit, Henry Luce, founder of the Time-Life empire, explained, in words that call out for pity for the powerlessness of the corporations that appear to rule the economy, that corporate enterprise is merely "a built-in hostage to ... the consumer's freedom of choice" (Luce 1950: 62).

According to the imaginary perspective of consumer sovereignty, any firm that is unsuccessful in adequately serving the consumer is doomed to fail. This rhetoric cleverly inverts the powerlessness of the majority of society. In reality, in a corporate society people as consumers exist to serve the needs of the corporations. But through the distorted lens of consumer sovereignty, corporate megaliths appear to be nothing more than the passive servants of the all-powerful consumer, despite the insignificant influence of the typical individual within corporate society.

## THE REAL MEANING OF INDIVIDUALISM

Within the myth of individualism, corporations diligently serve their kingly consumers, while these privileged consumers have the responsibility to earn the wages needed to participate in the market. Market society demands that individuals make their lives conform to the needs of the market, reducing the role of the individual in corporate society to two narrow dimensions: working diligently and consuming appropriately. Slacking off in either regard is unacceptable. Oh yes, the individual is also supposed to bring up a new compliant generation of well-behaved, hard-working, consuming individuals.

A quite different sort of individualism reigns supreme in the contemporary United States: corporate individualism. The giant corporations wield enormous power, enjoying all the rights of individuals with few of the responsibilities that ordinary individuals are expected to bear. In the world of corporate individualism, corporations are all but assured of success, while ordinary individuals are left to fend for themselves.

The people who own and run these corporations employ compliant legislators and regulators who then faithfully serve the corporate needs, often expecting a lucrative post in the corporate world after a sojourn in public service. So, in contrast to the powerless condition of ordinary private individuals, the giant corporations can deploy their enormous powers to redesign the economic and political landscape to meet their immediate interests.

As a result of this cozy relationship, these corporations enjoy subsidies, sweetheart contracts, tax breaks, limited liability for harms that they might impose on others, and every other imaginable sort of advantage. Despite the centrality of the corporation in modern American society, the economic and legal framework requires little of corporations in return for the benefits that they enjoy.

In short, while corporate leaders sanctimoniously proclaim the virtues of individual self-sufficiency, they have absolutely no intention of exercising this virtue in their own affairs. While the ethic of individualism demands considerable personal responsibility for working people, the economic and legal framework either absolves the corporate sector of its misdeeds or punishes it in an extraordinarily lenient fashion. Major corporations all too often effectively enjoy complete immunity from legal prosecution.

Even though the imagined rugged individualism of the American character includes a willingness to take risks, here too the standards for corporations are different. Despite the glowing corporate rhetoric about how society as a whole benefits from entrepreneurial risk-taking, the government covers much of the risk that the corporate sector faces.

Ordinary people, public institutions, the legal system, international policy, and virtually every other aspect of society must adapt to the needs of the giant corporations. Of course, this adaptation is not complete. Some choices still remain—choices more significant than "Coke or Pepsi." Even so, the most important choices in society lie far outside the realm of individual decision-making.

Corporations, however, rarely admit that they are exercising raw power when they make their demands. Rather than openly speaking in the name of the divine right of capital, corporations typically wrap their call for acquiescence in a mantle of public interest.

One of the most common ruses is to present their case in terms of jobs. Schools' primary purpose is to prepare students for jobs. The tax system must be modified to encourage the creation of jobs. Land use planning standards, designed to maintain or improve the quality of life, must give way to compromises in order to create jobs.

Unfortunately, the major corporations create relatively few domestic jobs. Indeed, they are far more energetic in transferring jobs to faraway places where crushing poverty forces people to accept subhuman wages. Besides directly cutting their wage bill, this strategy of relocating work abroad intensifies the competition among workers for the remaining jobs. In a final comic twist, job scarcity makes the corporate demands for concessions seem even more civic-minded.

This same corporate power produces a host of destructive outcomes. Corporate power intensifies inequality, at the same time that it reduces the quality of education, the media, and public participation, and threatens human health as well as the health of the environment. The rest of the book will address these problems and call for something better.

## BACK TO ADAM SMITH

Although the idea of consumer sovereignty did not originate with Adam Smith, we economists have a long tradition of tracing ideas back to that venerable figure. Writing at the dawn of the formal study of economics, Adam Smith laid out a powerful vision of the economy as an entirely voluntary process. At times, he went considerably further. For example, once while lecturing his students, Smith remarked:

an ordinary day-labourer, whom we false account to live in a most simple manner, has more of the conveniencies and luxuries of life than an Indian prince at the head of 1000 naked savages. His coarse blue woolen coat has been the labour of perhaps 100 artificers, the shearer, the picker, the sorter, the comber, the spinner, etc. as well as the weaver and fuller whose loom and mill alone have more of art in them than all the things employed about the court of a savage prince; besides the ship which brought the dies and other materials together from distant regions, and all the workmen, wrights, carpenters, coopers, smiths, etc. which have been employed to fit her out to sea and the hands which have navigated her. The iron tool with which he works, how many hands has it gone thro.—The miner, the quarrier, the breaker, the smelter, the forger, the maker of the charcoal to smelt it, the smith, etc. have had a hand in the forming it. How many have been required to furnish out the coarse linen shirt [which] he wears; the tanned and dressed-leather shoes; his bed which he rest(s) in; the grate at which he dresses his victuals; the coals he burns, which have been brought by a long land sea carriage; and other workmen who have been necessary to prepare his bread, his beer, and other food; besides the glass of which his windows are composed, production (of) which required vast labour to bring it to its present perfection, which at the same time excludes the wind and rain and admits the light, a commodity without which this country would scarcely be habitable, at least by the present effeminate and puny set of mortals. So that to supply this poor labourer about 1000 have given their joint assistance. He enjoys far greater convenience than an Indian prince. [Smith 1978: 338–9]

So, here we have a fanciful image of a poor, overburdened farmworker suddenly transformed into a sovereign consumer commanding a princely retinue of workers. Smith was writing at a time when social relations in Great Britain were turbulent to say the least (Thompson 1963). Were Smith's words meant to offer the poor some consolation, suggesting that they should be grateful for their affluence and put aside the revolutionary activities that troubled Smith's society? More likely, Smith was aiming at easing the consciences of the rich and privileged.

Smith's vision of consumer sovereignty mostly fell from view for a century and a half. By the end of the nineteenth century, workers were beginning to mount a powerful challenge to the existing order. Socialist parties were the fastest growing political organizations throughout the world. Economic and political leaders feared imminent revolution, just as they did at the time of Adam Smith.

In that environment, leading intellectuals began to counsel workers that they should not interpret their lives in terms of their unsatisfying existence as workers, but rather in terms of their experiences as consumers. The most famous call came from Walter Lippmann in his influential *Drift and Mastery* (1914):

> Many radical socialists pretend to regard the consumer's interest as a rather mythical one .... But we are finding, I think, the real power emerging today is just the mass of people who are crying out against the "high cost of living." That is a consumer's cry. Far from being an impotent one, it is, I believe, destined to be stronger than the interests of either labor or capital. [Lippmann 1914: 54]

So, workers may suffer indignities at the workplace, but as consumers they are sovereign—at least according to this comforting rhetoric.

## MARKETS UBER ALLES

Consumer sovereignty is a pleasant fiction designed to reassure the powerless. While business people might find such rhetoric useful for public relations, they speak a different language when they address each other. For example, Walter Wriston, former Chief Executive Officer of Citibank, described a future that was sure to delight his business readers in a book, tellingly entitled, *The Twilight of Sovereignty*. There, after asserting that information is the driving force in modern society, Wriston elaborated on his perspective of the world from the commanding heights of high finance:

> Today information about the diplomatic, fiscal, and monetary policies of all nations is instantly transmitted to electronic screens in hundreds of trading rooms in dozens of counties. As the screens light up with the latest statement of the president or the chairman of the Federal Reserve, traders make a judgment about the effect of the new policies on currency values and buy or sell accordingly. The entire globe is now tied together in a single electronic market moving at the speed of light. There is no place to hide.
>
> This enormous flow of data has created a new world monetary standard, an Information Standard, which has replaced the gold standard and the Bretton Woods agreements. The electronic global market has produced what amounts to a giant vote-counting machine that conducts a running tally on what the world thinks of a government's diplomatic, fiscal, and monetary policies. That opinion is immediately reflected in the value the market places on a country's currency. [Wriston 1992: 8–9]

In this new world order:

> capital will go where it is wanted and stay where it is well treated .... It will flee from manipulation or onerous regulation of its value or use, and no government can restrain it for long. [Wriston 1992: 61–2]

The consequences of capital rapidly fleeing a country can be catastrophic, as the Asian economies discovered a few years later in 1997. William McDonough, president of the powerful New York branch of the Federal Reserve Bank, was not exaggerating when he observed: "domestic policy mistakes elicit quick and harsh punishment on an economy from international sources" (McDonough 1995: 15).

So, Wriston was absolutely correct in announcing that the global marketplace "has produced what amounts to a giant vote-counting machine." This particular vote-counting based on dollars has the power to annul the will of the people. Yes, people may be free to vote as citizens however they may choose, but if their choice displeases those who sit in the trading rooms they will suffer dire consequences.

For example, two years after Wriston's book appeared, Bob Woodward, of Watergate fame, published his account of the Clinton administration. Woodward recounted a scene from the newly elected president's team meeting in Little Rock, Arkansas intended to shape the economic agenda for the incoming administration. Clinton had campaigned on the promise of a massive program to renew the country's deteriorating infrastructure of bridges, sewage treatment plants, water systems and the like, while creating a large number of jobs in the process. Now that the election was over, his advisors explained that the bond market would not approve if he were to follow through on his promise. Then Woodward paints the scene that followed:

> At the president-elect's end of the table, Clinton's face turned red with anger and disbelief. "You mean to tell me that the success of the program and my reelection hinges on the Federal Reserve and a bunch of fucking bond traders?" he responded in a half-whisper.
>
> Nods from his end of the table. Not a dissent.
>
> Clinton, it seemed to [Alan] Blinder, [whom Clinton later appointed as Vice Chairman of the Federal Reserve Board] perceived at this moment how much his fate was passing into the hands of the unelected Alan Greenspan [Chairman of the Federal Reserve Board] and the bond market.

[George] Stephanopoulos [Clinton's Communications Director in the 1992 campaign, realized that the administration's] first audience would have to be the Fed and the bond market. [Woodward 1994: 84]

Indeed, once Clinton took office, his Secretary of the Treasury, Robert Rubin, would give him daily briefings about the mood of the bond market.

Over and above the market forces that Wriston described, corporations have devised new legal systems to protect their interests against the will of the people. For example, prodded by corporate interests, the United States has led the way in creating trade agreements that allow business interests to challenge laws that supposedly restrain trade. For example, according to the North American Free Trade Agreement, food exporters from Mexico and Canada can sue federal, state, or local governments in the United States for such trade-unfriendly behavior as passing legislation banning pesticide residues on food. In theory, governments do not have to repeal the legislation. They merely have to pay the exporters for the profits that such legislation supposedly denies them. A committee that meets behind closed doors determines the penalty.

The World Trade Organization allows governments to take measures to punish countries that pass laws to protect the environment or the food supply. Unless a government can satisfy a secret World Trade Organization panel that its laws rest upon sound science, it must cease to enforce the law or else potential exporters can levy penalties on the offending country. So far, these tribunals, generally staffed by corporate-friendly personnel have been very unsympathetic to such regulation.

## FREEDOM OF SPEECH—FOR WHOM?

Although corporate interests are quick to claim for themselves extraordinary privileges, they wield their powers to deny the same rights to others. Consider the imbalance between free-speech for corporations and for individuals. Nike, the shoemaker, had a long record of having its shoes made in horrible sweatshop conditions that many commentators regarded as violations of human rights. Nike launched a public relations offensive defending its record. Mark Kasky, a Californian activist, sued Nike in a California court for violating the state Business and Professions Code, which prohibits false advertising. Kasky won his case, which was upheld by California Supreme Court (Greenhouse 2003).

Nike then appealed the decision to the Supreme Court of the United States on grounds that it has the First Amendment right to say what it wants, regardless of whether it is false or not. Companies, such as Microsoft, Exxon Mobil, and Pfizer, filed briefs on behalf of Nike. In the end, Nike settled without admitting any wrong doing, agreeing to pay $1.5 million to the Fair Labor Association, a workplace monitoring group. The fact that Nike insisted for so long that it had a free speech right to lie to the public in its advertisements shows how far free speech rights are supposed to extend to the corporations. I will briefly return to Nike's labor practices later.

Yet, the corporations are not the least hesitant to deny free speech to others. For example, another shoe company, Reebok, forged a deal with the University of Wisconsin, containing a "non-disparagement" clause that prohibited members of the university community from criticizing the athletic gear company. According to the contract:

> During and for a reasonable time after the term, the University will not issue any official statement that disparages Reebok. Additionally, the University will promptly take all reasonable steps to address any remark by any University employee, agent or representative, including a coach, that disparages Reebok, Reebok's products or the advertising agency or others connected with Reebok. [Klein 2000: 96]

In other words, companies are free to say what they like, but they are also free to sign contacts with universities, which are supposed to be bastions of free speech, with the purpose of restricting what people can say. One might admit that the University might legitimately agree to restrict what it might say, but to extend that restriction to its employees seems unconscionable.

Corporations take other strong measures to silence voices whose messages offend corporate interests. Corporations can threaten to withdraw advertisements from the media. They can file Strategic Lawsuits against Public Participation (SLAPP suits). For example, several environmental groups ran a newspaper advertisement in the *New York Times* on December 13, 1999, entitled "Global Warming—How Will It End?" The advertisement mentioned "coal" as a cause. Western Fuels Association, an arm of the power industry that purchases hundreds of millions of dollars of coal annually, sued the Turning Point Project, the International Center for Technology

Assessment, Friends of the Earth, Ozone Action, Earth Island Institute and the Rainforest Action Network. Western Fuels had contended that any statement in the media connecting "coal" with global warming should be construed as an attack on the Wyoming coal industry. The court eventually dismissed the suit.

SLAPP suits are relatively inexpensive for a wealthy major corporation or trade group, but they can cost dissident organizations or individuals dearly. Because of the expense involved in defending oneself against a corporation with a virtually unlimited budget for lawyers, the mere possibility of a SLAPP suit can be enough to force many organizations or individuals into silence.

Corporate interests have also framed laws intended to stifle free speech, such as the infamous "veggie libel laws," which prohibit speech which can harm the market for specified agricultural products. Although these laws have never withstood constitutional challenges, again defendants charged with such violations incur huge legal costs before they finally win in court. Lawrence Soley has assembled a valuable compendium of such corporate challenges to free speech in his book *Censorship, Inc.* (2002).

## THE PERVERSE CONSEQUENCES OF THE CORPORATE ABUSE OF POWER

One of the cruel ironies of corporate society is that in many cases the worse that corporations treat people the more support they win. Earlier, I mentioned how corporations tend to present their demands to society in terms of their potential to create jobs. Of course, many of the same major corporations have been most effective in stripping jobs from their payrolls. For example, the sales of the top 200 transnational corporations are the equivalent of 27.5 per cent of world economic activity, but these same corporations employ a mere 0.78 per cent of the world's workforce (Anderson and Cavanagh 2000).

Given the shortage of good jobs, major corporations demand huge concessions from state and local government in return for the promise of creating jobs or even just for not carrying through with threats to relocate existing jobs elsewhere. I am not referring to minor favors. Consider the case of Mercedes-Benz, which convinced the state of Alabama to provide $253 million worth of incentives in 1993— $169,000 for every job Mercedes promised the state (Brooks 2002).

Many companies never created their quota of promised jobs; some soon moved away after initially setting up; and worse yet, some never even built the promised facilities (LeRoy 1994). In those cases where the corporations actually do provide the jobs, some local governments are unable to afford to build enough schools to handle the growth that the new facilities required to accommodate the growth (Tomsho 1995). State and local governments are strapped for funds. Few can afford generous corporate subsidies.

Pensions offer another example of the perverse phenomenon of the corporate sector winning support by taking actions that harm individuals. Between 1979 and 1997, the share of employees with defined benefit plans—meaning that the plan promised a specific level of support—fell from 87 per cent to 50 per cent (Mishel, Bernstein, and Boushey 2003: 247). Under defined benefit plans, employers bear the responsibility to provide the promised pensions—a responsibility that they were more than happy to shed.

Today, about 85 per cent of private contributions are for defined contribution plans in which individuals decide how much to contribute, how to invest their assets in the plan, and how and when to withdraw money from the plan (Poterba, Venti, and Wise 2001). The level of support that the plan provides for individual workers depends upon their success in investing. These plans appeal to employers because they shift the risk onto the employee.

Money from pension funds was a major factor in fueling the stock market bubble of the late 1990s and the resulting appreciation of stock prices helped to fund the defined benefit plans. This mutual reinforcement came to an end with the collapse of the stock market bubble in 2000, accelerating the transition to the defined contribution plans.

One might expect that the disappearance of defined benefit plans might create attitudes less favorable to corporations. Although some workers may initially resent the disappearance of their traditional pensions, many people are certain that defined contribution plans will make workers identify with corporations. Largely because of these changes in pension plans, the number of individuals directly or indirectly owning corporate stock has soared. As a result, about 30 million individuals became stockholders in the 1990s. Today, more than half of the families in the United States own stocks (Aizcorbe, Kennickell, and Moore 2003).

In the new environment, no longer blessed with a relatively secure financial future, many workers are left to plan for their future as isolated individuals. Indeed, people whose retirement now depends increasingly on their holdings of stocks are more likely to feel that their fate is tightly bound up with corporate profits—even though the corporate lust for profits is typically responsible for their insecure financial situation. In the words of Michael Mandel, economics editor of *Business Week*: "In the high-risk society, workers, businesses, and communities must start thinking like investors in the financial markets" (Mandel 1996: 8).

Two economists from the Federal Reserve Bank of Dallas investigated how these changes in pensions may have affected domestic politics in the United States. They found that the mutual fund revolution has accompanied an increased Republican share of the popular vote in elections for the House of Representatives. They concluded that further legislation to make social security dependent on the stock market will reinforce people's feeling of dependence upon corporate success (Duca and Saving 2001).

Perhaps the most cynical example of the perverse consequences of political power comes from the strategy of purposefully defunding public institutions. One of the most outrageous examples of robbing public institutions to favor private interests is the treatment of the public school systems in the United States. Opponents of public education first starve schools of the funds necessary to operate efficiently. When these organizations inevitably fail to satisfy public demands for quality service, the proponents of private education play upon the growing dissatisfaction with public schools, claiming that private systems will operate more efficiently. Then the proponents of privatized education demand that the state distribute vouchers that subsidize private schools with state funds, even though these private schools are free to refuse to work with students that require special education.

To make matters worse, once education becomes privatized, not much time will pass before conservatives will demand that public support go only to those who cannot afford to pay for school on their own. By this means, public financial support for education becomes transformed into a form of welfare rather than a universal right. Programs for the poor inevitably become poor programs. A well-financed public outcry will almost certainly demand that hardworking taxpayers be absolved from having to pay for the education of families who are too lazy to earn enough on their own.

Similarly, in the case of public transportation, the lack of adequate funding forces fares to rise, discouraging the use of public transportation. Since costs do not fall proportionately to the number of riders, the cost per rider increases, allowing enemies of public transportation to declare that the system is hopelessly inefficient.

## PENSIONS AND INDIVIDUALISM

Why then did employers voluntarily offer defined benefit programs in the first place? The answer is that corporate power was not as strong at the time these plans began to proliferate. Unions then were able to muster considerable power. Defined benefit pensions offered a means to make workers see that their financial security would depend on the health of the corporate employer. Inducing workers to identify with the employer seemed to offer a mechanism to reduce workers' solidarity. In the process, workers might even be more inclined to see themselves more as individuals.

In 1950, Charles Wilson, the head of General Motors, set the standard for the new defined benefit pension system for the United Automobile Workers (UAW). Peter Drucker, the dean of modern business gurus, recognized the subtle corporate calculus that lay behind this system. Drucker claimed, probably not without reason:

> Wilson's proposal aimed at making the pension system the business of the private sector. And the UAW—in common with most American unions— was in those years deeply committed to governmental social security. Wilson's proposal gave the union no role whatever in administering the General Motors pension fund. Instead, the company was to be responsible for the fund, which would be entrusted to professional "asset managers." [Drucker 1976: 5]

According to Drucker:

> The union leadership was greatly concerned lest a company-financed and company-managed private pension plan ... would open up a conflict within the union membership between older workers, interested in the largest possible pension payments, and younger workers, interested primarily in the cash in their weekly pay envelope. Above all, the union realized that one of the main reasons behind Wilson's proposal was a desire to blunt union militancy by making visible the workers' take in company profits and company success. [Drucker 1976: 5–6]

Under defined benefit plans, workers were justifiably concerned that their employer remain solvent, but since these employers tended to be powerful corporations, the risk of failure seemed relatively small. Workers were shocked then in 1963 when Studebaker terminated its employee pension plan, leaving more than 4,000 auto workers at its automobile plant in South Bend, Indiana with little or none of their promised pension plan benefits. A little more than a decade later in 1974, Congress passed the Employee Retirement Income Security Act (ERISA), to partially guarantee workers' benefits in private pension plans. The current maximum is about $3,600 a month for those older than 65 at the time of the takeover, and less for those who are younger.

A wave of corporate bankruptcies left the government's Pension Benefit Guaranty Corporation with the obligation to provide partial coverage to so many workers that the agency accumulated a deficit of $11.2 billion at the end of fiscal year 2003. Eliminating this deficit will add an additional cost to the defined benefit plans, leading them to become still more rare.

Bankruptcies were not the only problem for the defined benefit plans. Rather than keeping their promises to workers, corporations have been using their pension funds as cash cows, pretending that overly optimistic investment returns in the future would be sufficient to cover promised pension benefits. This tactic let corporations divert billions from their pension plans, adding to their profits. For example, by 1999, General Electric's pension plan was adding more than $1 billion to its profit statement (Schultz 1999).

These financial manipulations, together with a general weakening of the U.S. economy, left private employer pension plans $400 billion short of assets needed to keep promises that they had made (McKinnon 2003). At the time of this writing, leading politicians are promoting legislation to limit employers' responsibility to keep such funds financially healthy. Even worse, as a front page *Wall Street Journal* story reported, corporations are actually suing retirees in order to demand reductions in the pensions that they had contractually promised (Schultz 2004).

So, if Drucker is correct, then the defined benefit pension plan was originally designed to make union members identify with their employer, undermining workers' solidarity. As workers became more disposable and jobs more temporary, such identification was no longer needed. In addition, workers no longer exercise nearly as much power as they did in the early postwar period, reducing the need to placate the labor force. So now, such pensions are disappearing, in part with the intent of making workers identify more with business in general rather than with a particular employer.

This individualism, unfortunately, will weaken society and promote the corporate agenda. This book is intended to lay the groundwork for a different approach.

# 2
# People as Consumers

## PEOPLE AS CONSUMERS

Business proudly proclaims, "The customer is king." Oh, really? Of course, the claim of consumer sovereignty is a charade. Anybody who needs to contact a seller after the purchase can attest to something considerably less than a royal treatment. The company realizes that after the completion of the sale, the customer is liable to move on to a different establishment. As a result, time spent on the customer is carefully rationed once the sale is complete. Some routinely treat the precious time of their previous customers as a free good, for instance, forcing them to waste countless hours of frustration navigating voice-mail mazes.

Then again, if consumer sovereignty were anything like a reality, certainly the government would be diligent in protecting consumers' interests. Sadly, such is not the case. Instead, the government places strict limits on consumer sovereignty, especially where any substantive consumer sovereignty might collide with corporate interests. Consider, for example, how shabbily the government treats consumers in regulating the food industry. In deference to corporate interests, government officials routinely refuse consumer demands to label genetically modified food or to inform consumers which processed food contains irradiated ingredients. In fact, labeling in general only came about after a long struggle.

Industry knows that the supposedly sovereign consumers might refuse to purchase such products. Consumers are also reluctant to purchase irradiated food. Because of their need to sell a product that people do not want, "industry leaders [in the biotechnology industry] view consumers ... as hostile forces threatening their economic viability" (Nestle 2003: 145).

The government allows industry to process meat in unsanitary conditions. It proposes to allow industry to use radiation to disinfect feces. Consumers, of course, would prefer having the meat packers prepare their produce more carefully rather than irradiating feces. After all, poop, even if irradiated, is not a particularly appealing ingredient (see Nestle 2003: 124). Withholding such knowledge helps to ensure the consumer's loyalty.

Nor can consumers know when farmers unwittingly have grown their food with fertilizer laced with toxic waste. The government approved that policy as a means of relieving corporations of the expense of safely disposing of their waste products (see Wilson 2001). The Environmental Protection Agency has even refused to regulate the dioxin in fertilizer made from sewage sludge (Pianin 2003b).

Efforts to require the food industry to display the country of origin on labels met a similar fate even though both the House and Senate approved such legislation. Retail grocery chains and food processors successfully pressured a conference committee that was supposed to reconcile the House and Senate versions of a spending bill to remove these provisions despite their prior approval. Because the committee had only a few legislators meeting without any public scrutiny, industry interests won out over the interests of consumers. The *New York Times* editorialized against this maneuver:

> Polls have shown overwhelming consumer support for origin labeling, which is already practiced by many of America's agricultural trading partners .... Instead, we got a chance yesterday to see exactly what the major food industry groups want for American consumers. They want ignorance. [Anon. 2004]

Government assurances that food products are safe must be taken with a grain of salt. For example, Dan Glickman, former Agriculture Secretary during the Clinton administration, supervised approval of several biotech products. In retrospect, he admits that he regrets that regulators largely ceded their watchdog role: "Regulators even viewed themselves as cheerleaders for biotechnology," he said. "It was viewed as science marching forward, and anyone who wasn't marching forward was a Luddite" (cited in Simon 2001).

Years later, after the momentum for genetically modified crops and animals had taken on a head of steam, the National Research Council, following a request from the Clinton administration, finally completed a study about one of the dangers of this technology—the unwitting release of organisms or, perhaps worse yet, their genes beyond where they were intended to be, potentially causing great harm. The study concluded that industry lacks the means to confine their product, but now the horse has left the barn (National Research Council 2004).

How seriously does the government take its responsibility in regulating the food system? After all, each year food-borne diseases cause an estimated 76 million illnesses and 5,000 deaths in the United States (Mead et al. 1999). These tragedies are only a small part of the cost of this unregulated food system. The United States produces as much as 50 million pounds of antibiotics each year—most of which is routinely given to farm animals, both to help counteract their unwholesome living conditions and to increase their weight gain. This routine application of antibiotics has accelerated the evolution of organisms that are antibiotic-resistant:

> Every year in U.S. medical institutions, 2 million patients contracted infections—bacterial, viral, and otherwise—and 90,000 died. Of those 90,000, many had drug-resistant bacterial infections, mostly S. aureus. The CDC estimated that 40,000 Americans died each year of those infections. [Shnayerson and Plotkin 2002: 15]

The inattention to sanitary conditions in the meat industry makes this situation even worse. Eric Schlosser, in his best-selling book, *Fast Food Nation*, described the gross conditions that prevail in the industry:

> A nationwide study published by the USDA in 1996 found that 7.5 per cent of the ground beef samples taken at processing plants were contaminated with Salmonella, 11.7 per cent were contaminated with Listeria monocytogenes, 30 per cent were contaminated with Staphylococcus aureus, and 53.3 per cent were contaminated with Clostridium perfringens. All of these pathogens can make people sick; food poisoning caused by Listeria generally requires hospitalization and proves fatal in about one out of every five cases. In the USDA study 78.6 per cent of the ground beef contained microbes that are spread primarily by fecal material. [Schlosser 2001a: 197]

> Nevertheless, the Reagan and Bush administrations cut spending on public health measures and staffed the U.S. Department of Agriculture with officials far more interested in government deregulation than in food safety. The USDA became largely indistinguishable from the industries it was meant to police. President Reagan's first secretary of agriculture was in the hog business. His second was the president of the American Meat Institute (formerly known as the American Meat Packers Association). And his choice to run the USDA's Food Marketing and Inspection was the vice president of the National Cattleman's Association. President Bush later appointed the

president of the National Cattleman's Association to the job. [Schlosser 2001a: 206]

In May 2002, two Agriculture Department veterinarians distributed a memo, "General Information and Conduct" for new meat inspectors at the Farmland National Beef Packing Company in Liberal, Kansas. This memo illustrates the degree to which the government limits its oversight of food safety (Becker 2002). A section on fecal contamination, warned the inspectors:

> stopping production for "possible" cross contamination is unjustifiable unless you can verify that there is direct product contamination. Verification is OBSERVATION of gross contaminate not SUSPECTED contaminate. This is the only criteria [sic] for justifying halting production.
>
> We will allow the company a chance to trim [feces, stomach contents, or milk] off on the moving lines unless it is so excessive, that it must be corrected with the line stopped. You are responsible for the time the line is off .... Remember, YOU are accountable for this very serious responsibility of stopping the company's production for the benefit of food safety verifiable ingesta or feces is as follows: a material of yellow, green, brown or dark color that has a fibrous nature. [Public Citizen 2002]

In other words, the administration warned inspectors against inconveniencing business operations, while downplaying their responsibility for protecting public health. The Bush administration has even gone so far as to refuse to sign a bill that informed the public about which stores received meat that was recalled because of possible contamination (Gersema 2003). In those cases where the regulators finally get around to taking action against meat processors after repeated violations, the courts typically protect the corporations rather than the consumers (E. Becker 2003a).

The government would prefer to turn to industrial solutions, such as irradiating food, rather than enforcing the modest regulations on the books. For example, the 2002 farm bill required the Agriculture Department to buy irradiated beef for the federal school lunch program, in effect subsidizing the nuclear industry by turning a radioactive waste product into a commercial product, which facilitates the consumption of contaminated food—a triple victory for industry.

When people do get sick, both government and business tend to blame the consumer for lack of adequate care in handling the food rather than pointing to the filthy, underregulated conditions in the slaughtering plants. The refusal of the government to protect the consumer's health and safety through its regulatory power underlies two facts: one, consumers cannot be kings if government and industry deprive them of essential information, and two, the interests of the consumer and those of the corporation are not congruent.

At times, the legal system even goes so far as to prohibit companies from giving consumers information that they might appreciate. For example, the government, bowing to corporate influence, allowed Monsanto to market a controversial bovine growth hormone to make cows give more milk, despite serious scientific concerns about the product's safety. In 1994, when Pure Milk and Ice Cream Co. of Waco, Texas and Swiss Valley Farms of Davenport, Iowa labeled their milk as free of the hormone, Monsanto sued, charging them with making false and misleading claims. Ben & Jerry's also began labeling its ice cream as being free from this hormone. In 1994, the state of Illinois threatened to seize its products sold with the offending label. Monsanto lawyers also sent letters to 2,000 retailers warning them against advertising that they carry "rBST-free milk," and sent a 30-page "legal memorandum" with a similar message to 4,000 food processors and dairy co-operatives (Gorelick 1998).

The companies made no health claim about their product. Nor did they make any allegations about Monsanto's product. They merely stated that it produced its ice cream from milk that was free from the hormone. Eventually, in 1997, Ben & Jerry's finally did successfully win the right in federal court case to inform consumers about the absence of the hormone in the production of its ice cream. Its victory came only after years had passed and the company had incurred substantial legal costs.

The dairies also settled out of court. They had to include a statement on their label to the effect that no difference has been found between milk containing the hormone and milk from untreated cows.

Then, in 2003, Monsanto struck again, suing a small milk producer in Maine for engaging in misleading and deceptive marketing practices by labeling its product to inform consumers that its milk did not contain the artificial growth hormone (Barboza 2003).

Given a choice, few people would like to sit down with a meal that contains irradiated feces, heavy metals, or perhaps even genetically modified organisms. So secrecy becomes an important marketing tool. In this respect, the federal government is more than willing to comply with industry's needs rather than the consumer's right to know. The United States Food and Drug Administration, one of the agencies charged with regulating the safety of these products, justified its decision to refuse to require labeling despite consumers' repeated calls for more information: "The Act requires that all labeling be truthful and not misleading. The Act does not require disclosure in labeling of information solely on the basis of consumers' desire to know" (U.S. Food and Drug Administration 1995). So much for consumer sovereignty!

In conclusion, the rhetoric of consumer sovereignty also implies that these sovereign consumers have adequate information about all the stuff that they buy. In fact, no typical working family could possibly have the time to evaluate all of their purchases rationally. Besides, as I already mentioned, the government supports the intentional withholding of information from consumers.

## THE FUTILITY OF EXCESSIVE CONSUMPTION

Over and above the deliberate withholding of information, consumers must contend with a deluge of misinformation in the form of advertising. In this sense, the attempt to advertise everywhere all the time occurs within the context of individual powerlessness. Think back to Walter Lippmann's suggestion that workers should seek to build their identity around their consumption rather than their work. Although his prescription might seem superficial, as a description of the emerging reality, his analysis was relatively accurate.

Few people in the United States today get the opportunity to develop a feeling of self-worth at their place of employment. Except for a few celebrities and professionals, most of us work in fairly insecure conditions, performing tasks we have little interest in, and helpless to change the content or goals of our work.

In part because of the turbulent job market, people rarely stay in the same geographic location throughout their lives. Because most people do not live in stable communities where people might get to know one another, they are reduced to distinguishing themselves by signaling their status to others through displays of consumption.

Identifying one's self with commodities is so strong in the United States that some parents are actually beginning to name their children after brands. For example, in 2000, families in the United States welcomed the birth of 353 Lexuses, 298 Armanis, and 269 Chanels (Kang 2003). In his remarkable book, *The Essence of Capitalism*,

Humphrey McQueen captures the paradox of consumption-driven identity:

> Consumption replicates the problems from which it is supposed to provide a refuge. It is the devastation of creative social labor, not the retreat into shopping that deserves to be criticized. The trouble with advertising is not so much that it deals with trivial or unreal issues but that it promises self-defeating solutions. Arising out of a pervasive dissatisfaction with the organization of work, mass marketing advises workers to seek fulfillment in commercialized leisure, to avoid involvement with unions, or to invest for their retirement (as Puritans once did for heaven)—thereby compounding the conditions that created the loss of on-the-job satisfaction in the first place. [McQueen 2003: 258–9; paraphrasing Lasch 1979: 64ff].

Unable to find their lives fulfilling, people attempt to signal their worth to others through consumption. Fred Hirsch has labeled this form of consumption as positional (Hirsch 1976). Ultimately, the attempt to distinguish oneself through consumption is not only futile, but inimical to the feeling of any human solidarity. I can only improve my relative standing by ensuring that someone else declines. In effect, then, the pleasure that I enjoy from consuming more comes at the expense of increasing the dissatisfaction of others.

Few people are content to be losers in this positional contest. People learn to envy those far above them and to delight in the misfortunes of others. For example, during the heady dot.com boom of the late 1990s, the *New York Times* ran an article describing "a wave of envy is gnawing at those near the top of the economic pyramid as they see others making even more. Most unsettled are successful corporate managers and professionals like doctors and lawyers earning $100,000 to $200,000 a year. Five years ago that made them feel privileged" (Kaufman 1998).

This jockeying to display one's status leads to a competitive attitude about positional goods and leads people to engage in never-ending rounds of consumptive one-upmanship. As one person advances in a display of distinctive consumption, others attempt to neutralize that effort through emulation.

Thorstein Veblen, an iconoclastic economist of the late nineteenth and early twentieth century, famously compared the wasteful competition during the ostentatious Gilded Age of the late nineteenth century to the legendary Potlatches of the Native Americans of the Northwest, in which Native Americans supposedly vied with one another by destroying goods in a display of wealth and power—a ceremony that tended to equalize wealth since it put the burden on the richest members of society. Veblen saw that since others will always attempt to ape the fashionable, the key to status will be to continuously discard old fashions and adopt new ones to remain ahead of others (Veblen 1899).

For Veblen, the masses, living in relative poverty, were largely excluded from this game, except insofar as the affluent went to great lengths to distinguish themselves from the less fortunate. For example, when the majority of people worked in the fields, affluent women would go about with parasols to shield themselves from sunlight as much as possible so that their pasty white skin would differentiate themselves from those who had to work. Later, when many of the poor began to take jobs in factories and offices, the affluent women would go out of their way to let the sun tan their skin.

The game of competitive consumption inevitably creates displeasure. As Karl Marx once wrote: "A house may be large or small; as long as the neighboring houses are equally small, it satisfies all social requirement for a dwelling. But let a palace arise beside the little house, and it shrinks the little house to a hut" (Marx 1849: 163). In a more humorous vein, H. L. Mencken once defined a wealthy man as one who earns $100 a year more than his wife's sister's husband.

This contest continues ad infinitum, much to the delight of marketers. As Coco Chanel, the successful fashion designer and perfume marketer, once insightfully observed, "Luxury is the necessity that begins when necessity ends" (Katz 1997: 17).

Consider the demand for the Hummer, a vehicle originally designed as an armored military transport vehicle capable of riding upon terrain that ordinary trucks would find impassable. For the most part, the market for this vehicle had been limited to those who needed the Hummer's special characteristics—namely, the military. Only after extensive prodding from Arnold Schwarzenegger did its manufacturer, AM General, even bother to produce a civilian model (Bradsher 2004: 362).

In December 1999, General Motors purchased the marketing rights to the Hummer from AM General. General Motors then dramatically ramped up the marketing reach of the Hummer, based on its discovery that "Hummers tend to appeal to people who never performed military service but wished they had" (Bradsher 2004: 370). With this insight, the company aimed its first push for this three and a half ton vehicle at the luxury market, especially in New York City.

Of course, few of the features of this vehicle would give drivers an advantage in a flat, but crowded city (except for the absurd special tax breaks that purchasers of very heavy vehicles enjoy). But the unique look and $100,000 price tag allowed the wealthy to conspicuously distinguish themselves from the less affluent, while perhaps somehow vicariously identifying with the wild adventures of those for whom the vehicle was originally intended. The game of positional consumption does little to make society better off, any more than the Hummers help their drivers to negotiate traffic jams in New York City.

## THE DEMOCRATIZATION OF THE POTLATCH

Out of necessity, modern capitalism has democratized Veblen's modern version of the Potlatch. In Veblen's day, the working class were too poor to participate in the Potlatch. Today, business needs them to join in.

Profit-maximizing companies attempt to lower costs—especially wage costs—as much as possible. At the same time, modern cost-reducing technologies tend to depend upon economies of scale—meaning that they can only achieve the cost savings by producing larger quantities of output. The limitation on wages, however, restricts the demand for these goods. As a result, the real problem that corporations face is not scarcity but an endemic shortage of demand.

In early capitalism, say before the age of Adam Smith, the great trading companies sought out markets abroad, more or less ignoring domestic demand. At the time, governments enforced sumptuary laws that prohibited poorer people from wearing anything even suggesting luxury. These laws initially served to distinguish the various ranks of society. Later, as the market became a more dominant force, these laws also helped to keep labor's monetary demands in check.

Once business became more dependent on domestic consumers, the sumptuary laws fell by the wayside. Now that the government no longer prohibited the poor from emulating their betters, marketers began to encourage such behavior. Josiah Wedgwood, the famous manufacturer of pottery in late eighteenth-century England, was a pioneer in developing a marketing scheme around the competitive emulation of fashion. He would go out of his way to ingratiate himself with the aristocracy, who would then become identified with his pottery. Although his aristocratic clientele may have bought their goods well below cost, Wedgwood's strategy made his products far more valuable to his less distinguished customers. As he deliciously observed: "Fashion is infinitely superior to merit in many respects" (McKendrick 1982: 108).

Wedgwood's strategy was fantastically successful. For example, even in the United States between 1898 and 1916, products for the table and the kitchen took up a surprising 13 per cent of the annual household incomes. Between 1922 and 1929 expenditures on China and glassware were still 6.8 per cent (Blaszczyk 2000: 130).

The automobile industry offers an even more dramatic example of the Potlatch. Henry Ford pioneered the mass market for automobiles. He standardized his cars, supposedly saying customers could have any car they wanted, as long as it was black (see Sloan 1964: 272). No company could compete with Ford on the basis of building a cheap, economical car, but Ford soon had this market saturated.

Used cars offered an alternative to an inexpensive new car. By 1927, two-thirds of all cars sold were used cars. General Motors and Ford attempted to restrict the competition from used cars by paying dealers for each used car they destroyed. This program took 650,000 cars off the market between 1927 and 1930. Dealers, however, often resold "junked" cars. For instance, one car went through the junking process six times (Gordon 1994; and Anon. 1938).

About this time, Hazel Kyrk published a prize-winning book, extending Walter Lippmann's vision by arguing that overproduction could be eliminated if the working class could be educated toward a more "dynamic" consumption of luxuries (Kyrk 1923: 278). In effect, not only should people content themselves by identifying as consumers rather than as workers, but their consumption could eliminate the problem of aggregate demand. She emphasized the importance of advertising in breaking down old habits—presumably meaning traditional patterns of consumption—in order to make consumers desirous of new needs (Kyrk 1923: 262–3).

General Motors' strategy was very much in tune with Kyrk's vision. It had already embarked on a massive advertising campaign to build up its market share (Marchand 1991). By 1920, the automobile industry, led by General Motors, already had accounted for one-quarter of all national magazine advertising (Gordon 1994: 42). Ford, in contrast, considered advertising a waste of money.

Even more dramatically, General Motors turned to designers to lure new customers into the marketplace. In the words of Alfred P. Sloan, under whose leadership General Motors wrested dominance of the industry from Ford: "The prevailing concept in the Executive Committee was to meet Ford more or less head on with a revolutionary car design" (Sloan 1963: 64). According to Sloan, "New styling features were introduced that were far removed from utility, yet they seemed demonstrably effective in capturing taste" (Sloan 1963: 278).

Sloan's vision was so successful that an ongoing policy of annual model changes made his design strategy a permanent feature of the industry. Symbolic of the importance of design for Sloan, in his book detailing his experience with General Motors, he devoted two of the 24 chapters to the subject of style (Sloan 1963, chapters 13 and 15). He ended the second of these chapters by describing how the P-38 fighter plane was the inspiration for the tail fin, emblematic of the non-functional flourishes intended to sell automobiles (Sloan 1963: 278). Sloan clearly understood that the proliferation of styles would confuse consumers, putting his company in a better position to extract profits from the public. As he cynically informed the corporate finance committee in the midst of the Great Depression in early 1931:

> Relatively inconsequential features will often influence a sale, adversely to the customer's interests with respect to other far more consequential features. No prospect [meaning customer] is intelligent enough to definitely determine the weighted value of all the elements that enter into any particular car. [Sloan 1963: 180]

Sloan's strategy proved hugely successful:

> Fins spawned finlets, Dagmars multiplied [protruding bullet-shaped objects on bumpers named for a busty Danish entertainer], and the auto-buying frenzy of the 1950s commenced, as if on signal. In 1955 new car sales totaled $65 billion, or 20 per cent of the Gross National Product .... General Motors became the first corporation to earn a billion dollars in a single year. [Marling 1994: 144–5]

But how could General Motors market so many cars if workers' earnings were held down in the interest of profit maximization? Gradual increases in earnings and the expansion of the middle class played a role, but central to General Motors' success was a massive dependence on credit.

Why would people take on so much debt just to acquire the latest style of tail fins or Dagmars? Charles F. Kettering, general director of General Motors Research Laboratories, whose name is more remembered today as the co-founder with Alfred Sloan of the Memorial Sloan-Kettering Cancer Center, offered a clue. In early 1929 he wrote an article in *Nation's Business*, entitled "Keep the Consumer Dissatisfied" (Kettering 1929). Coming only a few months before the stock market crash, the timing of the piece was interesting.

Kettering did not mention the growing debt burden of the public. Instead, he insisted that the key to economic prosperity is the organized creation of dissatisfaction. Kettering wrote as if his logic was self-evident:

> If automobile owners could not dispose of their cars to a lower buying strata they would have to wear out their cars with a consequent tremendous cutting in the yearly demand for automobiles.
>
> If everyone were satisfied no one would want to buy the new thing. [Kettering 1929: 79]

I will return to the question of dissatisfaction later to give this subject the attention it deserves. Before doing so, I want to discuss some other implications of the emphasis modern business gives to rapid style changes.

## PLANNED OBSOLESCENCE

The economy dissipates enormous energy in creating a steady stream of new products, most of which, like the finlets and Dagmars, offer no advantage other than novelty. In this vein, centuries ago, Adam Smith remarked:

> How many people ruin themselves by laying out money on trinkets of frivolous utility? What pleases these lovers of toys is not so much the utility, as the aptness of the machines which are fitted to promote it. All their pockets are stuffed with little conveniencies. They contrive new pockets, unknown in the clothes of other people, in order to carry a greater number. They walk about loaded with a multitude of baubles ..., some of which may sometimes be of some little use, but all of which might at all times be very well spared, and of which the whole utility is certainly not worth the fatigue of bearing the burden. [Smith 1759, IV.i.6: 180]

Smith concluded that the desire for luxury is little more than a "deception which rouses and keeps in continual motion the industry of mankind" (Smith 1759, IV.i.9: 183). Smith's contemporary, the philosopher Immanuel Kant, told a young Russian nobleman, "Give a man *everything* he desires and yet at this very moment he will feel that this *everything* is not *everything*" (Karamzin 1957: 40–1).

The self-deception and disappointment to which Smith and Kant pointed undoubtedly predates market economies. Even so, no previous economy has ever used this conundrum as a central organizing principle. At the time in which Adam Smith wrote, he had no idea that the deception he described would involve anybody but the upper classes, who without the prod of new demands would satisfy themselves with greater leisure. A century and a half later, the great advertisers have successfully encouraged the majority of the population to dissipate resources on "trinkets of frivolous utility."

Hemlines rise and fall in order to make people dissatisfied with last year's wardrobe. Fashions change so fast that secondhand stores, such as Goodwill or the Salvation Army, cannot keep up with the flow of discarded clothing, even though much of it is of high quality and relatively new. These agencies have little choice but to export much of their donated clothing to impoverished nations.

Nobody knows the horrendous resource cost of rapidly changing fashion, but again the experience of General Motors and the rest of the automobile industry is instructive. In a classic study of the economic costs of automotive design changes published in the conservative *Journal of Political Economy* the year before Sloan's account of his work with General Motors appeared, three quite prominent economists, Franklin Fisher, Zvi Griliches, and Carl Kaysen, estimated that more than 25 per cent of the selling price of a car came from the cost of model changes that were unrelated to performance (Fisher, Griliches, and Kaysen 1962). Since 1962, the speed with which new models of consumer goods proliferate has accelerated dramatically. The automobile industry pioneered planned obsolescence; it continues to push that strategy today. People who purchase a car can select from more than 1,000 models.

Nike offers a clear picture of how planned obsolescence has evolved. The first Nike shoe had a promotional life of seven years. By 1989, the marketing cycle was down to ten months (McQueen 2003: 187). Now, Nike creates 250 new shoe designs each season. The Swiss company that manufactures Swatch watches creates 140 different watch styles each year (Jenkins 1998). I doubt a new model watch is much more accurate than the model that preceded it. According to Jeffrey Madrick the Gap retail chain revamps its product line every six weeks, and changes its advertising frequently as well (Madrick 1998: 32).

The Productscan Online database counted 33,678 new food, beverage, health and beauty aids, household and pet products introduced during 2003, up from less than 22,000 in 1994 (Productscan 2003). Madrick reported that the number has increased fifteen- and twenty-fold since 1970 (Madrick 1998: 32). Relatively few of these new products actually represent an improvement; they are simply marketing strategies.

Paradoxically, constant style changes can actually limit the variety of products available to the public. When companies, such as Nike, go to great lengths to shower markets with a wide array of products, part of their strategy is to limit competition by filling the shelves with as many varieties as possible in order to prevent stores from stocking products from other brands. For example, when the Federal Trade Commission looked at five food products—bread, hot dogs, ice cream, pasta, and salad dressing—it found that a foodmaker could pay anywhere from $2,313 to $21,768 per item to get onto the ideal shelves in a major metropolitan area (Federal Trade Commission 2003). Small producers complain that this practice prevents them from competing.

According to the promise of consumer sovereignty this wide array of choices benefits the customer. The reality is somewhat different. Consider the 250 new shoe designs that Nike creates each season. From my personal perspective, this quest for novelty is quite detrimental. Writing as an aging basketball player with tender feet, I know that if I find a pair of shoes that fits well, I will never again be able to find a replacement with the precise feel and fit, since the style that I buy today will soon be discontinued. So, every time my shoes wear out, I must begin another search for a shoe that feels comfortable. Alas, in the end, consumer sovereignty turns out to be a quite constricted form of sovereignty.

These "search efforts" represent a serious cost. John Helliwell, an economist who has studied the relationship between economics and happiness, noted: "psychological studies show that increasing the range of product choice becomes costly to buyers at a fairly early stage: they find it harder to make decisions when faced with many alternatives, take longer to reach their decisions, and are more likely to later regret their decisions" (Helliwell 2002: 34).

For example, two psychologists set up tasting booths in an upscale grocery store, offering the opportunity to taste a number of jams—either 6 or 24. In the case of the 6-jam experiment, 40 per cent of shoppers stopped to have a taste and, of those, 30 per cent proceeded to purchase a jam. In the 24-jam experiment, a full 60 per cent stopped to taste, but only 3 per cent actually purchased a product. They described this difference as a "phenomenon of choice overload [in which] ... people ... are burdened by the responsibility of distinguishing good from bad decisions" (Iyengar and Lepper 2000: 1003–4).

Obviously, this problem is even more true when the commodity involves a more complex set of considerations than the taste of a jam sample. Think of the intense study required to select the best Health Maintenance Organization (HMO) plan. I doubt that many people find that experience particularly pleasurable. Perhaps more revealing, consumers, even the 40 million who do not have health insurance, never get to consider the choice of a national health care program that could avoid the excessive overhead costs of profit-making HMOs, especially when clear and reliable information is so hard to find.

So, in many, if not most cases, the number of new varieties offer no substantial advantage—just a variation in style. In fact, some companies are now finding that a reduction in the choices that they offer consumers actually increases sales (Iyengar and Lepper 2000).

## PROSPERITY AND HAPPINESS

I want to take a moment to consider what light economic theory might throw on the relationship between prosperity and happiness. Economists who believe in the harmonious functioning of the market construct beautiful theories to show how the economy works to maximize happiness and human welfare. Well, not quite. Because of the technical difficulties that economists encountered in elaborating this theory, they had to satisfy themselves merely by "proving" that a market will eliminate a very limited sort of inefficiency—that the market will never reach an outcome in which you could somehow give someone something without making someone else worse off. Even this modest "proof" requires a large number of assumptions that are never met in the real world.

In this theoretical context, within a market society, all individuals will attempt to maximize their happiness—economists use the term utility—given the limitations of their budgets. Firms will then adapt their business to accommodate individuals' desires. At the very least, because of economic growth over time in this world of consumer sovereignty, we should expect that each generation in advanced market economies would be far happier than its predecessor. Yet, nothing of the sort seems to be happening.

Most people would expect that an increase in a society's income would bring about an increase in happiness, but these expectations do not pan out. Instead, modern research seems to bear out Smith's intuition about the illusory utility of luxury. Societies do not seem to become happier with an increase in income after their basic needs are met. Instead, "once a country has over $15,000 per head, its level of happiness appears to be independent of its income per head" (Layard 2003; see also Frey and Stutzer 2002: 8; and Easterlin 1995). Germans and Nigerians seem to be equally happy. A similar equality holds for Cubans and Americans (Frank 1985: 31).

Of course, if the German standard of living fell to a Nigerian level, Germans would not be indifferent. German happiness does not exceed that of Nigeria because Germans have different material expectations than Nigerians do. These expectations shift as people experience a different standard of living. Similarly, if the Nigerians were brought up to a German standard and then fell back to their earlier level, their happiness would also decline below where it stands today.

In short, as people reach a higher level of prosperity, the standards by which they measure prosperity also increase. As a result, prosperity becomes an ever receding goal. For example, in 1986 the Roper polling organization asked Americans how much income they would need to fulfill all their dreams. The answer was $50,000. By 1994 the "dreams-fulfilling" level of income had doubled, to $102,000 (Schor 1998: 14; Stutzer 2004).

Corporations serve as a vehicle to accumulate wealth in an ever smaller number of hands. Those who enjoy the greatest wealth within this system raise the income aspirations for others. Corporations play a substantial role in fueling higher expectations. I might add another consideration in this discussion of happiness. A number of studies have found that nations with greater income equality enjoy better health, measured by longevity (Wilkinson 1997: 1–2). Even within the United States, people in those states with greater income equality live longer (see Kaplan et al.1996; Ross et al. 2000). I am fairly confident that the link between inequality, advertising, unfulfilled expectations, and poor health would be fairly strong.

I should add that just because societies do not report more happiness with increases in income beyond a certain threshold does not mean that money and income are unrelated to happiness for individuals within any society. Rich people do tend to be happier than the less affluent, but their happiness depends less on the extent of their riches than on how rich they are relative to others around them.

Nobody understood the relationship between money and happiness better than Thorstein Veblen. Although his ornate language makes for difficult reading, his analysis still holds:

> the end sought by accumulation is to rank high in comparison with the rest of the community in point of pecuniary strength. So long as the comparison is distinctly unfavourable to himself, the normal, average individual will live in chronic dissatisfaction with his present lot; and when he has reached what may be called the normal pecuniary standard of the community, or of his class in the community, this chronic dissatisfaction will give place to a restless straining to place a wider and ever-widening pecuniary interval between himself and this average standard. The invidious comparison can never become so favourable to the individual making it that he would not gladly rate himself still higher relatively to his competitors in the struggle for pecuniary reputability. [Veblen 1899: 39]

Such then is the "happiness" of the rich. Modern markets, however, may be particularly destructive of happiness. A number of social scientists have tried to analyze happiness. Their results are consistent. In the United States, happiness seems to have peaked in the 1950s. According to a report compiled in the mid-1990s, since 1957, the proportion of those telling surveyors from the National Opinion Research Center that they are "very happy" has declined from 35 to 29 per cent (Myers and Diener 1996; see also Lane 2000).

In the 1960s, people increasingly began to question the value of increasing material affluence. People who had never known the hardship and deprivation associated with the Depression were coming of age. For many young people, accustomed to a comfortable standard of living, merely accumulating more material goods seemed pointless. Many instead chose to distinguish themselves in a "counter culture" that shunned ostentatious consumption, although for the majority, this seemingly principled stance turned out to be a passing phase—or perhaps more accurately, a fad.

I should add that although material goods may not be a guarantee of happiness, one particular type of commodity may be an exception in its ability to ward off unhappiness—at least consumers seem to think so. In particular, many people turn to medication in an attempt to make their lives happier. In the 1960s, illegal psychedelics became popular. In the 1970s Valium topped the charts as the most widely prescribed drug in the United States, only to be replaced by Xanax in 1986. Today, Prozac is the world's most widely prescribed drug.

## MARKETS AND HAPPINESS

What might explain the seeming decline in happiness in the United States? Could markets themselves be responsible? Robert Lane suggests that markets may actually be antithetical to happiness (Lane 2000). He argues that markets put a premium on consumption, while tending to undermine those aspects of life that actually are essential to happiness—warm interpersonal relations, easy-to-reach neighbors, satisfying work, and a healthy family life. We saw some evidence about the way that markets can undermine happiness in the earlier discussion of the inordinate time demands that work makes on people.

Supposedly, a healthy economy requires a flexible workforce in which labor markets can shunt workers hither and yon at a moment's notice. The resulting job insecurity and unemployment associated with a flexible labor market are surely very destructive of happiness. The stress associated with this insecurity surely takes a serious toll on the economy, both in terms of increased health costs and the loss of potential creativity that is misdirected into worrying or looking for alternative opportunities.

We have seen that within the United States, the market has also required that families devote more and more of their time both to the job itself and to job-related activities, such as commuting. Certainly, in the United States, the decline of life associated with the reduction in leisure and the increasingly hectic demands of work must take a toll on people's perceived happiness.

While working conditions in Europe are more modest at this juncture, strong competitive pressures are building up to make European working conditions become similar to those in the United States. In effect, market forces are telling the Europeans that they must sacrifice their quality of life to remain competitive.

Now, let us change gears and look at the relationship between markets and happiness from the perspective of more abstract economic theory. Within the rhetoric of consumer sovereignty, firms exist to meet the needs of consumers. Insofar as consumers' budgets allow them to make commercial demands, firms supposedly stand ready to meet their every need.

Corporations, of course, are not simply passive servants waiting to meet consumers' needs. As I have already mentioned, corporations spend immense sums of money in order to create and manipulate these needs. Charles Revson, the founder of Revlon cosmetics, and a great admirer of General Motors, instituted the model change for his cosmetics, and, with it, planned obsolescence, although he compared his low-end product with a Pontiac. With a keen sense of psychology, he once quipped: "In the factory, we make cosmetics; in the store, we sell hope" (Tobias 1976: 107–8; also see McQueen 2003: 256). Does anyone believe that cosmetics actually deliver on the promises that they make?

Corporations also work to limit markets. Holding down wages to increase profits means that corporations have to struggle to expand their markets. Charles Kettering was impeccably clear that planned obsolescence was an integral part of that strategy. A tsunami of new styles is intended to make people dissatisfied with their existing possessions.

Society could vastly improve the quality of life in meaningful ways by diverting the time and energy devoted to these superficial makeovers of commodities to more productive activities—better health care or education, for example. Unfortunately, the supposedly sovereign consumer never gets to make that sort of choice.

Planned obsolescence is doubly destructive because it also undermines what economists consider to be the essential goal of economic activity: human satisfaction—what economists call utility. Conventional economic theory teaches that all value is subjective or even spiritual; that something has value merely because someone thinks that it does. Let me turn to a classic text, Arthur Cecil Pigou's *The Economics of Welfare*, which states quite clearly that "welfare includes states of consciousness only, and not material things" (Pigou 1920: 10).

The purchaser of a new commodity expects to derive a certain amount of future utility from the product. In many cases, the message delivered through advertisements influences those expectations, which are unlikely to be met. Disappointed hopes are less likely with a good that one consumes in a short period of time. Consumers of durable goods are far more vulnerable to disappointment. Albert O. Hirschman, an extraordinarily perceptive economist, suggested that by their very nature durable goods are likely to disappoint their purchasers:

any good that assures comfort or keeps discomfort at bay in a durable fashion, such as an automatic heating system or a refrigerator, will yield a comparatively low amount of pleasure. As long as it is in working order, such a good will satisfy a need once and for all, so that pleasure is experienced only once, when the good is first acquired and put to use ("turned on"). Thereafter, comfort is assured, but the pleasure that comes with traveling from discomfort to comfort is no longer available. [Hirschman 1982: 32]

Hirschman humorously suggested:

The Roman emperors knew, so it seems, what they were doing when they took care to supply the masses with bread and circuses: both vanish once you have taken them in, without leaving behind a corporeal shape on which consumers can vent any disappointment, boredom, or anxiety they may have suffered or may yet suffer. [Hirschman 1982: 29]

Hirschman charged that economists have not paid much attention to disappointment because they routinely assume perfect knowledge on the part of consumers (Hirschman 1982: 17). His charge is a bit too sweeping. After all, centuries ago, Adam Smith had acutely noted the disappointment of the owner of a watch that is no longer on the cutting edge of technology:

A watch ... that falls behind above two minutes in a day, is despised by one curious in watches. He sells it perhaps for a couple of guineas, and purchases another at fifty, which will not lose above a minute in a fortnight. The sole use of watches however, is to tell us what o'clock it is, and to hinder us from breaking any engagement, or suffering any other inconveniency by our ignorance in that particular point. [Smith 1759, IV.i.5: 180]

Both Hirschman and Smith missed an important factor that actively works to create disappointment: advertisements. Advertisers intend their message to make people more desirous of buying their products. One side effect of this fabrication of desire for new products is the reduction in the satisfaction with a consumer's existing goods.

## SABOTAGING HAPPINESS

Now, let us go back to the economists' idea about how the market allows people to maximize their utility. Part of their theory proposes that a durable object is expected to provide a stream of utility over its lifetime.

Imagine that you have just made a purchase of what seemed to be the very best product available. Now that you own this commodity, a barrage of advertisements announces a new, improved version that supposedly makes obsolete everything that has preceded it—whether it be a faster computer or better cup holders in a car. This advertising makes your possession now seem hopelessly deficient relative to the newest models on the market. In effect, this advertising campaign has undermined the stream of utility that you had expected from your purchase.

Probably the greatest power of advertising lies in its ability to create dissatisfaction. Business preys on human emotions with advertisements that appeal to the irrational part of the brain, especially by taking advantage of consumers' feelings of weakness, inadequacy, and insecurity. Symbolic of the extreme lengths to which marketers will go to manipulate consumers, BrightHouse Institute for Thought Sciences of Atlanta provides neuromarketing technology. It announces on its web site: "We use modern neuroscience methods to help businesses and organizations create better products, services and messages; and to improve society through a better understanding of human cognition." BrightHouse claims that their method can uncover "the unconscious as well as conscious determinants of behavior; much of what motivates our behavior occurs below the level of conscious awareness." Specifically, the company plans to use Magnetic Resonance Imaging (MRI) on volunteers to discover how the brain responds to being exposed to advertising or to new products. According to the company, this technology will reveal deep feelings of which the subjects themselves are unaware.

Similarly, the automobile industry is using neuromarketing to discover what part of the brain different models of cars activate. Gary Ruskin, executive director of Commercial Alert, has complained to the U.S. Office for Human Research Protection, an arm of the Department of Health and Human Services that MRI scanners are being used "not to heal, but to sell products" (Britt 2004).

Well before such advances in science, advertising had already been perfecting its ability to appeal to the subconscious. Not entirely surprisingly, Edward Bernays, Freud's nephew on both his mother's and his father's side of the family, was a pioneer in such advertising.

Advertising surreptitiously works to convince people that others will love, respect, or envy them only if they consume in an appropriate fashion. Conversely, if people's clothes are out of fashion or their car is shabby, then they might find themselves the object of ridicule. Advertising preys on the primitive fear of exclusion, exile, and abandonment.

In his book *Everyday Life in the Modern World*, the French sociologist Henri Lefebvre included a chapter entitled "Terrorism and Everyday Life." There he observed, "Not that fashion alone and independently causes terror to reign, but it is an integral/integrated part of terrorist societies, and it does inspire a certain kind of terror, a certainty of terror" (Lefebvre 1971: 165). In this environment, people who are uncertain of their position in the world stand in terror of being out of fashion—creating what you might call a "fashistic" world in which frightened consumers discard styles at breakneck speed to keep up with the latest style changes developed by companies, such as Nike and Swatch.

The continual need to keep up with fashion is the product of an impersonal world in which people frequently fail to see others in terms of their human qualities. Instead, we are reduced to communicating our status to each other by displaying fashionable possessions. So, while consumer sovereignty is touted to celebrate the power of the individual, this individuality is a mass-produced illusion.

Worse yet, marketers understand that people do not always consume as "sovereign individuals," but as part of a family. Using this knowledge, marketers often target their appeal to the most vulnerable members of the family—children—whom they know will often succeed in coercing their parents to purchase particular products.

Ultimately, then, this social act of consumption diminishes individuals, reducing them to compliant consumers in a process that would make Dr Pavlov proud. In the process, advertising-fueled consumption destroys the enjoyment that people had anticipated from their prior purchases. Under the influence of advertisements, goods that were originally intended to bring future pleasure quickly become objects of regret or embarrassment.

So, while one part of a corporation's efforts attempts to satisfy consumers' needs, in an effort to expand its markets through advertising, the same corporation may be creating substantial dissatisfaction. Economic theory devotes considerable attention to the way that business satisfies needs by providing goods and services, but it takes virtually no notice of the dissatisfaction created by advertising, except by occasionally mentioning the resources wasted in advertising costs.

This neglect is doubly destructive. Not only is advertising antithetical to happiness; some evidence suggests that happiness is a positive factor in creating economic growth (see Kenney 1999). If happier societies are indeed more productive, curtailing the destructive nature of advertising could accelerate economic growth, which, in turn, has the potential to generate more happiness, especially if society uses the fruits of that growth to fund socially productive activities, such as health care and education. Besides, since happy people are likely to consume less, even more resources would be available for such uses.

## CONSUMING CULTURE

I would like to shift gears for a moment and consider consumer sovereignty in the context of culture. In a sense, commodified culture is the inverse of most marketed products. For clothes or cars, advertisements are intended to sell the product. For commodified culture, the product exists to "sell" the advertisement.

A collection of 28 movie studios and television networks brought home this message in October 2001 when they sued ReplayTV and SonicBlue for marketing a product that let people view recorded programs while skipping the commercials. A few months later, Jamie Kellner chairman and CEO of Turner Broadcasting, explained the industry's logic in bringing suit: "Your contract with the network when you get the show is you're going to watch the spots. Otherwise you couldn't get the show on an ad-supported basis. Any time you skip a commercial ... you're actually stealing the programming" (Kramer 2002). Under the barrage of litigation, the company filed for bankruptcy. Its new owner, Digital Networks, now sells the product, but without the feature that allows consumers to skip advertising. So much for consumer sovereignty!

Just turn on your radio to see what commercial culture offers. Technically, radio could offer a bountiful range of programming, diverse enough to meet almost any taste. Instead, you will find no more than a dozen different formats over the entire commercial spectrum. Of these, none would dare to broadcast anything that might upset a potential sponsor. Where, then, is consumer sovereignty—especially for a consumer who would like something outside of the narrow range of available formats?

Instead of consumer sovereignty, commercial sovereignty reigns supreme. Serious reporting has almost entirely disappeared from the commercial media. Besides being expensive, investigative reporting could upset sponsors. Even cinema is becoming more dependent on uncredited sponsors who pay to have their products appear prominently in popular films. Tobacco companies, denied the opportunity to advertise on television, have successfully used Hollywood to have popular movie stars make smoking appear attractive to young people. For example, the Brown and Williamson tobacco company paid Sylvester Stallone $500,000 to feature personal usage of B&W products in *Rhinestone Cowboy*, *Godfather III*, *Rambo*, *50/50*, and *Rocky IV*, according to a letter from James F. Ripslinger of Associated Film Promotions to the actor, summarizing the agreement. <http://tobaccodocuments.org/youth/AmBWC19830614.Lt.html> Although Mr Ripslinger was probably mistaken about including *Godfather III* as one of the five films in question, the copy of the document reproduced on the Web originally came from the Brown and Williamson files.

Although the public has not been able to learn the details of more recent tobacco deals with the movie industry, smoking, which had become increasingly less prominent in films from 1950 through 1980–82, has recently surpassed its 1950s level (Glantz, Kacirk, and McCulloch 2004).

Even when the commercial product is offered for sale rather than serving as a vehicle for advertising, consumer sovereignty suffers. For example, because large chain stores increasingly dominate the book distribution system, small outlets that offer more offbeat publications are rapidly falling by the wayside. As a result, the range of published books significantly narrows—despite the growing technological capacity to expand the breadth of the industry's output.

Obviously consumers still have an apparently wide range of choices. A single supermarket may contain 35,000 differently priced items and a Wal-Mart store over 40,000 (Federal Trade Commission 2003; Boskin et al. 1998: 5). How meaningful these choices might be is an entirely different question. No matter what the Walter Lippmanns of the world proclaim, I cannot believe that people who must spend day after day in jobs that are meaningless or destructive or even dangerous would feel fulfilled just because they have the opportunity to choose among a few hundred different shoe styles or, worse yet, five brands of tainted meat.

# 3

# What Corporate Society
# Does to Workers

## INDIVIDUAL FREEDOM AND AUTHORITY IN THE WORKPLACE

Admittedly, although the widely-celebrated consumer sovereignty allows people to choose whether to consume Coke or Pepsi, nobody could even dream of suggesting that workers can act as sovereign individuals within their place of employment. Although ideologists mouth comforting platitudes that depict people as sovereign individuals in their role as consumers, obviously ultimate control of the workplace firmly resides with the employer. As Frederick Winslow Taylor, the father of scientific management proclaimed in 1911, just as the giant corporations were beginning to dominate the U.S. economy, "In the past the man has been first; in the future the system must be first" (Taylor 1911: 7).

Strangely enough, although the law in Britain and the United States evolved rapidly to allow for increasing freedom in the commercial sector, until relatively recently very ancient law regulated the obligations of workers to their employers. Karen Orren described the persistence of this archaic legal structure in her book, *Belated Feudalism* (1991). This legal framework dates all the way back to the Statute of Artificers (1563), the Statutes of Labourers (1349), and even earlier. The first of these laws was intended to reinforce employer control after the Black Death created a scarcity of workers. With fewer people available for work, laborers' bargaining position had improved. Rather than accept their temporary disadvantage, the rich and powerful passed the Statutes of Labourers, which codified earlier court decisions, seriously restricting the rights of laborers to change employers or location.

Of course, courts did not issue decrees that blatantly trumpeted their decisions, beginning with the words: "By the Statutes of Labourers ...." Instead, they based their decisions on later courts whose verdicts flowed from these ancient laws. Only in the late nineteenth century, when railroad strikes began to create serious interference with commercial activity, did the Interstate Commerce

Commission finally begin to apply a more modern legal theory. Over the next few decades, the legal system in the United States slowly began to break away from these ancient legal doctrines (see Orren 1991).

During the New Deal, popular pressure forced the law to evolve in a direction more favorable to unions. Since then the law has increasingly turned against the rights of unions, often on the grounds that unions violate the rights of individual workers.

The striking imbalance of power between individual workers and employers is so obvious that it requires no comment at all. Even our everyday language betrays the unequal distribution of power between the employer and the employed. The employers, being in a superior position, are said to "give" or "offer" work. For their part, employees should "accept" their jobs gratefully or find another suitable place of employment. In this sense, a sort of consumer sovereignty does actually operate in the workplace. There, the consumer—namely, the employer—enjoys nearly dictatorial powers over the seller—namely, the workers who sell their labor. Given the enormous stress associated with the labor market, no wonder so many people attempt to retreat into consumptionism.

Despite the obvious imbalance between workers and employers, some economists stubbornly insist on seeing only voluntary arrangements in the workplace rather than an exercise of power. For example, two highly respected economists—one of whom was the instructor in my freshman class in economics—compared the relation between employer and employee to that between shopper and grocer. They maintained that just as shoppers can fire their grocers by patronizing a different store, employers can chose to do business with different employees. "Telling an employee to type this letter rather than to file that document is like telling my grocer to sell me this brand of tuna rather than that brand of bread" (Alchian and Demsetz 1972: 778). The economists made no mention of the delicious irony that the relationship between the consumer of labor service (the employer) and the seller of labor services (the employee, represented in their example as a subservient grocer) may possibly be the strongest example of consumer sovereignty—that of the employers who purchase the services of their workers.

Other economists take this sort of fanciful thinking about voluntary arrangements in the workplace to an even more absurd level by claiming that workers preferred what were obviously coercive measures. For example, Greg Clark proposed that "factory discipline

[was] successful because it coerced more effort from workers than they would freely give .... The empirical evidence shows that discipline succeeded mainly by increasing work effort. Workers effectively hired capitalists to make them work harder" (Clark 1994: 128).

Greg Clark was referring to the sort of theory earlier proposed by Clark Nardinelli, who, presumably in all seriousness, declared that during the Industrial Revolution, children in the factories would voluntarily choose to have their employers beat them. In his words: "Now if a firm in a competitive industry employed corporal punishment the supply price of child labor to that firm would increase. The child would receive compensations for the disamenity of being beaten" (Nardinelli 1982: 289). Does any parent seriously believe that children would actually make such a calculation—especially when their parents pocketed their earnings? Similarly, Steven Cheung maintains that riverboat pullers who towed wooden boats in pre-communist China similarly agreed to hire monitors to whip them to restrict shirking (Cheung 1983: 5).

Perhaps those children defied all of our understanding of child psychology and chose to have themselves beaten to earn more money for their parents. Following that logic, we could extend our notion of voluntarism to slavery. After all, some people in impoverished nations, such as early China, Japan, and Russia, were so destitute that they sold themselves into slavery (see Patterson 1982: 130). Voluntary slavery exists today in some of the poorest parts of the world. Would any rational person see slavery as an indicator of freedom rather than absence of choice?

## FLEXIBILITY FOR WHOM?

Imagining the workplace as a network of voluntary relationships has dire political implications. For example, in 1997 a California state agency, the Industrial Welfare Commission, bowing to employer pressure voted to reinterpret an overtime regulation dating back to 1918. For almost eight decades, the state had mandated that employers had to pay overtime after eight hours of work per day. The agency ruled instead that henceforth employers should have to pay overtime only after workers have completed a total 40 hours of work, no matter how many hours they worked on any particular day. Under this new rule, an employer could demand that a worker stay on the job for regular pay for 12 hours a day or even longer just so long as the total workweek did not exceed 40 hours.

The agency, as well as the leading Republican politicians in the state, insisted that their intention was entirely innocent. They pretended to act in the workers' best interest. Given the choice, they argued, workers would prefer to have as much flexibility as possible, allowing them to adjust their schedule to meet their individual needs. I do not recall hearing a single worker speaking up in appreciation for their efforts. After all, if this option actually represented a choice for workers, why not let the workers choose that option.

Nobody denies that many workers could benefit from flexible hours. Indeed, one survey of British workers found that flexible working hours were more important than money for nearly a third of people looking for a new job (Department of Trade and Industry, United Kingdom 2002). Employers are less interested in workers' need for flexibility. Many employers prefer to have workers on overtime rather than hiring additional workers. Even though employers have to pay time and a half for overtime, employers actually save money by giving their workers the overtime premium. Providing benefits, such as pensions, health care or vacation time, to additional workers is more expensive than paying time and a half to some of the existing labor force. As a result, mandatory overtime is common in the United States (Golden and Jorgenson 2002). Of course, employers would prefer to keep their labor force working longer without having to pay a premium for overtime hours.

Everybody involved realized that the primary convenience that the Industrial Welfare Commission had in mind was that of the employers. While some exceptional employers might possibly use the new regulation to allow employees to schedule a more convenient work pattern, the basic thrust of the law would allow employers to reschedule work according to changing business needs. For example, if business slackens on a particular day, the employer could send the worker home early. If business picks up the next day, the employer could demand that the worker stay a few extra hours without any obligation to pay overtime.

Soon thereafter, the election of a Democratic governor meant that the new rule would not go into effect at the time. Undeterred, in 2002, after the Republicans won the U.S. Senate, they announced their intention to rewrite the federal overtime law along the lines that the California Republicans did, but then the government went further. The Department of Labor issued regulations that eliminated overtime protection for an estimated 8 million workers. To add insult to injury, the department then issued a report offering tips on how employers could avoid having to pay overtime (Strope 2004).

Overtime is a contentious issue for workers. Dissatisfaction with mandatory overtime is widespread, but far from universal. Many workers depend on the higher wages that overtime brings. Some need the overtime just to get by; others depend on overtime to enjoy a better lifestyle. Sometimes, this dependence seems to verge on the irrational. For example, the *Wall Street Journal* profiled a Chrysler auto worker, Bill Cecil, who, by working an average of 40 hours per week in overtime, earned $101,000 in 1995. Mr Cecil said that the extra pay allowed him to live comfortably, although the extra hours also led to his divorce (Lucchetti 1996). The paper covered Mr Cecil because his choice was so unusual. Few workers would want to live the life he has chosen.

Many workers do not have the option of working overtime because the time demands outside of work are too great. Eileen Appelbaum, a researcher who has devoted considerable attention to making workplaces more efficient for both workers and their employers, published a Mother's Day opinion piece in several newspapers discussing the growing time demands on workers. She observed:

> In 1979, middle-class married couples with children worked for pay just under 3,300 hours a year on average .... Today, as women's employment has increased, 60 per cent of married couples both work. Seventy-two per cent of women with children younger than 18, and 65 per cent of those with children younger than 6, are in the work force .... This is roughly equivalent to one full-time and one part-time job. In 2000, the latest year for which data are available, middle-class married couples with children were employed 3,932 hours a year. That is an increase of 650 hours, or 16 weeks, of work a year. It means that middle-class married couples with kids are working the equivalent of two full-time jobs. [Appelbaum 2002]

The majority of working mothers with children under age six work more than 30 hours per week. The time demands take a toll on the family. The U.S. Department of Agriculture Reported:

> Compared with children of nonworking mothers, children of full-time working mothers have lower overall HEI (Healthy Eating Index) scores, lower intake of iron and fiber, and higher intake of soda and fried potatoes, even after taking into account differences in maternal and other family characteristics .... Working mothers participate less in meal planning,

shopping, and food preparation. The children of working mothers are more likely to skip morning meals, rely more on away-from-home food sources, spend more time watching TV and videos, and face significantly greater risk of overweight. [Crepinsek, Burstein, and Ghelfi 2004]

For many of working mothers, obtaining childcare requires imposing on friends and family (Boushey 2003). Far too often, single mothers with young children have no one to whom to turn for childcare. From time to time, these unattended children get hurt or even die while their mother works. On the heels of this personal tragedy, prosecutors often charge such mothers with reckless endangerment—or even worse. For low income mothers without access to cheap childcare, the alternative would be to spend a very large portion of their salary for childcare, leaving them with insufficient income to survive.

Parenthetically, in 2003, the Senate Finance Committee following the wishes of the Bush administration voted down an amendment to the bill renewing welfare reform that would have added $11.25 billion in childcare money over five years for women coming off welfare. Senator Rick Santorum, a Pennsylvania Republican, waxed philosophical in speaking against offering assistance for childcare: "Making people struggle a little bit is not necessarily the worst thing" (Shogren 2003).

To make matters worse, workplace demands often continue even after working hours. Job-related activities are also taking up more and more time, especially when workers remain connected to the job with cell phones, fax machines, and e-mail. Commuting probably represents the greatest demand on workers' free time in the United States, especially because many people cope with the rising prices of housing by living far from their workplace. Traffic congestion makes the trip even longer. The average commute time is more than an hour in cities where the population exceeds 1 million people. Even in cities of less than 100,000 the average commute time is more than 40 minutes (Glaeser 1998: 151). The situation grows worse each year. For example, in 1999, the average Atlanta resident lost 53 hours to traffic delays, compared with only 25 hours as recently as 1992 (Krugman 2001).

Personal responsibilities make workers' lives even more complicated. With people living longer and medical insurance increasingly scarce, many married families strain under the burden of caring for their children and parents while each partner works two full-time jobs. Recall that two-thirds of mothers with children under age six are employed and, of these, the majority work more than 30 hours per week (Boushey 2003).

Given the rapid increase in the demands on individuals, flexible work schedules become more valuable for workers with each passing day—if those schedules adjust to the workers' own needs. But today flexibility mostly means that workers must adjust their schedules to the employer's needs. Especially for a two-job family, juggling family responsibilities with work is difficult enough, even with a relatively stable work schedule.

More and more, the presumption that most jobs would be 8 a.m. to 5 p.m. has become obsolete. In 1997, less than 30 per cent of all workers in the United States worked 35–40 hours per week, Monday through Friday on a fixed schedule according to a government survey (Presser 1999: 1778). No wonder that households report that they had just 19.8 hours left each week for relaxation, sports, hobbies, entertainment, and socializing in 1999, compared to 26.2 hours in 1973 (Burtless 1999: 18).

When flexibility becomes the exclusive prerogative of the employer, job demands can become incompatible with workers' other personal responsibilities. I get some idea of the extent of this problem with my students whose employers frequently demand that they shift their work hours with very little notice. Without advance knowledge of their schedules, workers have to expend considerable time, energy, and money to be able to balance their shifting work demands with family and personal responsibilities. They have to make on-the-spot arrangements for someone else to pick their children up at school or take a parent to the doctor. Such is the reality of our modern version of individualism in which commerce triumphs over all else!

Unexpected scheduling demands take an even more serious toll on family life. Not surprisingly, studies indicate that divorce and separation are more common among people working non-standard 8–5 jobs (Presser 2000). Ironically, many of the same conservative politicians who speak so earnestly about their deep dedication to family values applaud proposals to increase employers' flexibility as progressive policy—even though granting employers such flexibility is certain to disrupt the family lives of many employees.

Employers would even like to have workers' hours adjust to the fluctuating needs of their business. For example, some people must work split shifts, such as one shift in the early morning and another in the afternoon. In some rare cases, as with school bus drivers, split shifts are understandable. Split shift work, where employers expect people to report for work for two periods during the day, separated by unpaid time, to accommodate the peak demand periods, is becoming more common. This sort of employer flexibility is liable to abuse.

Now, take a moment to think about the nature of the time demands of the market economy. Modern technology should be lightening workers' burdens, not extending the hours of work, especially in the contemporary United States, where many of the most labor-intensive products come from sweatshops in poor nations. In fact, manufacturing employment is quickly disappearing from the United States. In addition, few people in America, still work in agriculture. Increasingly, people in modern economies work within what people once called the new economy. The time required to produce the essentials of a high standard of living is rapidly shrinking. Even so, work demands are increasing. What is going on?

The market now devotes more and more work for purely commercial reasons—advertising, marketing, extraneous packaging, financial manipulation, and bureaucratic bloat—none of which makes the typical citizen better off. These commercially oriented activities occupy an increasing part of the labor force. By minimizing such wasteful activities and concentrating on useful work, people could enjoy considerably more flexibility without any negative impact on their standard of living (see Perelman 2000b).

## UNEMPLOYMENT AS A DISCIPLINARY DEVICE

The mere mention of class conflict conjures up images of employers and workers engaged in direct confrontations. In fact, until the twentieth century, major corporations frequently employed private armies, sometimes the National Guard, and sometimes even federal troops to prevent workers from organizing to win better pay or working conditions.

Violent conflict between workers and their employer is uncommon today in the United States. When it does occur, a small employer rather than a giant corporation is typically involved. Employers have learned to employ other, less dramatic but equally effective methods to make workers afraid of challenging their employers.

Modern employers are not the first to discover the advantage of a climate of fear. For example, writing in 1786, the Reverend Joseph Townsend, who identified himself as a "Well Wisher to Mankind," proclaimed, "Hope and fear are the springs of industry" (Townsend 1786: 403). For Townsend, hope and fear operate in separate sectors of society: the wealthy respond to opportunity with their hopes of great gain; in contrast, Townsend insisted that fear had to be the primary motivation for the less fortunate: "The poor know little of the motives which stimulate the higher ranks to action—pride, honour, and ambition. In general it is only hunger which can spur and goad them on to labour; yet our laws have said, they shall never hunger" (Townsend 1786: 404). Fortunately, for Townsend and his compatriots, such laws were not frequently enforced.

Workers have good reason not to be optimistic about their prospects. They see few of their peers rise to positions of wealth and power. When they do, luck rather than industry gets them there. For workers with limited prospects, hope is probably an irrational emotion that sometimes induces them to take foolish actions, such as purchasing a lottery ticket in the vain hope of becoming rich.

Townsend suggested that fear must drive the poor because they are incapable of higher motives. In reality, business and its political representatives go to great lengths to construct the situations that give rise to fear.

Employers use different methods today to instill fear in their workers. Perhaps the most dramatic change in recent years is the degree to which business openly regards workers as disposable. The *Wall Street Journal* casually noted that "many management theorists" maintain that "the whole concept of a job—steady work at steady pay from the same employer—must be discarded" (Zachary 1995; see also Bridges 1994a and 1994b). For example, just after AT&T announced the layoff of 40,000 workers, James Meadows, the vice president for human resources and responsible for the policy, explained the corporate thinking about job mobility:

> In AT&T, we have to promote the whole concept of the workforce being contingent, though most of our contingent workers are inside our walls. Jobs [are being replaced by] projects [and] fields of work [are giving rise to a society that is increasingly] jobless but not workless.
>
> People need to look at themselves as self-employed, as vendors who come to this company to sell their skills. [Andrews 1996]

Within a few years, Mr Meadows' vision seemed to be coming to fruition. One report found:

> In fact, nearly one in five (18 per cent) of all American workers report they were laid off from a full- or part-time job during the 2000–2003 recession.

Among workers earning less than $40,000 a year, nearly one-fourth (23 per cent) were laid off from full-time work during this time. [Dixon and Van Horn 2003]

The business strategy of using unemployment is another example of what I earlier called the perverse consequences of the corporate abuse of power. Business uses its powers to harm the economy, making workers even more willing to grant concessions to their employers.

## COSTS OF JOB LOSS

This lack of job security imposes a heavy burden on workers. A recent British study showed that temporary workers have lower levels of job satisfaction, receive less training, and are paid less (Booth, Francesconi, and Frank 2002). Workers who frequently shift from job to job also have a difficult time in getting medical care and pensions.

Society still pays lip service to the sacred institution of marriage, despite the damage that job insecurity imposes serious burdens on family life. Many families break under the strain of unemployment. Even without the upheaval of unemployment, contingent employment imposes huge uncertainties on a household. Economic pressures often require both parties in a marriage to hold down a job. One spouse may have to relocate in order to maintain a career path. The family must face unpleasant choices in such a situation. Should the family separate or should one party sacrifice a career for the other spouse? Either choice imposes serious financial losses, over and above the personal costs associated with such a dilemma. The "trailing spouse" will have difficulty maintaining a successful career. Children have to adjust to new schools. Finally, for people who share custody of a child, the need for one to move can create additional hardships and extra expenses.

An interesting article suggests the difficulty of coordinating a dual career family in a slippery job market. The authors looked at households where both parties were college professors. They found that these families disproportionately locate in large metropolitan areas where the opportunity for both people to find jobs is higher. The authors suggest that this tendency reveals the difficulty of finding suitable employment for both parties in more remote locations. The article also reported: "The proportion of working 'power-couple' wives in such traditional female occupations as schoolteacher, nurse, librarian, or social worker fell from 72 to 43 per cent between 1940 and 1990" (Costa and Kahn 2000: 1291–2). One possible explanation for this decline would be that the wife in the family had difficulty finding suitable employment near the husband's job. Again, in the case of job instability, business imposes a cost on employees, while pocketing the profits that accrue from a flexible job market.

Over and above the time demands and emotional strain involved in relocation, moving imposes steep economic costs on workers. For example, for many families, homeownership represents their greatest material asset. Frequent relocation makes homeownership impractical since each round of buying and selling property entails substantial costs, not to mention the direct costs of moving one's belongings. In this sense, the risk of contingent employment is redoubled. To the extent that job insecurity makes people forgo purchasing homes, they lose the opportunity to profit from the appreciation in housing prices.

The costs associated with job insecurity go well beyond the cost and inconvenience of relocating. For many workers, a job loss can be traumatic. One study based on 1980 data estimated that raising the unemployment rate from 5 per cent to 9 per cent would lead to an additional 1,270 suicides (Sharipo and Ahlburg 1983). An earlier study found that a mere 1 per cent increase in unemployment rate will lead to 37,000 deaths if sustained over six years—not just from suicide, but from homicides and the deleterious effects on people's health (Brenner 1976). Unemployment scars other family members as well as the individual losing a job. To the extent that the effects of unemployment traumatize children, the costs of unemployment can carry over for decades.

Ironically, in the long run business will also pay a severe price for this supposedly efficient business strategy. Workers with long experience on the job develop valuable information, especially if management is intelligent enough to let them exercise judgment. By treating workers as disposable objects, business deprives itself of its capacity to draw upon workers' accumulated knowledge.

## MANIPULATION OF LABOR MARKETS

Manipulating the labor markets is a common, as well as effective technique for scaring workers. Business knows that if labor were to become relatively scarce, workers could take advantage of the situation to ask for better wages and working conditions. However, business has been able to rig the system to make sure that workers do not get such an opportunity.

Once workers seem poised to win higher wages—or even worse, to organize—business demands that the government institute policies in such a way that ensures business interests are served. For example, the government can open up the inflow of immigrant workers, whether it be for a Bracero program to strengthen farmers' bargaining position or to grant a large number of visas for immigrant computer programmers for the benefit of the high tech industries.

Business can also call upon the government to retard the pace of economic activity to prevent workers from taking advantage of a temporary scarcity of labor. This tactic changes the balance of scarcities in the sense that when the economy slackens, jobs rather than workers become scarce. This strategy ensures that workers enjoy a narrower set of options than investors do. So, by diminishing job opportunities, the government can augment the atmosphere of fear, undermining workers' confidence in demanding a better deal. With workers' aspirations limited, the government can accelerate economic growth once again.

Finally, business can take measures on its own, by shifting work to locations with abundant labor. For example, Jack Welch, once widely regarded as the most admired executive in the United States, shared his vision of the organization of the workplace when he was the CEO of General Electric: "Ideally you'd have every plant you own on a barge," meaning that he could easily move his operation if workers dared to demand better wages and working conditions (Weidlich 2002).

During the 1990s, the increasing lack of job security meant that employers needed far less unemployment to hold workers' demands in check. Alan Greenspan, Chairman of the Federal Reserve Board, began to speak to his colleagues at the Fed about the "'traumatized worker'—someone who felt job insecurity in the changing economy and so was accepting smaller wage increases. He had talked with business leaders who said their workers were not agitating and were fearful that their skills might not be marketable if they were forced to change jobs" (Woodward 2000: 163).

Greenspan has said as much publicly, but he uses language that is legendary for its obscurity. For example, the Chairman testified before Congress: "the rate of pay increase still was markedly less than historical relationships with labor market conditions would have predicted. Atypical restraint on compensation increases has been evident for a few years now and appears to be mainly the consequence of greater worker insecurity" (Greenspan 1997c: 254). The lack of clarity in this statement makes his words less harsh, but the meaning remains the same.

What Alan Greenspan says is not idle speculation. He is arguably the single most influential person in determining the level of overall economic activity. In addition, Greenspan has incredible access to the very best information available. For example, the Federal Reserve System employs literally hundreds of economists.

Greenspan is not alone in appreciating the benefit of low unemployment without wage increases. One of the governors at the Federal Reserve Board, Edward W. Kelley Jr. spoke up at a meeting of the Fed's Open Market Committee, its most important policy center, about "the good results that we are getting now":

> I don't know how much, [sic] has to do with the so-called traumatized worker. How long is the American workforce going to remain quiescent without the compensation increases that it thinks it should get? When employment is as strong as it is right now, I don't think we can depend on having permanently favorable results in that area. This has been a rather big key to the present happy macro situation where we have a high capacity utilization rate and a relatively low inflation rate. We all feel rather good about that. [Kelley 1995]

Kelley's "we" was not a very inclusive "we." Even so, Kelley and his circle welcomed a situation where economic growth was increasing profits, while wages were stagnating. I recall overhearing a conversation at an economics conference around 1992. I thought that I recognized the voice of the speaker behind me. I looked over my shoulder and confirmed that I was hearing Milton Friedman, the doyen of conservative economists, and Nobel Prize winner, enthusiastically explaining the implications of the prospects of trade with China.

Friedman made no mention of China's political and economic characteristics, which you might think would make close relations with China less than desirable in his eyes. Instead, he extolled the potential effect of expanded trade with China on U.S. labor markets. Friedman predicted that the potential addition of about 1.5 billion Chinese workers, many of whom would be producing for the U.S. market, would impose a decidedly negative effect on wages in the United States. Of course, China is not the only less developed economy whose products are supplanting those from the United States. China probably captured Friedman's interest only because of its immense size, comprising almost one-fourth of the world's population.

A few months later, the *Wall Street Journal* reported on Friedman's continuing enthusiasm for Chinese trade in a story about how workers were falling behind at the time: "It's not widely recognized how enormous this effect is," said Milton Friedman. "You've got a billion people in China who suddenly are available for use with capital. You have half a billion behind the (former) Iron Curtain" (Zachary and Ortega 1993).

A decade later, Friedman's expectations were more than borne out. Chinese goods pour into the United States, while the ability of Chinese consumers to purchase U.S. goods is modest, at best—at least for the time being. For example, in 2002 the difference between what China exported to America and what America exported to China stood at more than $100 billion worth of goods. As companies shift their production to China, Mexico, or any of the other far-flung regions that supply the United States, many Americans must "reinvent" themselves into work that is more insecure, worse paid, or even nonexistent.

Personally, I don't believe for a moment that the displacement of domestic labor is the primary purpose of the present U.S. trade policy. But, as the Friedman conversation suggests, that its effectiveness in creating a climate of fear was not absent from the policy considerations.

Free trade has the potential, as any economics text shows, to improve the well-being of humanity—especially, if the government provides those displaced by trade with the education and training to upgrade their skills to work productively in other sectors of the economy. Although existing legislation does authorize some modest retraining, distressingly little has been done in this regard. Instead, trade serves to "recruit" more workers into what Karl Marx called the reserve army of the unemployed.

Marx's metaphor in no way conflicts with Milton Friedman's analysis. Marx's military imagery, however, connects the ultimate effect of the earlier more violent methods of keeping labor in check with the more polite techniques that business uses today.

Labor is not unmindful of the stakes in this struggle. A study published by the Institute for International Economics, intended to address the public's qualms about corporate globalization, found that unskilled workers, who are most likely to be displaced by international trade, are the most antagonistic to globalization. Moreover, workers' attitudes do not seem to vary with the degree to which their industry is vulnerable to trade, perhaps suggesting that they see their situation in terms of their class status (Scheve and Slaughter 2001: 9).

The facts seem to bear out these workers' suspicions. Even though the Gross Domestic Product of the United States grew from $4.1 trillion in 1973 to $9.3 trillion in 2001, hourly wages corrected for inflation in 1982 dollars declined from $8.55 in 1973 to $8.17 at the end of 2001 (President of the United States 2002, Table B2: 322 and Table B 47: 376).

### MONETARY POLICY TO MAINTAIN UNEMPLOYMENT

Trade policy is a relatively indirect tool for keeping labor in check. Besides, governments cannot manipulate trade policies quickly enough to respond to the ebb and flow of the economy. Monetary policy is ideal in this regard, because the Federal Reserve Board can alter its policies at a moment's notice.

The Federal Reserve has a long tradition of using tight monetary policy to discipline labor when wages begin to rise. Similarly, when labor is relatively weak, the Fed is more willing to stimulate the economy by making money more available. For example, Alan Greenspan told the Senate Budget Committee on January 21, 1997:

> As I see it, heightened job insecurity explains a significant part of the restraint on compensation and the consequent muted price inflation .... The continued reluctance of workers to leave their jobs to seek other employment as the labor market has tightened provides further evidence of such concern, as does the tendency toward longer labor union contracts .... The low level of work stoppages of recent years also attests to concern about job security .... [However] we must recognize that ... suppressed wage cost growth as a consequence of job insecurity can be carried only so far. At some point in the future, the tradeoff of subdued wage growth for job security has to come to an end .... [E]ven if the level of real wages remains permanently lower as a result of the experience of the past few years, the relatively modest wage gains we've seen are a transitional rather than a lasting phenomenon. The unknown is how long the transition will last. Indeed, the recent pick-up in some measures of wages suggests that the transition may already be coming to an end. [Greenspan 1997a]

Greenspan's predecessor, Paul Volcker also emphasized the importance of using monetary policy to keep wages in check: "in an economy like ours, with wages and salaries accounting for two-thirds of all costs, sustaining progress will need to be reflected in the moderation of growth of *nominal* wages" (Volcker 1982).

Edwin Dickens, an economist from Drew University, has written a series of articles analyzing the minutes of the meetings of the Open Market Committee of the Federal Reserve Board back as far as the 1950s. He reports numerous occasions when participants voted to tighten the money supply with the specific intent of forcing employers to be less generous with their wage offers (Dickens 1995 and 1997).

Of course, permanent massive unemployment would be self-defeating. Relatively high levels of employment are necessary to maintain markets at a profitable level. Only after economic momentum improves workers' bargaining power does business call for tighter monetary conditions. So business calls for a balancing between the need for unemployment as a disciplinary device and the profits associated with a rapidly growing economy.

To make matters more complicated, government policies create what is often called a political-business cycle. When a new administration comes into office, it typically tends to tighten economic conditions, blaming its predecessor for making such actions necessary. As elections approach, the government makes serious efforts to boost the economy, thereby curtailing unemployment (see Soh 1986). In addition, although unemployment may be effective in disciplining workers on the job, unemployment often encourages people to vote for candidates who may be less sympathetic to business.

## THE WAGES OF FEAR

Fear, of course, can be a great motivator. In some circumstances, fear is a very useful condition. It can condition us to avoid hazardous conditions and can startle us to warn us of impending dangers. Fear can also be counterproductive. Consider the following example. Most people can easily walk for 50 feet on a narrow plank that lies on the ground. Let that same plank span a ravine with a 1,000 foot drop and the same walk can become terrifying. Why? Once we look down, we begin to think about the consequences of a misstep. The more we think, the more difficult the next step becomes. We begin to question our own abilities. Eventually, we can become consumed with doubt and can even end up confirming our worst fears.

In this vein, Amitai Etzioni noted: "A large body of research shows that under stress people's decision-making becomes less rational" (Etzioni 1988: 73). As long as business relies on fear to motivate workers, their performance will be less than optimal.

## RISKS OF WORKING

While unemployment is dangerous, working is even more so. One study found that, despite the undeniable health costs associated with unemployment, the net effect of increasing unemployment was an improvement in the overall mortality rates, in large part because of the decrease in work-related mortality and the falling off of alcohol consumption, which people use to release the stress of working (Ruhm 2000).

Besides being mind-numbing and unpleasant, work is often downright dangerous. For example, during the period 1980–98, approximately 109,000 civilian workers died from work-related injuries, an average of 16 deaths per day. In 1998 alone, 3.6 million workers were seen in hospital emergency rooms in the United States because of injuries that occurred on the job (Centers for Disease Control 2002). While less immediate than deaths from injuries, deaths caused by occupational diseases run almost ten times as high, at about 60,000 per year in 1992 (Leigh et al. 1997). In 1990, the American Public Health Association estimated that each year 350,000 new cases of occupational diseases develop from toxic exposures (Landrigan 1992).

Some work is obviously dangerous, but the combination of speedups, excessive overtime, and employer efforts to economize on safety has made the workplace far more destructive than it needs to be. In 1969, during the Vietnam War, the Secretary of Labor, George Schultz, later to become the Secretary of State and Bechtel Group President, remarked: "During the last four years more Americans have been killed where they work than in Vietnam" (Linder 1994: 57). No wonder, one early economist referred to those "killed and wounded in the industrial battle" (Marx 1977: 552).

Despite the enormity of the human toll, the government is lax in collecting data on the extent of deaths from occupational injuries and diseases (Linder 1994). The estimates of workplace injuries and diseases exclude the health costs associated with stressful working conditions. People who spent more than five hours per day in front of a computer screen tend to complain of headache, eyestrain, joint pain, and stiff shoulders (Nakazawa et al. 2002).

The continuing high rate of occupational deaths is extraordinary considering the massive deindustrialization that has been underway over the last few decades. Work in mines and factories is obviously more dangerous than white- or pink-collar jobs involving research, marketing, sales or accounting. Yet, despite the shrinkage of jobs in such risky occupations, the death toll remains shockingly high.

Despite the impression you get from watching evening news shows, far more people die from workplace injuries and diseases than from homicides. For example, the Federal Bureau of Investigation counted 13,752 murders and involuntary homicides in 1998, representing less than one-third as many deaths as the numbers of fatalities from occupational injuries and work-related diseases (United States Department of Justice 2002, Table 3.118).

Yet the deaths from occupational injuries and diseases go virtually unnoticed. When is the last time you watched a news feature about a worker who died on the job, unless some crazed fellow-worker with a gun caused that death? In contrast, the corporate media gives considerable detail to homicides. Some murders only appear on the local news. Other sensationalized cases receive endless coverage in the media.

The dangers that workers face are nowhere to be seen on the media, except, when a rescue team dramatically saves workers from a dangerous predicament. Typically, the report will focus on the rescue itself without commenting on the immediate cause of the workers' plight.

What explains the deafening silence regarding these tragedies of workplace death and disease? In part, the reason for the silence is that many of those who fall to occupational accidents and diseases are poor. Information about such occupational deaths may embarrass a potential sponsor or make the program seem anti-business. Not surprisingly, the corporate media tends to tread lightly on white-collar crime of all sorts, especially if it is responsible for workers' deaths.

Take as an example, the mostly immigrant labor force that works in slaughtering houses. According to the Bureau of Labor Statistics, meatpacking is the most dangerous occupation in the United States. According to Eric Schlosser:

In 1999, more than one-quarter of America's nearly 150,000 meatpacking workers suffered a job-related injury or illness. The meatpacking industry not only has the highest injury rate, but also has by far the highest rate of serious injury—more than five times the national average, as measured in lost workdays. If you accept the official figures, about 40,000 meatpacking workers are injured on the job every year. But the actual number is most likely higher. The meatpacking industry has a well-documented history of discouraging injury reports, falsifying injury data, and putting injured workers back on the job quickly to minimize the reporting of lost workdays. [Schlosser 2001b]

For example, the logbooks at the IBP Dakota City, Nebraska recorded 1,800 injuries and illnesses, but the logbook of the Occupational Safety and Health Administration (OSHA) recorded only 160 (Schlosser 2001a: 179–80).

The government does an abysmal job of protecting workers. To begin with, the Occupational Safety and Health agency is hopelessly understaffed. A couple thousand inspectors cannot possibly regulate the 6.7 million worksites in the country. Overworked inspectors often have little choice but to accept the employer's word.

To make matters worse, enforcement is excessively lenient. For example, an incident resulting in death or serious injury resulted in a median penalty of $480. An early study by Richard Zeckhauser and Albert Nichols observed that in 1975 federal inspectors visited an estimated 2 per cent of approximately 5 million workplaces. The average fine per violation was only $26. A 2 per cent chance of paying a $26 fine represents an expected cost of a mere 52 cents—hardly much of a deterrent (Zeckhauser and Nichols 1978: 205 and 208).

Despite the minimal costs of the fines it imposes, one study indicates that OSHA has the potential to be quite effective, finding that if an Occupational Safety and Health inspection results in a penalty, the plant experiences a 22 per cent decline in injuries during the next few years. The same study found that, despite its weak enforcement, OSHA is still responsible for about a 2 per cent decrease in the total number of injuries (Gray and Scholz 1991).

To put the weakness of the regulation of job safety into perspective: A 1992, AFL-CIO report noted that during the 1972–90 period the U.S. government spent $1.1 billion per year to protect fish and wildlife. In the same period, the government spent $300 million to protect workers from health and safety hazards on the job (see Reiman 1996: 70).

Job safety hardly appears in political dialogues. Instead, governments try to cut back on workers' compensation insurance payments to help injured workers. The media gleefully reports incidents of workers defrauding the system by falsely claiming injuries, but such deceit is not widespread. For example, the Ohio Bureau of Workers' Compensation employed 80 investigators to ferret out cases of fraud in 1994. The investigation led to 51 convictions and uncovered $52 million of fraudulent claims, or about 2 per cent of all the dollars going to compensation (Leigh et al. 2000: 195).

Many work-related deaths and injuries are avoidable. Frequently, the responsible employer was cutting corners, trying to get a little bit extra out of workers or just resisting a modest outlay for safety. Not infrequently, the employer is willfully flaunting the laws intended to protect workers' safety. Calls for enforcement are met by the claim that regulations are job killers rather than protection against killer jobs.

Symptomatic of that attitude was an article that *Government Executive* published in 1982, entitled, "White House Stop-Using-Drug Program—Why the Emphasis Is on Marijuana." According to this article: "While OSHA was created (in itself, a result, in part, of political pressure in Washington by anti-Big Business activists) and gushing regulations having to do with workplace machines and procedures, corporations themselves began attacking a major part of the problem where it really was—in alcohol and drug use by employees" (cited in Baum 1996: 188).

## THE PAIN OF SERVITUDE

Workers who manage to avoid the direct hazards of the workplace do not necessarily remain unscathed. Animal studies indicate that across a wide range of species, creatures that find themselves in subordinate positions suffer higher levels of stress, which has serious consequences for their health (see Sapolsky 1994: 261ff). Subordinate workers seem to suffer a similar fate.

Just as animals impose stress on subordinates by continually flaunting their dominance, something similar happens in the workplace. Most jobs require substantial conformity over and above the competent completion of tasks. Besides demanding a certain degree of deference, employers frequently expect workers to dress and to behave according to certain norms, even when these have nothing whatsoever to do with objective job performance.

Not infrequently, bosses get pleasure in dominating their subordinates in the workplace just as an alpha male would in the wild. Some psychologists even go so far as to identify sub-criminal psychopathic behavior in the workplace as an important subject of study. One study described how such bosses "can mask their antisocial traits" while acting out upon their subordinates (Babiak 1995: 172).

Subordination takes a toll on workers, even when the circumstances might seem reasonable. One study found that workers with little control in their jobs were 43 to 50 per cent more likely to die during a period of five to ten years than other workers who had high-stress jobs but more decision-making responsibilities. The authors suggested another possible pathway besides the direct toll that stress takes: "Passive work could represent work depleted of meaningful content. This alienating work could result in social disengagement and/or adoption of high risk behaviors that lead to mortality" (Amick et al. 2002: 378). Needless to say, although the government collects data on workplace safety, this more subtle toll on workers escapes the official statistics.

When I was young, I remember being struck by the number of symphony conductors and famous concert soloists who seemed to be quite vigorous at an age that I considered to be very old. In later years, as I reconsidered my observation, I realized that they probably had challenging work that they regarded as rewarding. Even later, I appreciated that they also had a great deal of control over their work, unlike the majority of employees. Obviously, no society could consist solely of symphony conductors, but even so, to the extent that working conditions can be made closer to those of symphony conductors, the health benefits would probably be greater than any possible scientific advancement.

Subordination is not the only cause of stress on the job. Recall how the threat of unemployment is used to keep workers in a continual state of fear. Traditionally, business absorbed much more of the risk of economic instability. Often, workers in jobs with frequent layoffs earned more per hour to compensate them for their periodic bouts of unemployment. The new emphasis on contingent employment means that now workers must absorb a great deal of the risk involved in business, over and above the other risks associated with working.

Rather than compensating workers for their lack of job security, average wages have been declining. Reductions in benefits have been even more extreme. Considering the other costs of job insecurity, such as the cost of relocation and the stress and strain on family life, workers' conditions are even more unfavorable. These factors must also take a serious toll on their health.

## THE LETHAL ECONOMY OF TIME

Many factors contribute to stress in the workplace, not least of which is the continual speedup common in many industries. Consider the example of the automobile industry:

> In the Mazda plant at Flat Rock, a suburb of Detroit, the application of just-in-time introduced production times never seen before in the United States. In the early 1980s the usual work pace at the Ford, General Motors and Chrysler plants covered between 40 and 50 seconds per minute, while the remaining 10 to 20 seconds were waiting or idle time ("dead" time, in terms of increasing the value of capital). Mazda, however, which at its Hofu plant in Japan manages to attain a saturation of working time close to 60 seconds a minute, at Flat Rock set—and achieved—the goal of keeping its workers working for 57 seconds of every minute. It thus gained a considerable advantage over its competitors, since working 12 seconds more per minute is equivalent to 12 minutes more every hour, 96 minutes per 8-hour working day, 8 hours per 5-day working week, which amounts to about 400 hours more per year for every single worker.
>
> The miracles performed by Toyota at the NUMMI plant in Fremont, California, a joint venture with General Motors, are even more astounding. Here, Toyota took an auto factory with low productivity and an even lower quality product and turned it into a super-productive factory, modeled on the Takaoka plant in Japan. The average number of seconds worked per minute jumped from 45 to about 57, and the rate of absenteeism was slashed from the 25 per cent of the old plant to between 3 and 4 per cent—which means that real hours rose overall by 40 per cent, without taking into account the further lengthening of hours intrinsic to Toyotaism (workers going in early to work, working overtime, taking part in quality circles and other after hours company activities). [Basso 2003: 63–4]

Such speedups are not merely a matter of making workers do their jobs more efficiently; they can result in crippling repetitive motion disorders, or even worse. For example, because of rapid line speeds at a Nissan plant in Smyrna, Tennessee workers experienced twice as many injuries per worker compared to the automobile manufacturing plants in the United States run by the Big Three—General Motors, Ford and Daimler-Chrysler (Welch 2003).

In other industries, the mayhem is even more extreme. For example, consider the slaughtering houses where cattle whisk by workers at breathtaking speeds. According to Eric Schlosser: "The typical line speed in an American slaughterhouse 25 years ago was about 175 cattle per hour. Some line speeds now approach 400 cattle per hour" (Schlosser 2001a: 173). The employees are expected to cut through pieces of this rapidly moving flesh and bone with sharp instruments. Life-threatening injuries, as I already noted, are commonplace. Those workers who escape serious injury must still feel considerable stress, especially when they see the physical consequences for their less fortunate fellow workers.

Even in less dangerous work, speedups can cause stress. For example, employees in call centers know that supervisors monitor their calls. Management expects workers to shave off milliseconds by avoiding the use of extraneous words, such as please and thank you. Yes, some businesses do script such niceties in situations where they believe that such exchanges might help to make a sale, but when such efforts would not add to profits they are discouraged.

For example, a journalist with *Wall Street Journal* reported how pleased managers were that they could train greeters at Wendy's Old-Fashioned Hamburgers to say, "HimayItakeyourorderplease?" —"a triumphant two seconds faster than is suggested in Wendy's guidelines" (Ordonez 2000). For many call center workers, repeated failures to follow scripts that can cut back on time spent with customers can result in termination.

A century and a half ago, Karl Marx observed that all economics ultimately reduces itself to the economics of time (Marx 1857–58: 173). In a slave economy, the masters organize the time of the slaves. In market society, the employers or their representatives organize the time of the employees. They also must ensure that the employees use this time efficiently—otherwise valuable profit opportunities can slip away.

The economy of time need not be such that everybody must work every second. Leisure can also be a valuable use of time, although those who profit by the work of others may not agree. In many precapitalist societies time, as such, was not a particularly scarce resource. During certain peak times, say at harvests, people would have to work long and hard. In between those intervals, time demands were minimal. For example, an eminent economic historian, Joan Thirsk, estimated that in the sixteenth and early seventeenth centuries, about one-third of the working days, including Sundays, were spent in leisure (cited in Thomas 1964: 63; see also Wilensky 1961). Karl Kautsky (1899: 107) offered a much more extravagant estimate that 204 annual holidays were celebrated in medieval Lower Bavaria.

Prior to the Industrial Revolution, the rich and powerful had largely succeeded in using the power of the state to take away the peasantry's traditional access to land. Once poor people in the countryside could no longer support themselves on the land, they had little choice but to attempt to work for wages. The hours were long and the work demanding. Even so, the political economists of the time still railed against what they considered to be widespread sloth on the part of the workers (Perelman 2000a, Chapter 1).

With the arrival of the Industrial Revolution, employers came to regard the normal working day as 10 hours or 12 hours or even longer. The more time workers spent in factories, the more profits they made for their exploiters. In this spirit, a British factory inspector in the mid-nineteenth century reported that a highly respectable master told him, "If you allow me to work only ten minutes in the day over-time, you put one thousand a year in my pocket." The master went on to add, "Moments are the elements of profit" (cited in Marx 1977: 352).

In effect, employers at the time saw the length of the working day rather than the tempo of production as the key lever to extracting more profit from their workers. In this new world of capital, people naturally came to equate time with money.

A central part of Karl Marx's *Capital*, first published in German in 1867, emphasized the role of labor time. Marx went into great detail about the way in which longer hours translated into higher profits for capital. For this reason, although many professors found the book virtually incomprehensible at the time, Marx's analysis of the extension of the working day resonated among workers, more so than any other part of his book.

Indeed, workers devoted considerable energy to resisting the long hours as best they could. By the late nineteenth century, workers enjoyed some modest success as the length of the working day began to fall. Just before World War I, workers in the United States experienced an unparalleled drop in the workweek. Workers were less successful in raising wages during that period. The increase in wages, adjusted for inflation, was one of the slowest on record (Hunnicut 1988: 17–18).

The changing nature of the workforce helps to explain the modest decrease in the workday. A rush of immigrants from southern and eastern Europe began to form a sizable portion of the workforce. These immigrants were not inclined to labor such long hours. As a result, workers frequently came to work irregularly or quit their jobs after a short time. For example, at the Ford plant in 1913, on a typical day, an average of 10.5 per cent of the workers would not show up. The annual turnover rate was 370 per cent, meaning that the company had to hire an average of more than three workers per year to staff one position (Slichter 1919: 266 and 243–4).

At the time, business was of two minds regarding shorter hours. Some business leaders warned that greater leisure would lead the workers into depraved lifestyles. Others were convinced that the extra leisure would allow workers to become more civilized. Presumably, such civilization would include developing a more "responsible" work attitude among the labor force (Hunnicut 1988: 20 and 28).

Finally, business was coming up against another barrier to profitability. Workers could pump out far more goods than people could afford to buy. The threat of underconsumption was an almost obsessive concern for business. A number of institutions offered prizes for the best essay capable of reassuring business that the problem of underconsumption was illusory. In 1921, Hazel Kyrk's book, already mentioned in the last chapter, won the prestigious Hart, Schaffner & Marx prize of $1,000 for her previously discussed essay on the subject, although the award was open to any subject. Her idea that workers could principally identify with their life as consumers resonated with a large share of the leadership of big business.

This part of the business community recognized that shorter working hours could open up a new market serving the recreational needs of the population. The automobile market, bolstered by a combination of freely available credit and a flood of advertising, was poised to take advantage of this market, as I discussed in the last chapter regarding General Motors. During the Great Depression, once the demand for automobiles had collapsed, even the stonyhearted Henry Ford, in an article entitled "The Fear of Overproduction," published in the popular *Saturday Evening Post*, declared "leisure [was] a cold business fact .... [W]here people work[ed] less they buy more [since] business is the exchange of goods. Goods are bought only as they meet needs. Needs are filled only as they are felt. They make themselves felt largely in the leisure hours" (Ford and Crowther 1930: 3; cited in Hunnicut 1988: 45–6).

Such concern about the quality of the workers' lives, even when it was commercially motivated, had its limits, as we shall see.

## SOVEREIGNTY IN THE WORKPLACE

Although ideologues of market society proclaim the centrality of consumer sovereignty, they did not seem to want consumer choice to extend to leisure. Of course, while in the workplace, workers are supposed to be workers rather than consumers. Certainly, they are not supposed to exercise their individual choice. When they do, leaders look upon them unfavorably.

Douglas Fraser, past president of the United Automobile Workers, used to tell a story about a young employee at the Twinsburg, Ohio stamping plant. A young man faithfully labored for four days a week, but he never came for the fifth day. The plant was loath to fire this worker because labor markets were so tight at the time. In fact, management was on a seven-day schedule because of widespread absenteeism. Finally, the plant manager confronted the young man, demanding to know why he regularly worked four days a week. The worker responded, "Because I can't make a living working three days a week" (Halberstam 1986: 488). Fraser, the union leader, disapproved of the young worker. He wanted his workers to earn high salaries so that they could purchase lots of consumer goods, but he did not want them to have the choice of more leisure.

As workers gradually won a shorter working day, employers became more intent on exercising their legal right to try to squeeze every second of effort out of their employees. A union carpenter in late nineteenth-century Chicago captured the workers' perspective on this stage of the economy of time. Asked about the new eight-hour day, he responded favorably: "yes; but if we won seven hours, half of us would be dead" (Linder and Nygaard 1998: 13; citing Cross 1989: 53–4).

Building on the philosophy that "Moments are the elements of profit," employers attempt to harvest profit from every available second. These free seconds represent leisure, but they can also be a physiological necessity.

Normally, these corporate conquests of time pass unnoticed, but occasionally when employers' excesses reach the point of absurdity or inhumanity, the public gets a view of the interior of the workplace. The actions of the Jim Beam Co., a producer of whiskey, recently came to public attention. The company instituted a new policy for workers on its Clermont, Kentucky bottling line that prevented workers from going to the bathroom more than once a day, except during scheduled breaks and lunchtime (Tejada 2002).

Parenthetically, the Jim Beam policy is somewhat ironic. After all, despite the attractive rhetoric of consumer sovereignty, the government typically seeks to restrict the access of supposedly sovereign consumers to mind-altering substances, presumably because such products erode the work ethic.

Much of the press could not resist the bathroom humor of the Jim Beam case. In fact, the restrictions on bathroom use are not humorous at all. Nor are they unique to Jim Beam. In fact, they are relatively common. Marc Linder and Ingrid Nygaard wrote a fascinating study of this subject, entitled *Void Where Prohibited: Rest Breaks and the Right to Urinate on Company Time* (1998). He is a prolific legal scholar and economic historian; she, a urogynecologist.

They show that the consequences of such restrictions go well beyond the temporary discomfort of postponing natural processes:

> A urogynecologist's practice is filled with women suffering from bladder problems, many of which could be alleviated or prevented by more humane policies. It is, of course, not only the bladder specialist who builds a practice based in part on the vicissitudes of employment. The orthopedist, chiropractor, or rheumatologist treats multitudes of patients with repetitive stress injuries such as carpal tunnel syndrome; the neurologist or ophthalmologist cares for patients with headaches or changes in vision; the gastroenterologist aids patients with severe constipation—the list goes on and on, all health problems related at least in part, if not wholly, to lack of opportunities to void, rest fatigued muscles, drink adequate fluids, and defecate. [Linder and Nygaard 1998: 9–10]

Linder and Nygaard describe an even more dramatic case of bathroom restrictions than that imposed by Jim Beam:

> At a Nabisco plant in Oxnard, California, which manufactured A-1 steak sauce, the world's supply of Grey Poupon mustard, and Ortega salsas, female workers filed suit in 1995, complaining that they had developed bladder and urinary tract infections from being forced to wait hours for permission to use the restrooms. When confronted with a supervisory ukase "to urinate in their clothes while working on the production line" or face three-day suspensions for using the toilet ... they "finally resorted to wearing diapers." Those unable to spend $41 per week on incontinence aids and laundry "wore

Kotex and toilet paper," although such make-shift protection is harmful when drenched in urine. [Linder and Nygaard 1998: 49]

The workers finally sued. A right-wing journalist, Emmett Tyrrell, ever mindful of the importance of personal responsibility, "thoughtfully counseled them to avail themselves of the special diapers that owners of Central Park's horse-drawn carriages had used for their horses" (Linder and Nygaard 1998: 49; referring to Tyrrell 1995).

Lunch breaks also make an inviting target for those intent on squeezing more working time from the day: According to Linder and Nygaard:

The world's most spectacular example of a shorter but less porous workday was, again, Ford's conversion of his Highland Park, Michigan, plant from two nine-hour shifts to three eight-hour shifts in 1914 in connection with his introduction of the $5 daily wage. By permitting lunch wagons to enter the factory, Ford was able to reduce the meal period to [a] "10 minutes gift"—including the time for washing hands and fetching food—just long enough for "a pick-up sandwich," which workers ate at "their places." By the 1920s, workers complained that only by applying Fordist methods to eating would it have been possible to gulp down lunch in the few minutes before they had to return to the line—often with an all-too predictable "Ford stomach." [Linder and Nygaard 1998: 16]

Given a choice, I assume that most workers would trade a loss of a few moments' wages in return for the right to relieve themselves when necessary or even to eat a meal without being under duress. But employers do not offer them such choices.

Employers' own choices, however, are not necessarily wise. The human body is limited in its ability to adjust to the relentless demands of industrial rhythms. As a result, a little accommodation on the part of the employer has the potential for significant payoffs in productivity.

In Germany, researchers have been studying the science of work since the late nineteenth century. Long ago, German studies showed that the all-out assault on workers' natural processes was actually self-defeating (Linder and Nygaard 1998: 20–1). Even Frederick Taylor, the father of scientific management who attempted to make a science out of driving workers as hard as possible, realized that periodic rests increased workers' productivity (see Kanigel 1997: 302–4, 331). More recently, studies have confirmed that the lack of rest breaks increases the risk of industrial accidents (Tucker, Folkard, and Macdonald 2003). On the whole, American employers have rejected such findings out of hand, undoubtedly, in part, because they will not tolerate any challenge to their unlimited command in the workplace.

So, sadly, whether on the job or unemployed, a worker's lot is not always an enviable one. No wonder that Walter Lippmann advised workers to identify with their lives as consumers!

## THE RETREAT TO CONSUMPTION

Lippmann's idea that people should judge their lives from their perspective as consumers rather than as producers certainly fell on fertile soil in the United States. Unlike Europe, where class lines were hardened, in the United States, at least outside of the South, they were somewhat more fluid. Several factors contributed to this situation besides the oft-noted absence of a traditional aristocracy. To begin with, the economy was growing relatively rapidly, allowing people to move up socially. Since the founding of the United States, rapid economic expansion caused skilled workers to be in short supply. By developing specific skills that were in demand, workers, especially from England or northern continental Europe, had a far greater chance of significantly increasing their standard of living than comparable workers in Europe.

In addition, waves of new immigrants were always available to take the lowest paying jobs. By keeping unskilled wages low, employers could afford to pay their skilled workers better wages, while economic growth allowed a fair number of the unskilled workers or their children to move up to better jobs.

So, in contrast to European workers who tended to see themselves as members of a class without much possibility of advancement, skilled American workers were more likely to identify with their specific craft rather than with their class. As a result, the European labor movement was able to put together a far more effective political strategy than its U.S. counterpart.

By the late nineteenth century, much of European business worked within a system of cartels. Frequently, unions helped business to enforce these cartels. Also in the United States, some businesses used unions to help them keep competition in check. However, in contrast to Europe, by the late nineteenth century the legal system in the United States frowned on cartels. The law did, however, permit a large part of U.S. business to combine. As a result, a huge merger wave almost completely transformed the economic landscape. Because the dominant corporations faced relatively little potential competition, they had no need for unions to help them stabilize their industries (see Robertson 2000, chapter 4).

While Lippmann was writing about the future of the working class as consumers, the giant corporations were investing in new technology that made obsolete many of the skills on which workers had pinned their hopes. So, between the late nineteenth century and the 1920s, big business felt confident enough to launch a strong anti-union campaign. In many industries, small business had difficulty competing with the giant corporations. In a desperate effort to survive, small business became even more anti-union than its large corporate counterparts.

In this environment, workers' ability to wield organized power as workers through unions was virtually destroyed. Workers no longer had the power to organize effectively to demand better working conditions, the way that European unions did. Nor did they have the clout to influence the political environment.

By the time Lippmann proposed that workers should console themselves with consumption, class lines in the United States had begun to become more rigid, but, of course, not absolutely fixed. Lippmann advised workers not to challenge the existing society. Instead, workers should work within the current system in the hopes that they could share in the fruits of future economic growth.

The enormous technical progress that has occurred since Lippmann wrote should have made a good life possible for all. Nothing of the sort happened. Once the Cold War began, about three decades after Lippmann's work appeared, the union movement had become so tame that it began to collaborate actively with the government to undermine unions in other countries that did not fall in line with the foreign policy of the United States (see Shorrock 2003).

As unions' strength disappeared, wages failed to keep up with productivity. For example, between 1979 and 2001 while the real Gross Domestic Product increased by about 88 per cent, the median family income in the United States increased from $44,255 to $51,407—only a 16 per cent increase (Mishel, Bernstein, and Boushey 2003, Table 1.1: 37). During the same period, the average hours worked by a married couple with children, where the head of household was between the ages 25 and 54, increased by almost 12 per cent (Mishel, Bernstein, and Boushey 2003, Table. 1.27: 100). So, as a very rough approximation, longer hours explain almost all of the increase in the median family's income.

These averages hide a perversity about working hours. In some families, wage earners are unable to find full-time work. Instead, they must satisfy themselves with part-time work, which often provides inadequate income. Others must work far longer hours than they would prefer because of mandatory overtime. Each extreme causes its own hardships, which average measures conceal.

The norm today for a married family is that both partners must work. For example, as Doug Henwood pointed out in his *After the New Economy*, a worker earning the average manufacturing wage would have had to work 62 weeks to earn the median family income in 1947. By 1973, 74 weeks were required; by 2001, 81 weeks (Henwood 2003: 39). As the work requirements continue to expand, by necessity, the typical American family begins to resemble that of Bill Cecil, the Chrysler employee mentioned earlier in this chapter, who worked an excessive number of hours in order to consume more.

Sadly, the market has done nothing to ensure an equitable sharing of the benefits of technology. In 1930, John Maynard Keynes speculated that productivity increases should make a three-hour workday possible in the near horizon (Keynes 1930: 329). Since then potential productivity has probably accelerated more than Keynes could have imagined.

Adding insult to injury, relatively little of the total working time in the United States actually goes to productive work. Instead, more and more time goes into activities that do little to improve the quality of life—work such as marketing, advertising, and financial speculation. I explored this subject in more detail in an earlier book, *Transcending the Economy: On the Potential of Passionate Labor and the Wastes of the Market* (Perelman 2000b). As a result, people who find themselves working increasingly long hours have little to show for their efforts.

## IMAGINE

Consider what would happen if society nurtured people instead of allowing business to drive workers as hard as possible. Imagine how productive the economy would be if schools were designed to encourage creativity. In a more rational society in which schools fostered creativity, some of the young people who are today languishing in unemployment or wasting away in prison instead could be excelling as scientists or teachers or in other productive endeavors.

Stephen J. Gould called attention to this potential almost a quarter of a century ago. Not long before, scientists had removed Albert Einstein's brain from his corpse, hoping to discover the source of his enormous creativity. The scientists found nothing unusual in the physical characteristics of the brain. Gould put his finger on the heart of the matter, remarking: "I am somehow less interested in the weight and convolutions of Einstein's brain, than in the near certainty that men and women of equal talent have lived and died in cottonfields and sweatshops" (Gould 1980: 151).

Think back to the GI Bill after World War II—perhaps the best investment the government ever made. People who would never have had the chance to get an education went to colleges and universities. Thousands and thousands of veterans took advantage of this opportunity, then used that education to contribute to society.

We can get a feel for the profound importance of the GI Bill for lower-class citizens from the account of a reunion of the 1944 high school class from Turtle Creek, Pennsylvania, a poor working-class community. Edwin Kiester, Jr., himself a beneficiary of the bill, wrote that his class had 103 male graduates in a high school class of 270. He reported with some evident pride that

> thirty earned college degrees, nearly ten times as many as had in the past; 28 of the 30 attended college under the GI Bill of Rights. The class produced ten engineers, a psychologist, a microbiologist, an entomologist, two physicists, a teacher-principal, three professors, a social worker, a pharmacist, several entrepreneurs, a stockbroker and a journalist [Kiester himself]. The next year's class matched the 30-percent college attendance almost exactly. The 110 male graduates of 1945 included a federal appellate judge and three lawyers, another stockbroker, a personnel counselor, and another wave of teachers and engineers. For almost all of them, their college diploma was a family first. Some of their parents had not completed elementary school—a few could not read or write English. [Kiester 1994: 132]

The experience of the Turtle Creek students was replicated throughout the country. As Kiester noted:

> the first GI Bill turned out 450,000 engineers, 240,000 accountants, 238,000 teachers, 91,000 scientists, 67,000 doctors, 22,000 dentists, 17,000 writers and editors, and thousands of other professionals. Colleges that had

languished during the Depression swiftly doubled and tripled in enrollment. More students signed up for engineering at the University of Pittsburgh in 1948 (70 percent of them veterans) than had in five years combined during the 1930s. By 1960 there were a thousand GI Bill-educated vets listed in Who's Who. [Kiester 1994: 130]

Nobody to my knowledge, certainly no economist, has ever tried to take account of the full impact of the GI Bill, either for people such as Kiester's classmates or for the nation as a whole. Such a work would be daunting, to say the least, because the ramifications of this transformation are so extensive. Of course, the impact of the bill goes far beyond the terrain that economists typically navigate.

Thomas Lemieux, a Canadian economist, and David Card, a fellow Canadian who teaches at the University of California, Berkeley and a recipient of the John Bates Clark award from the American Economic Association, have studied the Canadian version of the GI Bill, although from a relatively narrow perspective. The Canadian law did not affect Quebec as much as the rest of Canada since the French-speaking universities made no provision for returning veterans. By comparing labor productivity in Quebec and Ontario, they were able to estimate the effect of the Canadian version GI Bill on labor productivity. As would be expected, they found that productivity rose considerably faster in Ontario than Quebec (Lemieux and Card 1998).

This measure certainly understates the effect of the Canadian GI Bill in part because their methodology assumes that the improvements in Ontario would not affect Quebec. Certainly, some of the productivity improvements in Ontario would have filtered into Quebec, either because workers moved from one province to another or because of the spread of technology developed in Ontario.

In any case, we should not confine our interpretation of the GI Bill to the direct effect on labor productivity. The bill promoted a more egalitarian society by offering opportunities to people who could not otherwise have enjoyed them. To this extent, it promoted a sense of justice, as well as all the favorable outcomes associated with a sense of justice. It may well have contributed to the spurt in productivity that the industrialized countries enjoyed, beginning a decade or so into the postwar period after the beneficiaries of the GI bill had time to rise to strategic positions.

# 4

# Corporate Accountability

## CORPORATIONS AS INDIVIDUALS

In one sense, the United States has indeed witnessed the triumph of the most bizarre sort of individualism imaginable—corporate individualism. Some background to this assertion will be useful.

Corporate power has always been an important part of the United States. Corporations, such as the Massachusetts Bay Company, established a number of the original colonies that later formed the United States. At the time, however, the public viewed corporations with considerable distrust; governments only chartered corporations in return for an expectation that they would serve some public purpose. Even Adam Smith was leery of corporate power. He prided himself on his attack in *The Wealth of Nations* on the largest corporation of the day, the British East India Company. I might mention that he also tried to use his influence with powerful friends to land a job with the company.

In 1791, the government chartered the Bank of the United States. Just after the charter expired in 1811, the War of 1812 destabilized the financial system. In response, the government chartered the Second Bank of the United States in 1816. After Andrew Jackson successfully vetoed the recharter 20 years later, states began to grant corporate charters to banks more freely than they had been doing before, laying the groundwork for a more liberal attitude toward corporations in some quarters.

Soon thereafter states began competing with each other in luring corporations with lenient conditions for corporate charters. Even so, widespread distrust of corporations remained common among much of the population.

At the end of the Civil War, Congress passed the Fourteenth Amendment to the United States Constitution for the ostensible purpose of freeing the slaves. Representative Roscoe Conkling, one of the framers of the Fourteenth Amendment, claimed that he and his fellow legislators drafted the amendment with a secret purpose in mind. According to Conkling, they had intended all along that their handiwork would lay the groundwork for the corporate-sympathetic courts to grant corporations the same rights as individuals (Hacker 1940: 387; Beard and Beard 1933: 112–13; and Allen 1937: 83–4).

Indeed, the courts soon ruled that on the basis of this amendment, corporations were entitled to enjoy all the rights of individuals, over and above the rights that they enjoyed by virtue of their corporate charters. Oddly enough, these rulings actually were unfounded, since the original Supreme Court decision regarding corporate personhood, upon which all these later rulings supposedly rested, as I will discuss later, never happened.

In 1882, the same year that John D. Rockefeller formed his Standard Oil Trust, the Southern Pacific Railroad sued Santa Clara County, California regarding its tax bill. In the course of the proceedings, the railroad proposed that it should be afforded the full rights of an individual on the basis of the Fourteenth Amendment. Here, Conkling registered his claim about the original intent of the amendment. In its final decision, the court supposedly granted corporations Fourteenth Amendment rights. In fact, the decision actually said nothing about the amendment; however, the court recorder took it upon himself without any authority to insert the extension of Fourteenth Amendment rights to corporations. Although his words had no legal standing, other courts accepted them as if they were part of the decision, creating a body of precedents that have further reinforced corporate rights (Hartmann 2002: 99–125; Graham 1968).

A number of progressive historians lent credence to Conkling's claim that the supposed ruling in the Santa Clara case was exactly what the framers had originally intended. After all, Conkling and others on the congressional committee had been railroad attorneys (Hacker 1940: 387; Beard and Beard 1933: 112–13; and Allen 1937: 83–4).

Conklin's testimony has not stood up to modern scrutiny. The great jurist, Oliver Wendell Holmes, forcefully rejected Conkling's interpretation (Fairman 1987: 724–8). Modern historians also bristle at Conkling's admission (Graham 1938). In fact, Conkling, who by that time was actually in the pay of the railroads, had "resorted to fraud and misquotation" (Graham 1968: 17).

In the decades that followed, an immense merger wave began to spawn the system of giant corporations that rules society today. The courts ruled time and again that efforts to regulate corporations were unconstitutional on the grounds that such regulations would deny them rights guaranteed to individuals. The amendment was far less successful in promoting its original intent. By 1892, the Supreme

Court ruled in *Plessy* v. *Ferguson* that, in effect, the Fourteenth Amendment did not grant Blacks the same rights as other citizens. In the words of Barrington Moore: "the Fourteenth Amendment has done precious little to protect Negroes and a tremendous amount to protect corporations" (Moore 1966: 149). Another commentator was more specific, observing that "a property minded Supreme Court in the era culminating in *Lochner* v. *New York* in 1905, applied the 14th Amendment in ways that denied equality to blacks while developing a highly privatistic version of property rights" (Scheiber 1988: 142; see also McCurdy 1975).

Just what does it mean to treat corporations as individuals? Although corporations obviously are not human, they can wield enormous power well beyond what any human being could dream. Their charters grant them a possibility of immortality not available to ordinary human beings. A distinguished English jurist of the seventeenth century took a far more realistic view than modern jurisprudence, finding:

> a corporation ... is invisible, immortal, and rests only in intendment and consideration of the law .... They cannot commit treason, nor be outlawed, not excommunicate [sic], for they have no souls, neither can they appear in person, but only by attorney .... A corporation ... is not subject to ... death. [Coke 1612: 973]

Unfortunately, the law granted an artificial personhood to the corporations. How have modern corporations been able to use their particular version of personhood to stand above the law?

## CORPORATE CRIME AND PUNISHMENT

Ambrose Bierce, an acerbic journalist of the late nineteenth and early twentieth century, defined corporate status in his *Devil's Dictionary*: "Corporation: an ingenious device for obtaining individual profit without individual responsibility" (Bierce 1958: 25). Indeed, Milton Friedman, perhaps the most influential defender of the market, implicitly advocates antisocial behavior by insisting that "there is one and only one social responsibility of business—to use its resources and engage in activities designed to increase its profits so long as it stays within the rules of the game, which is to say, engages in open and free competition, without deception or fraud" (Friedman 1962: 133). Later, as I will show, Friedman's colleagues even dropped this minor qualification to the otherwise unlimited objective of profit maximization.

Of course, corporations' ability to get away with antisocial behavior does not depend on the power of academic writings—even when the writer is as influential as Milton Friedman. Corporations can muster more than enough economic and political influence to stifle the voices of those harmed by such behavior.

No matter what the cause, the government takes corporate crime so lightly that it does not even bother to publish statistics on this subject. A corporation is most likely to face indictment if it acts in a way that harms shareholders' interests. In those exceedingly rare cases when the courts do find a great corporation guilty of a different category of crime, the penalty is usually a modest fine that is pitifully small compared to the resources at the disposal of the corporation, even when willful violations of safety regulations causes the deaths of ordinary human beings.

Recall the earlier discussion of the obscene numbers of deaths caused by occupational injuries and diseases. Of course, the employer is not always to blame, but all too often they are. In fact, so many people have died at some firms that one might be forgiven for suspecting that a serial killer was at work. For example, nine people have died working at factories operated by the McWane Corporation, a company that has repeatedly flaunted safety regulations, according to an exposé by the Public Television Program *Frontline* and the *New York Times* (Barstow and Bergman 2003a; 2003b; and 2003c). Shockingly, the company had yet to face a serious penalty before the national media took up this case. Although the glare of publicity did eventually cause the government to charge the plant manager, maintenance superintendent, engineering manager, production superintendent, and a former human resource manager—no senior executives face prosecutions (Barstow 2003a).

McWane, however, hardly ranks among the corporate giants. In fact, relatively few large corporations ever face indictment, even when they create wholesale devastation. Even the tobacco firms faced only civil penalties for all the deaths that they helped to inflict on society.

Perhaps part of the disinclination to indict the mammoth organizations reflects the difficulty of winning a case in court. The great corporations can marshal far more powerful legal resources than government prosecutors can—especially when the government is anything but zealous in pursuing corporate felons. In addition, these corporations employ powerful public relations agencies who can effectively shape public opinion.

So even when the government charges a major corporation, winning a criminal conviction is almost impossible. For example, at least 200,000 workers have died from occupational injuries since 1972. These deaths resulted in only 151 referrals for criminal investigations. A mere eight people have actually served any time for these deaths, the longest sentence being six months. All but two of these convictions involved relatively small construction-related companies. The jail sentences for all of these deaths totaled less than 30 years. Of these 30 years, 20 were from a single case, a chicken-plant fire in North Carolina that killed 25 workers in 1991, in part because the owner had locked the exits, preventing the workers from escaping the blaze. In no case was a major corporation involved (Frontline 2003; Barstow 2003b).

The likelihood of convicting a major corporation for lesser crimes is even more slim. Of the 1,283 corporations convicted of federal crimes from 1984 through 1987, only about 10 per cent crossed the threshold of $1 million in sales and 50 employees; less than 3 per cent of the convictions concerned firms big enough to have traded stock (Cohen 1989: 606).

Those corporations that escape conviction suffer no consequences for the harm that they do. For those corporations that do face monetary sanctions, the penalty is light. Total monetary sanctions imposed on the small number of corporations that are convicted represent an average of only 33 per cent of the estimated monetary value of the harms caused. If we only include direct fines, then the ratio of fines relative to monetary value of the harm falls to a mere 10 per cent (Cohen 1989: 618: Table 6).

Whether in terms of the size of the corporation or the enormity of the crime, the smaller perpetrators are more likely to face higher sanctions than corporate criminals that practice grand larceny. This perverse relationship, commonly observed in the treatment of ordinary criminals, also applies to economic crimes. You can see a strong inverse correlation between the size of the harm done and the sanction as a percentage of the magnitude of that harm (Cohen 1989: 617–68). One study found:

a firm causing up to about $50,000 in harm can expect to pay about twice that amount in criminal penalties and restitution. However, a firm causing over $1 million in harm is likely to pay less than the harm it caused in criminal fines and restitution. [Cohen 1989: 658]

Consider the pattern when the government imposes penalties on military contractors for defrauding the government. One recent study revealed just how little such fines affect the value of their stock. For one of the top 100 defense contractors the penalty caused a statistically insignificant decline of 0.39 per cent in value of the firm, judging by the stock market. For firms that are not among the 100 largest, the mean effect is more than ten times as large, at 4.46 per cent (Karpoff, Lee, and Vendrzyk 1999).

In addition, corporations found guilty of some crime can negotiate what are called deferred prosecution agreements. Under such arrangements, the government need not publicize the outcome. If the corporation merely ceases its illegal activities, the charges are dropped after a period as short as a year (Mokhiber and Weissman 2003).

Knowing that the probability of a serious penalty is virtually nonexistent, corporations see little reason to be overly concerned about violating laws and regulations. Economists even apply what they call a "rational cheater" model to describe such behavior (Nagin et al. 2002). For example, employers regularly fire union supporters, in flagrant violation of the law. They jokingly characterize the back-pay awards made to reinstated labor activists as a "hunting license" fee (Norwood 2002: 247).

One case stands out as an exception to usual leniency for corporate crimes. In 1961, the government convicted Westinghouse and General Electric for price fixing. These companies, along with some lesser firms, met to conspire to rig their bids and then falsified records (Mokhiber 1988: 217). F. F. Loock, president of the Allen Bradley Company, one of the corporations indicted by the Philadelphia grand jury in the price-fixing conspiracy case, displayed the arrogance of the conspirators, commenting about a meeting the corporate representatives attended in order to set prices: "No one attending the gatherings was so stupid that he didn't know that the meetings were in violation of the law. But it is the only way a business can be run. It is free enterprise" (Mokhiber 1988: 218; citing Smith 1961: 178).

As might be expected, the judge imposed relatively trivial fines compared to the earnings of the giant corporations. General Electric, which faced the largest judgment, had to pay only $457,000, an amount that represented only one-tenth of 1 per cent of its earnings over the five-year period that the conviction covered (Herling 1962:

319). As noted by John Herling, the author of a book concerning the case, General Electric was hardly a first time offender:

> In December, 1961, the Justice Department ... listed 39 antitrust actions against GE, 36 of them since 1941. These included 29 convictions, seven consent decrees, and three "adverse findings" of the Federal Trade Commission. To the Justice Department this indicated "General Electric's proclivity for persistent and frequent involvement in antitrust violations" in all branches of industrial production. Westinghouse could show almost as cluttered a record in antitrust violations. [Herling 1962: 320 fn]

Can you imagine what would happen to a shoplifter who was determined to ply his trade time and again? While the monetary dimensions of this judgment were insignificant, the penalty did have one unusual feature that made this verdict unique. The judge sentenced three vice presidents to spend 30 days in jail (Mokhiber 1988: 220). I recall the reactions of business people at the time who were absolutely shocked that respectable executives could find themselves in prison, even for a few days.

The "harsh" penalties paid by the three executives seemed to send a message to the corporations. The prices of turbine generators and other heavy electrical equipment that they conspired to inflate soon fell by nearly 70 per cent (Keller 1977: 74).

Alas, nothing similar has happened for four decades. Executives of major corporations no longer have any reason to fear that they will face incarceration for carrying out illegal policies to maximize corporate profits, except possibly when the victims are rich investors or other corporations.

### THE CORPORATE OBLIGATION TO COMMIT CRIME

Not only do corporations not have to face the same consequences as human beings, but many people in power actually encourage corporations to ignore the law. In contrast, the state frequently incarcerates human beings for fairly minor infractions. Repeat offenders face especially serious consequences. For example, in 2003 the Supreme Court upheld a California law that sentences people previously convicted of a serious crime to life imprisonment for petty offenses, such as minor shoplifting.

No corporation—not even one that has defrauded the public of billions of dollars—has ever faced anything comparable to a day of prison time—not even for repeated offenses. The death penalty for corporations is unthinkable, no matter how many deaths that a corporation might cause. Instead, defenders of the corporations insist that society does not have the right to prosecute corporations for criminal activity.

During the height of the scandal involving Enron's multibillion-dollar frauds, a *Wall Street Journal* opinion piece entitled "Corporations Aren't Criminals" noted: "Under the common law, a corporation could not be guilty of a crime because it could not possess mens rea, a guilty mind" (Baker 2002). Sadly, the author was correct—at least insofar as the current courts are concerned.

In the eyes of some judges, the law goes even further than merely ruling that corporations that violate the law lack a guilty mind. They insist that corporate managers, who do possess a *mens rea*, actually have an ethical responsibility to violate the law when doing so will prove profitable for stockholders. Corporate executives might face penalties if they illegally harm their corporate employer, but if their actions harm others, they can rest easily. Conservative legal scholars applaud such leniency.

For example, Frank H. Easterbrook and Daniel R. Fischel, the former a federal judge as well as a senior lecturer at the University of Chicago School of Law, wrote:

> It is not true, however, that there is a legal duty to enforce every legal right .... Managers do not have an ethical duty to obey regulatory laws just because those laws exist. They must determine the importance of these laws. The penalties Congress names for disobedience are a measure of how much it wants firms to sacrifice in order to adhere to the rules: the idea of optimal sanctions is based on the supposition that managers not only may, but also should violate the rules when it is profitable to do so. [Easterbrook and Fischel 1982: 1171 and 1177 n]

Richard Posner, another influential federal judge, who is also a prolific author and a senior lecturer at the same University of Chicago School of Law as Fischel, made a similar assertion (Posner 1986). When Milton Friedman, the University of Chicago colleague of these legal scholars, had proposed that the only responsibility that corporations have is the duty to maximize profits without taking any social concerns into consideration, within the bounds of the law, his position was controversial. A few decades later, federal judges now propose that the obligation to earn profits overrides the law, their position does not stir up protests. So we should not be surprised that reputable economists find Posner's article praiseworthy. As one article in the Chicago Law School's prestigious *Journal of Law and Economics* suggests:

Even when top managers have direct knowledge about the fraudulent activities, they may be pursuing projects that, prospectively at least, have positive net present value. That is, managers can commit frauds as part of a value-increasing strategy. As Richard Posner suggests, incumbent managers' comparative advantage may derive in part from their willingness to commit or tolerate fraudulent activities. [Agrawal, Jaffe, and Karpoff 1999: 315]

The University of Chicago has a long tradition of contemplating the economics of crime. In 1968, Gary Becker, long associated with Chicago and like Friedman a Nobel laureate, wrote his famous article, "Crime and Punishment: An Economic Approach" (Becker 1968). He proposed that the appropriate method of preventing crime is to increase penalties. To my knowledge, nobody within the Chicago orbit ever proposed to make the penalties more stringent.

The management of the firms caught in the recent spate of corporate scandals—Enron, WorldCom, Tyco, etc.—may have deluded themselves into believing that they were increasing the value of their firms, even as they were enriching themselves. They may not even have believed that they were engaging in criminal activity. The sort of calculations that Easterbrook and Posner seem to have had in mind was a situation in which management knew that they were doing serious harm, but persisted because the prospective profit outweighed the penalties.

Easterbrook and Posner reflect a more common view that business is by definition an activity that allows people to operate unconstrained either outside authority or by their own conscience. In the words of one commentator:

A red light, or the upraised palm of a traffic policeman, brings people to stop (at least in places where people tend to obey them) not by the exercise of power—neither a light nor a hand can stop a moving automobile—but by the exercise of authority .... Many citizens who would unhesitatingly stop for a red light, even at a deserted intersection at 2:00 a.m., would painstakingly calculate the relative cost and benefits of breaking laws against environmental pollution, insider trading in securities, of failing to report income to the

Internal Revenue Service, and then obey or violate the law according to how the calculation worked out. [Fields 1990: 113]

The classic case of a corporation calculating that the probable economic penalties would not threaten potential profits concerns the Ford Pinto. From 1971 to 1976, Ford placed the fuel tank of this car only six inches from the rear bumper. In even a minor rear collision these tanks were liable to be punctured by bolts protruding from the differential housing. Any spark from a cigarette, ignition, or scraping metal could then engulf both cars in flames (Estes 1995: 196–7; see also Dowie 1977). By conservative estimates Pinto crashes caused 500 burn deaths to people who would not have been seriously injured if the car had not burst into flames. Mark Dowie's classic article on the Pinto suggested that the figure could be as high as 900 (Dowie 1977).

Ford was aware of the dangers. Crash tests showed that a simple rubber bladder inside the gas tank could have prevented fuel from spilling from ruptured tanks. The cost of rectifying the problem would have been a mere $5.08. Another effective change would have cost a mere $11. However, Ford's cost-benefit analysis showed that the resulting deaths and injuries avoided would be insufficient to justify an outlay of $11 per car (Estes 1995: 196–7).

Ford is not alone in weighing the costs and benefits of lethal design failures. In 1973, General Motors was making a similar calculation, expecting that the company could save money by paying out the costs of 500 deaths from its vehicles rather than fixing its defective fuel tanks at a cost of $8.59 per vehicle (Court 2003: 16; Bakan 2004: 61–3).

You might find such calculations despicable. I do, but apparently not everybody does, including federal judges. Just imagine the outrage if some foreign terrorists had conspired to kill more than a thousand people. But, in the business world, knowing that the likelihood of a penalty is small and that the likelihood of a serious penalty even smaller, firms have little reason to fear the consequences of their actions.

In conclusion, although people who defend corporate rights are commonly quick to call for individual responsibility, they are less inclined to demand a comparable degree of corporate responsibility. Instead, they ignore corporate crime or find legalistic excuses for corporate misbehavior. So, if corporations are individuals in the eyes of the law, they are individuals with a special privilege to ignore the law.

## RESPONSIBILITY AND TORT REFORM

Given the absence of criminal penalties for corporate misbehavior, society needs an alternative means to protect itself against corporate abuses. Ideally, effective regulation might help to keep corporations in line, but the regulatory structure in the United States is embarrassingly weak.

Part of the problem reflects the political organization of the United States. The framers of the Constitution deliberately constructed a fragmented government with limited powers, impeding the creation of effective regulatory mechanisms. In contrast, the governments of Western Europe have stronger and more unified bureaucracies that more actively regulate economic activity. As a result, the European public depends more on the government to handle what in United States must be subject to litigation.

In the absence of criminal sanctions or effective regulation, the civil courts represent perhaps the last, and sadly all too often the only avenue of protection for Americans (Burke 2002: 8). With the massive deregulation of business during the last two decades, the need to rely on the courts has become even more extreme.

Admittedly, litigation creates an enormous waste of resources. To get a rough handle on the overall economic cost of litigation, one study of 35 countries used the presence of physicians as an indicator of productive labor. The authors found that the more lawyers per physician in a country, the slower growth would be (Magee, Brock, and Young 1989: 119–20).

Since the likelihood that a corporation will obey the law depends on the likelihood of potential sanctions, only huge judgments can deter business from cutting corners, even where public safety is put at risk. Reducing the costs that corporations face obviously increases their incentive to ignore legal requirements. For example, Ford never faced criminal charges in the Pinto case. Instead, those who suffered injury or their loved ones could only sue the company for damages in civil court.

In an effort to cut off this last avenue of redress, corporate interests loudly complain about the excessive costs of litigation. A frequently cited actuarial study prepared by Tillinghast-Towers Perrin indicates that tort costs rose from $67 billion in 1984 to $152 billion in 1994

(United States Congress 1996; citing Tillinghast-Towers Perrin 1995). The press, echoing the corporate public relations machine, often gives the impression that the majority of these cases involve product liability, but Ralph Nader's Public Citizen's web site reports that this category accounts for only about 400,000 of about 19.7 million civil cases filed annually according to the National Center for State Courts (Conlin 1991; Public Citizen 1998).

Michael Rustad, a law professor who reviewed the available empirical studies of product liability cases, reported that each and every one of these studies concluded that punitive damage verdicts are rare (Rustad 1998: 54). In addition, he found that "[a] typical defendant in a products liability case is a national corporation, not a small business. The majority of primary defendants assessed punitive damages in medical malpractice cases are corporate defendants such as nursing homes, hospitals or health care organizations" (Rustad 1998: 54).

Business is not immune from the hysteria about tort reform. In 2004, when Democratic presidential candidate John Kerry chose John Edwards, a trial lawyer, to be running mate, business reacted with anger, even though Edwards' voting record was hardly anti-business. The *Wall Street Journal* reported:

> there is nothing that makes America's CEOs see red these days like America's trial lawyers. "It's visceral," says one person who works with a group of chief executives. "You can feel it in a room." The nation's top executives view the plaintiff's bar as modern-day mobsters, shaking down corporations by bringing endless lawsuits that are too costly and too dangerous to litigate and that result in settlements costing billions to the corporate bottom line. The antipathy, while not new, has never been greater. [Murray 2004]

The so-called tort reform movement effectively uses expensive (but misleading and sometimes even fictitious) examples to argue against an individual's right to sue corporations. In fact individuals rarely win their cases and even when juries award individuals huge sums to plaintiffs, they rarely see that much money. Instead, appeals or prior agreements between opposing lawyers reduce the actual payment (see Hallinan 2004).

Yet, corporations themselves do not hesitate to initiate litigation. Recall, for example, our earlier discussion of SLAPP suits designed to intimidate individuals from participating in political activity.

Suits between corporations occupy far more of the court's time than product liability cases do.

Rarely does the public hear about such corporate abuse of the legal system, even though the stakes are far larger in corporate proceedings. The suit between Texaco and Pennzoil is emblematic of the costs of massive corporate litigation. From 1984 to 1988, these two corporate giants battled one another in the courts. Pennzoil initially won a judgment of more than $10 billion, but the ultimate settlement was reduced to a mere $3 billion. In the aftermath of the suit, Texaco's value fell by far more than Pennzoil's rose because of the money that the litigation consumed. In addition, the corporations had to devote time and energy to the litigation over and above what the lawyers cost. Not surprisingly, the combined equity of the two firms fell by about $21 billion, many times more than the legal fees incurred in the course of the litigation (Cutler and Summers 1988).

In the end, the public pays for this litigation. The cost of administering the legal system for these trials absorbs public money that could be used to fund education or healthcare. In addition, corporations pass their own litigation costs on to the public.

Despite the relatively small size of most product liability suits, they do represent a considerable threat to a few industries that work with hazardous materials, such as tobacco and asbestos. Other than such rare exceptions, product liability suits mostly are a nuisance, but they do not threaten the economic foundation of industries. However, if product liability suits were more effective, the hazards that corporations pose would be far less dangerous.

In public, corporate executives complain loudly about the costs of liability suits; in more private outlets, they tell investors that such costs are inconsequential. For example, Frank Popoff, CEO of Dow Chemical, has warned that product liability costs are "a killer for our global competitiveness." Yet Dow's annual report to its investors blandly declares, "It is the opinion of the company's management that the possibility that litigation of these [products liability] claims would materially impact the company's consolidated financial statements is remote." Similarly, Monsanto's vice president for government affairs has charged that liability litigation "clogs our courts, curtails American innovation and creativity, drives up the costs of consumer products, and prevents some valuable products and services from ever coming to market." Yet Monsanto's report to shareholders concludes that "while the results of litigation cannot be predicted with certainty, Monsanto does not believe these matters or their ultimate disposition will have a material adverse effect on Monsanto's financial position" (Stefancic and Delgado 1996; citing Nader 1995).

Nonetheless, since political influence is so inexpensive compared to the potential savings that such influence offers, many corporations generously contributed millions of dollars to the tort reform movement, which aims at curtailing product liability suits (see Alliance for Justice 1993: 52–69). For example, the Manhattan Institute solicited contributions from corporations that could profit from its extensive ability to shape the debate about corporate liability:

> The think tank claimed to make "the rhetoric of liability reform incorporate transcending concepts like consumer choice, fairness and equity"; and ensure that the "terms of debate remain favorable" by paying scholars to write books that articulate the corporate position and are then read by judges, commentators, and talk-show hosts. The think tank boasted, "Journalists need copy, and it's an established fact that over time they'll 'bend' in the direction in which it flows. If, sometime during the present decade, a consensus emerges in favor of serious judicial reform, it will be because millions of minds have been changed, and only one institution is powerful enough to bring that about .... We feel that the funds made available will yield a tremendous return at this point-perhaps the 'highest return on investment' available in the philanthropic field today." [Court 2003: 42–3]

Two senior fellows at the Manhattan Institute, Peter Huber and Walter Olsen, have been among the most prominent figures in the campaign for tort reform. According to Huber, lawyers cost the economy more than an astounding $300 billion a year in indirect costs (Huber 1988). How did Huber come up with such a number? It was easy:

> From a single sentence spoken by corporate executive Robert Malott in a 1986 roundtable discussion of product liability, Huber, in his 1988 book *Liability: The Legal Revolution and Its Consequences*, adopted an unsubstantiated estimate that the direct costs of the U.S. tort system are at least $ 80 billion a year—a number far higher than the estimates in careful and systematic studies of these costs. Huber then multiplied Malott's surmise by 3.5 and rounded it up to $ 300 billion—and called that the indirect cost of the tort system. The 3.5 multiplier came from a reference in a medical journal editorial concerning the effects on doctors' practices of increases in their malpractice insurance premiums. Huber's book contained no discussion

of the applicability of this multiplier. It would appear that Huber, who has recently taken to lecturing on the dangers of "junk science," certainly knows whereof he speaks. [Galanter 1992]

Despite such shoddy research in one of the key documents in their campaign, corporations and the think tanks that represent their interests have been remarkably successful in promoting their one-sided version of tort reform. For example, even before the Republican takeover of Congress in 2002, the American Tort Reform Association listed some of their numerous victories:

Since 1986, 45 states and the District of Columbia have enacted ATRA-supported tort reforms into law. Thirty states have modified the law of punitive damages; Thirty-three states have modified the law of joint and several liability; Twenty-one states have modified the collateral source rule; Twenty-nine states have penalized parties who bring frivolous lawsuits; seven states have enacted comprehensive product liability reforms; Medical liability reforms have also been enacted in most states. [http://www.atra.org]

President George W. Bush has adopted the cause of tort reform as a high priority. He repeatedly interjects the following statement in his talks: "Frivolous lawsuits drive up the cost of health care, and they therefore affect the Federal budget. Medical liability reform is a national issue that requires a national solution," as if frivolous malpractice suits are a major problem in the health care crisis that plagues the United States today (Bush 2004).

In addition to modifying unfriendly laws, corporations have been very successful in engineering the defeat of elected judges who are sympathetic to consumers. This tactic intimidates judges who will be careful not to offend corporate sensibilities.

More recently, the tort reform movement scored an even greater victory. In 2003, the Supreme Court in *State Farm Mutual Automobile Insurance Co.* v. *Campbell et al.* limited punitive damages on the grounds of the Fourteenth Amendment—a further indication of the extent to which this amendment has defended corporations rather than real individuals. The court ruled that punitive damages must be proportionate to the actual losses suffered by individual plaintiffs. Although the court did not set an outright cap on damages, it noted that a ratio of more than 4-to-1 "might be close to the line of constitutional impropriety" (Court 2004).

This decision severely restricts punitive damages. Just imagine that the penalty for bank robbery would be that individual depositors could sue for four times the value of their account. Would that arrangement deter bank robbery?

This State Farm decision will strongly limit corporate liability in the future. One conservative supporter of the decision reported: "The effect of State Farm v. Campbell on ... blockbuster punitive damage awards was almost immediate" (Viscusi 2004: 16). Lowering the liability for damages has several effects. With reduced potential liability, those suffering harm will have more difficulty in finding attorneys willing to take their cases on contingency. As a result, corporations will face fewer lawsuits. Even if the firms lose their case the costs will be much less. So, under the new rules, corporations will have little incentive not to put the health and safety of the public at risk.

In the same session that the Supreme Court decided the State Farm case making large punitive awards from corporations more difficult, it also upheld California's three strikes law that allows life sentences for shoplifting. The coupling of these two decisions is indicative of the imbalance between corporate rights and human rights in the United States today.

Not satisfied with rewriting the law, corporations are increasingly developing their own private tort reform by requiring their customers, often unwittingly, to sign away their right to sue. Any grievance goes to an arbitration board instead of the court. All too often, the corporations themselves get to select the arbitrators.

In short, corporations demand for themselves freedom from criminal sanctions, freedom from civil liability, and freedom from government regulations—all the while demanding for themselves all the rights and privileges of a real life person.

In closing, I might mention one towering irony in the tort reform movement. Recall the pious—almost mystical—belief in consumer sovereignty espoused in powerful circles. Within the context of consumer sovereignty, the individual consumer is supposedly intelligent enough to be the best judge of how to operate in the economy. The same conservative interests that credit consumers with great rationality in one sphere of activity—namely, consumption—would have us believe that as jurors, these same people suddenly fall into wild fits of irrationality, awarding claimants in product liability suits obscene amounts of money. I cannot understand why these otherwise intelligent people would suddenly change the moment that they sit in the juror's box.

## SUBCONTRACTING

Corporations use a number of tactics in order to avoid responsibility, even when criminal liability is not at issue. Because corporations can spawn new corporations with relative ease, they can use these subsidiaries to shield activities that they prefer not to be exposed to public scrutiny. This technique is particularly effective when their corporate offspring exist offshore.

Outsourcing provides an even more convincing form of plausible deniability. For example, companies that spend millions and millions of dollars to create an attractive image for consumers would be embarrassed if the public were to learn that they ran abusive sweatshops. Recall the suit against Nike's claim that the company made sure that its products were produced under humane conditions. Nonetheless, corporations want to enjoy the immense profits made possible by underpaid labor. By putting this work out for bid to outside contractors, they can deny that they have responsibility for the poor treatment of the workers.

To further insulate themselves from responsibility, corporations often require the subcontractors to sign contracts, agreeing to create relatively benign conditions for their workers. The subcontractors who submit the lowest bid will win the contract. Since the work to be done is quite unskilled and the potential for technological savings is limited, the corporations know full well that the subcontractors will only be able to profit through a ruthless exploitation of their employees. Nonetheless, corporations routinely demand lower and lower bids from their subcontractors, virtually forcing them to violate workers' rights. In the event of public exposure of the working conditions in the sweatshops, the corporations can claim ignorance, pretending that they demand that each and every one of their subcontractors adhere to the highest ethical standards.

Such practices are not only limited to sweatshops in far off lands. Corporations use subcontracting to cut the costs of unskilled labor in the United States, hoping that the invisibility of these people might absolve them from responsibility. For example, companies, including some that otherwise have relatively good relationships with labor, have begun to hire janitorial firms to clean their premises.

These subcontractors frequently hire undocumented workers. For example, taking advantage of these powerless immigrants, unscrupulous employers often refuse to pay for overtime hours. Again, the company that hires the subcontractor can deny all responsibility for any such abuses.

Corporations use numerous other subcontracting-like techniques to avoid responsibility. For example, if a corporation wants to pursue a shady deal, it can set up another company, a Special Purpose Entity in another location beyond the reach of U.S. regulations. Unless some unexpected event, such as a bankruptcy, brings it to the attention of the regulators, the corporation can avoid accountability. The ultimate purpose of many of those Special Purpose Entities is often to avoid regulation or to confuse potential investors (see Portnoy 2003).

# 5

# Accountability vs. Responsibility

### INTRODUCTION

Accountability has become an increasingly popular term for conservatives in recent years. The rhetoric of accountability differs from the rhetoric of responsibility. Responsibility seems to apply to individuals who make choices on their own. Accountability applies to individuals working within a bureaucratic framework, especially one that corporate interests want to change.

One could be forgiven for believing that American society has elevated accountability into a religious doctrine. The term, accountability, has an authoritarian twinge, in a sense that those who speak of accountability rarely suggest a parallel commitment to support those whom they hold accountable. People in authority generally impose accountability standards only when it is convenient for them. In other words, superiors hold their subordinates accountable. Subordinates rarely, if ever, get the opportunity to apply those same standards of accountability to their superiors. So, while demanding accountability from others, those in power consider themselves above accountability, apparently because they already know how wonderful their performance is.

In private, corporate executives are more candid about their ethical standards. As CEO of RJR-Nabisco, Ross Johnson famously enunciated the three rules of Wall Street: "Never play by the rules. Never pay in cash. And never tell the truth" (Burrough and Helyar 1990: 489). In this spirit, corporate executives commonly lavish goods on themselves without any accountability, except when some event, such as bankruptcy, causes outsiders to scrutinize their behavior. For example, the once-admired, ex-Tyco CEO Dennis Kozlowski had the corporation supply him with a $15,500 sewing basket, a $6,000 umbrella stand, and a $6,300 wastebasket, among other things. None of these items seem essential to a well-functioning corporation.

The government also seems to be allergic to accountability. Take, for example, the case of missile defense, a centerpiece of the military budget of the George W. Bush administration. Although noted scientists have repeatedly warned that this technology is probably impractical and certainly not cost effective, leading purveyors of weapons are heavy contributors to the campaigns of elected officials. So, in early 2003, in its rush to get this technology in place, the administration of George W. Bush inserted language in its 2004 budget proposal granting the Defense Department the right to ignore its normally-required responsibility to first test the effectiveness of a weapons system before deploying it (Firestone 2003). In other words, accountability was to be absent and yet government support for this scientifically flawed project was abundant.

Now, compare the lax accountability in military spending with the recent fad in educational reform supposedly built around increased accountability. In this case, accountability means nothing more than evaluating teachers and schools on the basis of their students' test grades on multiple-choice exams. The advantage of this policy is that every level of administration can say that it is actively pursuing policies to ensure quality education by pressuring teachers and schools to improve test scores, whether or not those in power are supplying the resources to make that improvement likely.

Unfortunately, test scores are a very poor indicator of the quality of education. Even if test scores were an accurate reflection of an individual student's achievement, they are a bad measure for ranking schools. The problem here is that, for statistical reasons, small schools have an enormous variability, creating serious distortions in the data (Kane and Staiger 2002). However, in any case, people who have experience in teaching know that such exams can not capture what education, at its best, should offer.

Sadly, the emphasis on tests will actually harm education. Because of the pressure to improve test results, teachers must redesign their curricula to prepare students for tests rather than to actually educate them. Can you imagine any student being inspired in a subject by being programmed to answer multiple-choice questions?

Even if tests were an accurate barometer of education, this system of accountability still can not accurately measure teachers' work. These comparisons stack teachers working in poorly equipped schools with large numbers of disadvantaged students against those who teach in affluent communities that supply their schools with the very best equipment. You can know in advance where most teachers in a school with many poor children are going to rank.

Of course, some teachers from the same schools will do better than others in terms of their students' test scores. To the extent that test scores have any bearing on education, those results might give some hints about where teachers might make improvements. However, the test scores by themselves are more likely than not to be misleading.

To make matters worse, these tests are expensive. As a result, schools must divert badly needed money to pay for costly testing services—money they could use to improve the classroom experience (see Kronholz 2003). To the extent that accountability involves interpretation, schools employ layer after layer of bureaucracy, to put their test results in the best possible light, consuming still more money.

Worst of all, high stakes testing encourages schools to act in ways that harm students. For example, teachers will use precious classroom time to prepare their students for the tests instead of teaching what is most valuable. Some schools even go so far as to script teachers to ensure that they are emphasizing the tests.

Schools also resort to cruel bureaucratic maneuvers to improve their test scores. For example, schools can expel students who are less likely to perform well on the tests or they can encourage them to drop out.

Of course, many conservatives' motives for advocating educational reform are unrelated to the quality of education. Some see a potential market for private education. Others want to use educational reform as a tactic for hobbling the teachers' unions, which tend to support more liberal politicians (see Miner 2004).

The virus of accountability is infecting higher education, where more and more administrative resources go into developing supposed evidence of learning. While no one can doubt that effective teaching is important, mechanically-applied tools that can accurately measure learning are nonexistent. Those tools that are at hand are, at best, misleading.

I suspect that part of the appeal of accountability in education reflects an intense desire on the part of corporations to find new markets. Following the example of health care, many business interests have a vision of the widespread creation of educational maintenance organizations, EMOs, modeled after health maintenance organizations, HMOs. Accountability standards allow public agencies favorable to privatization of education to identify low performing schools and then call upon businesses to operate them. Poor communities, disappointed by the shabby public education offered to them were expected to be relatively receptive to private education.

Since private schools have options not open to public schools, they are thought to have a better chance to raise test scores and still turn a profit. Private schools do not have to respect unions for the staff and teachers. They do not have to offer services to the community that public schools do. For example, in San Francisco, the privately run Edison school had fencing around the playground, preventing the neighborhood from using the facility after the school lets out. This move may have lowered maintenance costs, but it did so at a price to the community.

More important, private schools do not have the obligation to serve all students. They can choose not to educate children with expensive needs, such as those with disabilities. Private schools can expel difficult or even slow children. By cherry picking better students, private schools should be able to appear efficient, producing higher test scores at a cost below that of public schools, which are left to serve the most expensive, difficult children. Unfortunately, even with their substantial advantages, private schools have not been able to fulfill even their limited promise of raising test scores at a price comparable to public education.

## THE VIRTUAL IMPOSSIBILITY OF ACCOUNTABILITY

The ultimate irony of accountability is that at the same time that the objective of accountability is becoming more popular, it is becoming less possible. Let me explain what I mean. During the heyday of classical capitalism, most economic activity involved manipulating materials in order to fashion them into a final product. Leather became shoes. Cotton became cloth.

Capitalists did everything they could to break down the traditional craft-based production traditions so that they could control the production process. This objective was slow in coming, often because the employers themselves did not understand the underlying technology. Some traditional work practices, like those of the puddlers, who were the key figures in the steel mills, lasted through most of the nineteenth century.

Once managers succeeded in establishing their control, each worker was supposed to have relatively limited individual responsibilities. Employees were merely to follow orders. Employers had the responsibility to discover market opportunities and then to monitor their workers to make sure that they operated efficiently. This last responsibility presumed that employers had the capacity to be able to define jobs with a considerable degree of precision and then to monitor their workers effectively.

Few businesses have been able to organize their work so completely—McDonald's fast food workers come to mind. But for a good many jobs—especially those associated with modern technology—management has no choice but to give their workers more discretion (see Prendergast 2002).

Consider the difference between a worker on an early assembly line and a computer programmer. In the former case, a casual visual inspection might tell whether a worker was doing his job or not. Yet, even in this type of job, workers' actions are not always transparent. Stanley Mathewson reported the tactic of an automobile worker's finding a loophole in a job description:

> A Mexican in a large automobile factory was given the final tightening to the nuts on automobile-engine cylinder heads. There are a dozen or more nuts around this part. The engines passed the Mexican rapidly on a conveyer. His instructions were to test all the nuts and if he found one or two loose to tighten them, but if three or more were loose he was not expected to have time to tighten them.
>
> [A supervisor who was puzzled that so many defective engines were passing along the line eventually] discovered that the Mexican was unscrewing a third nut whenever he found two already loose. [Mathewson 1939: 125]

After all, loosening one nut required less effort than tightening two. I wonder how much time passed before the supervisor discovered the worker's trick or if a less observant supervisor would have even noticed.

In the case of the computer programmer, individual responsibility may be all but invisible. Many programmers are part of large teams. An individual programmer may have responsibility for a small module in a complex program. The smallest error in a program can have disastrous consequences.

Peter Neumann's unsettling book, *Computer Related Risks*, lists 15 serious problems that occurred in the United States manned space program. Of these, nine seemed to involve a software problem (Neumann 1995: 32). One of the best-known of these spacecraft catastrophes occurred with the Mariner I spacecraft, the first U.S. space vehicle designed to visit another planet (Venus). On the morning of 22 July 1962, the space vehicle rocketed from the launch pad and four minutes into its flight began moving on an erratic path. NASA had to destroy it in the air before it could do any serious damage. A single incorrect character in the equations of motion encoded in a huge FORTRAN guidance program was responsible for the failure (Campbell-Kelly and Aspray 1996: 200).

More recently, NASA lost a $125 million Mars Climate Orbiter because of a software glitch. The problem resulted from Lockheed Martin Corp. engineers and navigators using commands based on English measurements (feet, inches, etc.) while engineers at NASA made their calculations using the metric system. The spacecraft flew too close to Mars and is believed to have burned up in the Martian atmosphere (Anon. 1999).

When a program does malfunction, supervisors often have great difficulty in discovering the exact source of the problem. In the case of the Challenger program, the fact that the problem was in such an obviously vital part as the O-ring, undoubtedly made discovery much easier. In other cases, the solution may be nothing more than a crude fix that seems to avoid the problem, even though nobody knew exactly what caused the malfunction in the first place.

Even if a program seems to work, how do you judge the effort of the individual programmer? Do you count keystrokes or lines of code? Or do you rely on evaluation of other members of the team? Or do you wait for a catastrophe?

## CLEANING UP THE MESS

An apocryphal story illustrates the difficulty of discovering the cause of a system failure. A woman who cleaned hospital rooms was unable to find an unused electrical outlet to run her buffer. When she ran into this problem, she would simply unplug a cord from one of the outlets, complete her job, and then methodically reattach the cord, but not before patients on life support had expired.

Tracing this simple problem would not be a trivial matter. Presumably, the affected patients would have only two things in common: reliance on electricity for life support and a shortage of electrical outlets in their room. The first is obvious; the second is not. Who would think to check for the absence of a spare electrical outlet when assessing the cause of death?

In the case of the person who cleaned the room, a hospital could publish a set of guidelines. If the hospital management were somehow to think through all the contingencies, it could develop a standard procedure that would prevent the cleaner from making a fatal decision.

No self-respecting hospital administration would be able to anticipate all contingencies. I suspect that the spare outlet problem would be among the possibilities that management would be likely to overlook. Besides, cleaners are "invisible" parts of the hospital, people without responsibility, often working for an outside contractor. Given that one small mistake on the part of one of a large number of workers can result in a disaster in many complex systems, employers in such cases might be expected to pay premium wages in order to attract the best workers and to keep them motivated (Kremer 1993). The story, of course, is unrealistic. After all, even an untrained worker in a hospital would probably be careful not to interfere with life support equipment.

In the case of a complex computer program, an individual programmer might not have any idea about the overall impact of a particular module. Here management definitely has the responsibility to ensure coordination. Recall how NASA lost its spacecraft because Lockheed engineers wrote their commands in English measurements while NASA engineers used the metric system.

When a serious problem does occur invariably corporations place the blame on an individual's mistake—typically someone quite low on the totem pole, like the hypothetical hospital cleaner. Yet, when workers do point out dangers, they themselves often face some sort of retribution.

For example, a mechanic for Frontier Airlines found himself charged with damaging an airplane because he put a piece of rubber in the engine. He was not some sort of saboteur; on the contrary, he was worried that the plane was unsafe. The plane was being pushed off from the gate to take off with 130 passengers. Since he thought that his supervisors were not taking his safety concerns seriously, he took matters into his own hands, forcing the company to double check the problem (Gutierrez 2003).

As a passenger, I feel that I have far more to fear from shoddy maintenance than from terrorism. Had the plane crashed without the mechanic's intervention, the corporation would have likely placed the blame on the ground crew, perhaps even the same mechanic.

### GLOBALIZATION AND CORPORATE ACCOUNTABILITY

Accountability becomes all but impossible in a corporately globalized world economy. For example, in late 2002, the tanker ship *Prestige* broke up, causing the largest oil spill in the history of the world, poisoning the beaches of Spain with thousands of tons of foul sludge. The over 70,000-ton oil cargo appears to have been ultimately headed for Singapore. (This account closely follows Willmore 2002.) The aged, single-hulled ship's owner was a Liberian company called Mare International. Liberian law makes it hard to be certain who really owns Mare, but according to the British newspaper the *Independent*, the secretive Greek Coulouthros shipping dynasty may be the owner.

The owners of the *Prestige* registered the ship with the Bahamas Maritime Authority, which is not based in the Bahamas, but in the City of London. An oil trading company called Crown Resources, formed in Gibraltar in 1996, owned the oily sludge. At least five of Crown's Directors are British and one (Joe Moss) is a former Gibraltar Government Minister. In July, the company moved its headquarters to Zug, Switzerland.

Crown Resources is in turn owned by a fascinating Russian conglomerate called the Alfa Group Consortium. The Chairman of the Supervisory Board of Alfa Group is Mikhail Fridman, one of the powerful oligarchs who control the Russian economy. According to *Forbes*, he was the 68th richest person in the world in 2003, worth $4.3 billion. One of his firms is under investigation for Mafia connections.

Given this confusing network of control, who will be held accountable for the disaster? The total accident insurance on the ship was £15 million, which will come nowhere near covering the damage that the spill has caused. For example, a Greenpeace study reports that the much smaller *Exxon Valdez* spill clean-up cost $400 million (Caballero 2003: 6). Should those injured by the spill sue in Russian courts? Or should they sue in Switzerland, Liberia, England, Gibraltar, the Bahamas or Greece?

Even if the injured parties successfully sue, collecting damage awards will be problematical, at least judging by the experience of the *Exxon Valdez* catastrophe, which dumped 11 million gallons of crude oil—about half as much as the *Prestige* did—into Prince William Sound, Alaska in March 1989. Exxon Mobil managed to keep the major suit tied up in the courts rather than pay damage awards. For example, 13 years after the accident, in December 2002, a federal judge finally ruled that $4 billion was an appropriate judgment for the approximately 32,000 plaintiffs—including fishermen, communities, businesses and landowners—but the verdict displeased the company, which planned to appeal once again. More than 1,000 of these plaintiffs have died (Gumbel 2004).

Unlike the *Prestige* spill, the line of authority was clear cut in the case of the *Exxon Valdez*. In the case of *Prestige*, the various responsible parties will probably be able to play different jurisdictions against each other, forestalling penalties even more effectively than Exxon Mobil.

As globalization becomes more entrenched, complex international deals will make arrangements, such as those surrounding the *Prestige*, more common. As a result, keeping a tighter leash on corporate power is more necessary than ever before.

# 6
# The Role of Risk

INTRODUCTION

In 1986, Walter Wriston published his book, *Risk and Other Four-Letter Words*, where he wrote:

> The men and women who founded our country were ... adventurers who took personal risks of the most extreme kind .... Today, however, the idea is abroad in the land that the descendants of these bold adventurers should be sheltered from risk and uncertainty as part of our national heritage .... At bottom, democracy itself rests on an act of faith, on a belief in individual responsibility and the superiority of the free marketplace. [Wriston 1986: 219–20]

People unfamiliar with Wriston's career might not fully appreciate the delicious irony in his words. Wriston had already capped his career as Chief Executive Officer of Citibank when this book appeared. At the time, Citibank had recently become deeply enmeshed in the Latin American debt crisis, so much so that Citibank had been getting nearly 50 per cent of its revenue from its loans to Latin America.

Citibank had been intent on "selling"—many used the term "pushing" (see Darity and Horn 1988)—as much credit as possible to Latin America. It made these loans without much thought about the ability of Latin America to repay them or without putting adequate reserves aside to cover potential defaults. Citibank never outwardly expressed much concern about the risks of such loans. In fact, in 1982, a month after Mexico had defaulted on its foreign debt, Wriston wrote an op-ed piece for the *New York Times*:

> Countries don't go out of business .... The infrastructure doesn't go away, the productivity of the people doesn't go away, the natural resources don't go away. And so their assets always exceed their liabilities, which is the technical reason for bankruptcy. And that's very different from a company. [Wriston 1982]

Wriston's theory was full of holes. In fact, many of his business allies were critical of this piece (Zweig 1995: 765–6). Wriston may have also realized how inappropriate the position he adopted in the piece was. At any rate, a few years later when he published his book with his high-sounding words about "bold adventurers," he did not see fit to include this stellar article on bankruptcy.

This reticence certainly was justified. By 1991, some Citicorp debt had been reduced to junk-bond status. Public figures, as diverse as Rep. John Dingell and Ross Perot, described Citibank as insolvent (Zweig 1995: 867 and 872).

The Federal Reserve had to dispatch the president of the New York branch of the Federal Reserve Bank to Saudi Arabia to arrange for Prince Alwaleed Bin Talal Alsaud to invest another $1.2 billion in the bank in late 1990. The Federal Reserve also had to be sure to keep interest rates down long enough to salvage the bank (Woodward 2000: 73).

Evan so, the rescue was not a certainty. Wriston's biographer commented:

Citibank may not have been insolvent, but its condition was clearly a cause for alarm. In August 1992, it was forced to disclose that regulators had demanded that it sign a "memo of understanding"—an "MOU" in regulators' shorthand—admitting that its difficulties were critical enough to require intensive regulatory supervision. Examiners, one Citibank officer said, regularly took over the boardroom to go through the loan portfolio piece by piece. In fact, [John] Reed [Wriston's successor] admitted later, Citi came "very close" to the abyss in December 1991, when the comptroller of "the Currency declined to sign off on Citi's reserve levels. But Citi was deemed "too big to fail." [Zweig 1995: 974]

Despite the dire straits in which Citibank found itself, the confidence that Wriston exuded in his op-ed may have been justified after all. While the company's objective business situation was grim, to say the least, Citibank did not face much risk that Latin American countries would declare bankruptcy, but not for the reasons that Wriston gave. Instead, Citibank's "bold adventurers" realized that they would be "sheltered from risk and uncertainty" after all. In short, Citibank survived because the bank had powerful friends in high places.

Later, as more Latin American economies faltered, many economists and investors wondered how these poor countries could ever hope to repay their crushing debts. But then, the United States, in part through the International Monetary Fund, forced a brutal austerity on Latin America to squeeze as much repayment as possible out of these loans. Decades later, Latin America still had not recovered from these policies, but Citibank, which after a series of massive mergers became known as Citigroup, prospered mightily. Shamelessly, the corporation even earned substantial profits from fees for restructuring those Latin American loans.

In short, the loans, issued with little concern for any underlying economic rationale, involved serious risks, but those who bore the brunt of the risk were the poor of Latin America who are still suffering the consequences. Recall how Wriston reveled in the idea that capital markets will hold countries responsible if they run afoul of the standards preferred by capital markets. No such fate awaited Wriston and his executives. Instead, as James Grant, a conservative investment analyst, observed:

> In its 1990 annual report, Citicorp would suggest that it was really nobody's fault. Neither the market nor the regulators had anticipated the "adjustment of asset values or the drop in U.S. real estate values." The "corporation was essentially in no worse shape than the market" and "[to] an important degree, we are in the hands of the economy and nobody is very secure in predicting its performance." [Grant 1996: 170]

Reading Mr Wriston's sermon about the value of personal responsibility and a willingness to accept the consequences of risk in light of this history certainly requires a healthy sense of humor. Neither he nor those who followed him at the corporation ever accepted any responsibility for their actions nor, to the best of my knowledge, ever made a single gesture to the millions of people harmed by their irresponsible loans.

Little has changed since Wriston originally published his book about risk. Almost 20 years later, Vice President Richard Cheney echoed Wriston's lofty sentiments about the importance of entrepreneurial risk-taking: "The president and I understand that the government does not create wealth and it does not create jobs, but government policies can and should create the environment in which firms and entrepreneurs will take risk, innovate, invest and hire more people" (Bumiller 2003).

Indeed, President George W. Bush—whose own early business career consisted of a series of failed enterprises, which were then rescued by his father's business friends and Washington cronies—introduced the annual *Economic Report of the President* with an almost identical statement as his vice president's (President of the United States 2003: 4). These sentiments are ironic for an administration whose budget counts $600 billion in loan guarantees (Office of Management and Budget 2004b).

Even more so than Wriston, Mr Cheney has personally benefited from government largesse. After building a career in government culminating in his tenure as secretary of defense during the presidency of George H. W. Bush, Mr Cheney, who had no prior business experience, became the CEO of Halliburton, a company that had long profited handsomely from government contracts. Not surprisingly, what Mr Cheney lacked in business experience, he more than made up for with his government connections. Under his watch, Halliburton's government contracts soared. As a token of its gratitude and a practical desire to continue its circle of political influence, Halliburton was very generous to Mr Cheney. The company arranged that when Cheney returned to government service as vice president, he left the company with a $35 million severance package.

During the 2000 election campaign, in a debate with the Democrats' vice-presidential candidate, Cheney insisted with a straight face that "the government had absolutely nothing to do with" his financial success over the previous eight years. In fact, the vice presidency no doubt can provide Mr Cheney with even more political connections for future business ventures if he decides that he needs to augment his wealth even more by returning once again to the private sector.

Unfortunately for Halliburton, Mr Cheney was not a completely positive influence. Although Halliburton's government contracts proved highly lucrative, the company fell into a number of fiascos, including bribery scandals, trading with forbidden countries, and money-losing deals. Daniel Gross, who writes the Moneybox column for the online magazine *Slate*, described one of Mr Cheney's missteps:

> Cheney midwifed the Barracuda-Caratinga Project, which is gnawing a hole in the company's balance sheet. Under the $2.5 billion deal, announced in January 2000 when Cheney was CEO, Halliburton was supposed to develop two offshore oil fields in Brazil by December 2003 and April 2004, respectively. But the project has turned into a fiasco, with huge cost overruns and bad schedule misses. As of June 30, 2003, the project was 75 percent complete—and more than a year behind schedule. By that date, Kellogg, Brown and Root, the responsible subsidiary, had already recorded a pretax

loss of $345 million on the project, with the possibility of greater losses to come. [Gross 2003]

Mr Cheney also had the company acquire Dresser Industries, a company previously very close to the Bush family, for $7.7 billion in 1998. George Herbert Walker Bush wrote in his autobiography that Neil Mallon, the former president of Dresser Industries, was a mentor second only to his father. The first president Bush even named one of his sons Neil Mallon Bush.

Dresser Industries had owned another company, Harbison-Walker Refractories, which produced a product that was one-third asbestos. Workers would mix the asbestos-laden concoction with water then spray the solution as a liner for industrial blast furnaces. The heat in the furnace would break down the liner every few months, creating dust clouds, exposing even more workers to the lethal substance (Grimaldi 2002). Because of numerous asbestos-caused deaths and diseases Harbison-Walker Refractories faced enormous liabilities.

Taking on Harbison-Walker Refractories unintentionally exposed Halliburton to risks, but this deal hardly qualifies as the sort of bold risk-taking that Mr Cheney advocated. To my knowledge, Mr Cheney never encouraged Halliburton to act like a bold risk-taker. Nor did he behave as a bold risk-taker in facing the company's responsibilities. Instead, Halliburton engaged in a series of complex maneuvers to limit its liabilities.

In November 2003, Halliburton agreed to pay $4 billion dollars— $2.8 billion in cash and the rest in stock—to cap current and future payments to asbestos victims. While these amounts might appear to be staggering at first sight, the company is responsible for many thousands of people who have suffered exposure to asbestos. The monetary judgments per person possible under this cap are much less than awards have been for other people suffering comparable harm.

Without recent court decisions that have severely limited corporate liability in class action suits, Halliburton's offer would have had to have been substantially greater. Halliburton's plan also included shielding itself from most of its liability by placing only part of its KBR subsidiary into bankruptcy, alongside Harbison-Walker Refractories, which was already in bankruptcy. Then again, Halliburton may have other options in mind, especially because this company seems to thrive more on government connections than business acumen.

Besides, Halliburton is not alone in its asbestos liabilities. Even though the lethal qualities of asbestos were already known during the 1930s, companies continued to work with it, exposing countless people to the deadly fibers. One study estimated that nationwide:

> Legal claims for injuries from asbestos involve more plaintiffs, more defendants and higher costs than any other type of personal injury litigation in U.S. history. As of the end of 2002, 730,000 individuals had filed lawsuits against more than 8,400 defendants, and the total amount that defendants and insurers had spent on resolving claims—including all legal costs—was estimated to be $70 billion …. Estimates of the total number of people who will eventually file claims range from 1.0 million to 3.0 million, and estimates of the eventual cost of asbestos litigation range from $200-$265 billion. [White 2004: 183]

No wonder that Justice David Souter lamented in the U.S. Supreme Court case *Ortiz* v. *Fibreboard Corporation* about "The elephantine mass of asbestos cases." Not surprisingly, friends in high place have been sympathetic to the plight of Halliburton and the other corporations facing asbestos liability. For example, Utah Senator Orrin Hatch, chairman of the Senate Judiciary Committee, sponsored legislation to limit liability from future asbestos injury claims, leaving asbestos victims holding the bag.

Illinois Senator Richard Durbin countered that the legislation amounted to "a windfall" for corporate defendants, such as the Halliburton Corp., citing an analysis that concluded its asbestos liabilities would shrink from more than $4 billion to $420 million. He said a number of defendant companies' share prices have moved sharply higher as the committee has progressed toward a deal (Gordon 2003).

Between 1997 and mid-2000, Halliburton's Political Action Committee donated almost $500,000 to members of Congress. The company was especially generous to those politicians who supported this legislation to limit its potential liability—legislation that opponents dubbed the "Asbestos Industry Relief Act." Zelma Branch, a company spokeswoman, said that the company's donations were innocent enough. In her words, "Our PAC has made contributions without regard to the pending asbestos legislation. Any similarities between the supporters of such legislation and the recipients of contributions from our PAC is (sic) purely coincidental" (Schneider and Olsen 2000).

Ultimately, the point of such legislation is to protect the company from shouldering responsibility while leaving the dead or debilitated workers with relatively little compensation for the risk that they bore from working with the asbestos. This story has an even happier ending for Halliburton since the invasion of Iraq left the company with more than $2 billion dollars in contracts for the rebuilding of the Iraqi infrastructure, including one worth $1.22 billion that the government awarded on a non-competitive basis.

I suspect that these contracts will do more to restore the financial health of Halliburton than the economy of Iraq. Although Vice President Cheney has strenuously maintained that he has cut his ties with Halliburton, he received deferred compensation of $147,579 in 2001 and $162,392 in 2002, with payments scheduled to continue for three more years. He also holds 433,333 unexercised stock options. A recent Congressional Research Service report concluded that federal ethics laws treat Vice President Cheney's deferred compensation checks and unexercised stock options as a continuing financial interest in the Halliburton Co. (Allen 2003).

Returning to Wriston's original proposition, if by adventurers, he meant those who invested in business, he was also mistaken on historical grounds about their willingness to accept personal risks. In fact in the United States, government promotion of industry was commonplace, especially in the early years of the republic. Government offered tariff protection, subsidies, and even the right to hold lotteries to encourage new industry. All these actions reduced risks.

Corporate charters also shielded business from risk. Until the mid-nineteenth century corporate charters were not freely available in the United States. Instead, they were special privileges that frequently provided business with the safe harbor of monopoly rights. In the case of railroads, the key national industry of the nineteenth century, loans and subsidies from local, state, and federal government—including the gift of almost 200 million acres of public land—were essential to inducing "adventurers" to "risk" their funds. Most of the private financial backing for this investment came from abroad—especially from Britain—rather than from citizens of the United States.

The greatest protection from risk may have come after corporate charters became freely available in the middle of the nineteenth century. These charters offered limited liability for investors—meaning that if their business failed, they would be safe from the risk that creditors might hold them personally liable for the corporate debts (see Moss 2002). Without that protection, as well as Halliburton's lucrative new contracts awarded under Cheney's vice presidency, the company's future would be doubtful at best.

## RISK, UNCERTAINTY, AND PROFIT

Despite Wriston's questionable credentials as an objective advocate of requiring individuals to accept the adverse consequences of risk, virtually every economist accepts the fact that risk plays a central role in market economies. How could the situation be otherwise? However, as I will show, more often than not it is private individuals or society at large that bear the risk, while corporations enjoy the rewards. Before addressing that subject, I will first discuss the nature of risk, and a related term, uncertainty.

By risk, economists mean something that can be assigned a specific probability, such as flipping a coin. I do not know when I flip a coin whether it will come up heads or tails, but I can be fairly certain that if I do so 1 million times, tails will come up in close to half the flips.

In the case of the coin flip, suppose that you are betting that you get two coins if you get heads and nothing if you lose. The expected payoff of the bet is one-half of two plus one-half of zero—or a total of one.

Obviously, reality is far more complex than a simple coin flip. Even so with more complex bets where all the odds are known, you can still calculate the expected payoffs. Life insurance is based on this sort of calculation. So, assuming that people are rational and known odds are known, analyzing risky situations is not much more difficult than evaluating decisions where the outcome is certain.

Economists distinguish between risk and what they call uncertainty. Uncertainty is something altogether different from risk. Uncertainty refers to conditions in which nobody can possibly know what the likelihood of an event may be. For example, the late Danish physicist, Per Bak, capped his career by studying the seemingly trivial subject of the physics of sand piles. You can continue to build a pile of sand until a point comes at which a particular grain will set off an avalanche. Bak showed the impossibility of predicting which grain will trigger the event or how high the pile will have to be before it occurs (see Bak 1997). Similarly, nobody can know what the next outbreak of a new disease will be. Fifty years ago, who could have predicted the AIDS epidemic?

Of course, people are not rational at all in managing personal risk. People often avoid slight risks, yet take wild gambles.

Risk does not present a great complication for the smooth running of a market economy, but uncertainty does. So, to be precise, we should translate the risk Wriston refers to as uncertainty. Within the context of market economies, uncertainty is pervasive. In a market economy, producers have no legal mechanism to coordinate their actions with other producers. Without knowledge of the intentions of consumers and competitors, business cannot reduce uncertainty to calculable risk.

True, as information accumulates, people may be able to transform some uncertainty into risk. For example, over the centuries people learned about certain regularities in weather patterns. Yet, despite the ability to predict weather patterns more accurately, the extent of uncertainty does not recede because the growing complexity of the forces that influence our lives creates entirely new uncertainties.

Frank Knight's *Risk, Uncertainty, and Profit* is the classic work on the subject. According to Knight, the key figure in market economies is the entrepreneur, who acts as the major bearer of risk, just as Wriston suggested. From his perspective, capitalism is "the system under which the confident and venturesome 'assume the risk' or 'insure' the doubtful and timid by guaranteeing to the latter a specified income in return for an assignment of the actual results" (Knight 1921: 269–70). Knight went on to explain:

Under the enterprise system, a special social class, the business men, direct economic activity; they are in the strict sense the producers, while the great mass of the population merely furnish them with productive services, placing their persons and their property at the disposal of this class; the entrepreneurs also guarantee to those who furnish productive services a fixed remuneration. [Knight 1921: 271]

So, according to Knight, entrepreneurs are those people who are confident enough in their own vision that they are willing to invest in uncertain enterprises. These entrepreneurs then contract with other agents in the economy, guaranteeing them a fixed reward. For example, they offer labor a specified wage and suppliers of materials agreed-upon prices. The entrepreneur's profit represents what is left over after paying these predetermined expenses. In effect then, according to Knight, most of profit represents a reward for successful entrepreneurial risk bearing—or to be more precise, successful coping with uncertainty. In Knight's words: "Profit arises out of the inherent, absolute unpredictability of things" (Knight 1921: 311).

## KNIGHT: ON CLOSER EXAMINATION

In actual fact, entrepreneurs are hardly the great risk takers that either Knight, Wriston, or economic theory makes them out to be. In reality, more and more, the market has been rigged so that individuals, especially those with the least resources, find themselves forced to take on the most risk. For workers, years of education and experience can suddenly become worthless in the job market. Worse yet, workers face serious risks of workplace deaths and injuries.

Duration represents an important aspect of risk. Consider the relationship between the entrepreneur and an employee. Even if an entrepreneur promised an extraordinary wage of $1,200 per hour, such employment might not be particularly attractive without assurance of a sufficient duration. If the work terminated after a couple of seconds, the time and effort of coming to work might not be worth the trouble. The earlier discussion about the growing importance of flexible workers suggests that this example, while extreme, is not entirely hypothetical. To the extent that finding a new job might involve relocation, a further cost comes into play. Workers, not employers, must bear the risk of this cost.

Indeed, corporations have become extremely sophisticated in shifting risk onto others. In the process, workers, consumers, and society at large all turn out to be major bearers of risk, with little to show for their involuntary or unwitting risk bearing.

Recall my earlier discussion of pensions. The initial structure of defined benefit pensions certainly seemed to conform to Knight's idea of the entrepreneur as risk taker. Companies took on the obligation to provide for their workers during their retirement—presumably taking on the risk associated with that obligation.

During the 1970s, speculators began a technique known as leveraged buyouts. Speculators would purchase major corporations using the assets of those corporations as collateral. Pension plans were one of the most attractive assets. Once the transaction was completed, the speculators could liquidate the existing pension plan, replace it with a cheaper plan, pocketing a handsome profit. From that time on, many corporations began to regard their pension plans as profit centers.

In recent decades, as I have already mentioned, companies have been shying away from defined benefit plans and turning instead to defined contribution plans, in which workers shoulder the risk by taking the responsibility for investing their own funds.

Many major companies that retained defined benefit programs behaved irresponsibly, manipulating their pension programs for corporate profits. One particular tactic was to assume that they could earn an unrealistically high rate of return on their pension funds. Based on this premise, managers could withdraw money from the funds since they could assume that future profits would be more than adequate to cover their obligations (see Schultz 2003). As a result, the government agency that guarantees defined benefit pension plans, the Pension Benefit Guaranty Corporation, now faces a deficit of $11.2 billion as of January 2004—an increase of $7.6 billion over the previous year (Pension Benefit Guaranty Corporation 2004).

When, despite its numerous advantages, a major corporation does stumble, more often than not, the government stands ready to bail it out. Large corporations have much more access to such risk protection than small-business. Lobbying and generous political campaign contributions are obviously part of the equation, but government representatives typically claim that the failure of a major corporation could threaten the health of the entire economy. For example, in late 1979 the government rescued the Chrysler Corporation. Not surprisingly, part of the package required substantial sacrifices on the part of workers.

Even though such massive rescue packages are relatively rare, the very fact that the government stands ready to offer such protection provides a cushion against uncertainty that represents a substantial subsidy because banks are aware of their bailout potential. As a result, such favored corporations can pay less to obtain funds by borrowing or through the stock market because both lenders and investors know that their risk is more modest than it would be in dealing with lesser businesses.

In conclusion, Knight's appealing proposition that entrepreneurs earn profit as a reward for relieving risk for the rest of society does not seem to hold up under close scrutiny. Interestingly, if profit mostly represents a reward for risk bearing, then profitability should have declined with the diminution of risk. Such has not been the case. On the contrary, shifting risk to others has been a major source of corporate profits. Despite having to shoulder less risk, the bulk of economic rewards still flow to the rich and powerful.

## PROTECTION AGAINST BUSINESS RISK

Let us return to my suggestion that despite the fact that profits are supposedly a reward for shouldering risk—more properly called uncertainty—government goes a great way to protect business from both risk and uncertainty. Earlier, I made a brief mention of how governments have traditionally offered business refuge from uncertainty in the form of tariff protection and subsidies. In addition, Governments also grant firms monopoly status to provide them with relatively risk-free markets. Government regulations frequently protect business from the dangers of strong competition. For example, the underlying purpose of the Interstate Commerce Commission was to hold railroad competition in check (see Kolko 1965).

Despite the best efforts of the government, from time to time competition becomes more heated, especially when the economy slows down. Once these slowdowns occur, the government stimulates the economy through monetary and fiscal policy. Economic stimulation minimizes the possibility that competition may become too harsh (Perelman 1999). Loosening of monetary controls also helps to protect speculators against losses.

The U.S. government generously offers corporations more direct protections from risk. Consider the role of agencies, such as the Overseas Private Investment Corporation, which has supported nearly $145 billion of investments since 1971, or the Export-Import Bank, which authorized a total of $10.1 billion in loans, guarantees and export credit insurance to corporations in fiscal year 2002.

The Congress also grants corporations direct protection against risk. The infamous Price-Anderson Act that shields the nuclear power industry from most of the liability arising from serious accidents is a good example. If we are to believe the public relations communiqués of the nuclear industry, this law is unnecessary. Why should the nuclear power industry worry about liability from catastrophes? After all, the industry and its protectors repeatedly assure us that the technology is virtually free of risks; when addressing the government, however, the industry turns around and demands protection from the risk of accidents. In particular, nuclear power generators insist that the generous protection from risk that the Price-Anderson Act provides is an absolute necessity. Without this legislation, the industry's insurance costs would be prohibitive.

Why would insurance be expensive if risks were virtually nonexistent, as the nuclear industry claims? Taking the nuclear industry at its word, insurance companies should be flocking to the power companies offering to insure them against an almost impossible event, since they could collect fees without having to worry about ever paying out any claims.

Instead, fearful of the risks involved, insurance companies generally take care to exclude nuclear accidents from homeowners' insurance. What, then, do the insurance companies know about the risks that the nuclear power industry prefers not to tell the public?

In fact, the nuclear industry realizes that insurance carriers do not share the industry's confidence about safety. Insurers would expect hefty premiums to cover the risk of a catastrophic nuclear accident. This expense would make the production of nuclear power unprofitable, even with numerous other public subsidies. As a result, the government has stepped in to limit the liability of the industry.

Under this legislation, each of the 103 reactor operators is responsible for taking out a $200 million insurance policy. In addition, in the event of an accident that causes more than $200 million in damages, all 103 nuclear reactor operators in America are liable for additional payments capped at $88 million per reactor. The total of the $200 million insurance policy plus the $88 million per reactor is $9.3 billion. The nuclear industry has no responsibility for any damages in excess of this $9.3 billion. Of course, $9.3 billion is not a trivial amount of money, but it would not come anywhere near the costs of a major nuclear accident. For example:

In the wake of the 1979 Three Mile Island accident, the federally-funded Sandia National Laboratory prepared a report on behalf of the Nuclear Regulatory Commission (NRC). This 1982 study estimated that damages from a severe nuclear accident could run as high as $314 billion or more than $560 billion in 2000 dollars. Since that study, the NRC has developed "more realistic" modeling improvements to the agency's probabilistic risk assessment. A review of their 1982 study "found that property damages would be twice as much as those calculated in 1982, solely on the basis of the modeling improvements made." In addition, the Chernobyl catastrophe has cost the nations of Russia, Ukraine and Belarus $358 billion. This Chernobyl total, however, is vastly understated, since it does not attempt to estimate the costs to other nations, which also experienced health costs from the far-reaching nuclear fallout. [Public Citizen. Critical Mass and Energy Project 2001]

The Chernobyl comparison understates the cost of a catastrophic nuclear accident for another reason. Prices in Eastern Europe are far less than in the United States.

Based on the estimate of $560 billion, the $9.2 billion provided by private insurance and nuclear reactor operators represents less than 2 per cent of the potential costs of a major nuclear accident. Considering what commercial insurance costs would be without the liability cap, the Price-Anderson Act provided an estimated annual subsidy of $32 million per reactor at 2001 prices (Dubin and Rothwell 1990).

The Price-Anderson Act is part of a double whammy on individual homeowners whose insurance policies typically contain the common exclusionary clause that protects the insurer from liability in case of a nuclear accident. Again, the public at large will absorb the cost, either as taxpayers footing the bill or as uncompensated victims.

Well, maybe I should have said triple whammy, because the industry will expect individuals as ratepayers to protect them from risk. For example, following the Three Mile Island disaster, a writer in *Barrons* worried about one of the potential victims of the incident in an article entitled "Nuclear Threat: Three Mile Island May Yet Claim Further Victims." Rather than expressing concern about the neighbors of the plant, the author feared that the Pennsylvania public utilities commissioners would not raise rates enough to protect Metropolitan Edison from financial fallout. Without any intended irony, the author exclaimed: "In the generation of nuclear energy, manmade hazards seem unavoidable, but bankruptcy strikes us as a needless risk" (Bleiberg 1981).

The nuclear industry is not alone in enjoying protection from liability. For example, in the wake of the attack on the World Trade Center and the Pentagon in September 2001, Congress passed far-reaching legislation authorizing the creation of the Homeland Security Department. At the last minute, the conference committee inserted language authorizing protection from liability for companies that manufacture thimerosal, a mercury-based vaccine preservative. The same bill also shielded any company that is deemed by the government to be making products needed for the war on terrorism from all product liability lawsuits.

Advocacy groups charge thimerosal has been responsible for a surge of autism in children (Allen 2002). Before 1980, diagnoses of autism in children stood at about one in 10,000 children; now the frequency has risen to one in 250 (Fuentes 2003: 15). Only after an outcry did the Congress repeal the thimerosal provision, but not the more far-reaching protection for companies producing products for homeland security.

Why was protection against thimerosal suits a matter for national legislation in the first place? Eli Lilly is the largest maker of thimerosal. In 2000, Lilly was the pharmaceutical industry's largest donor to congressional candidates at $1.6 million, with 80 per cent going to Republicans. Mitch Daniels, who was the powerful White House budget director at the time, was a former president of North American operations for Eli Lilly.

Economists have adopted the insurance term "moral hazard" to explain how protection against risk encourages undesirable changes in behavior. Imagine a driver who receives a lifetime insurance policy that will cover the cost of any automobile accidents. Such a person would be likely to exercise less care in driving than a person who feared having to cover the cost of accidents.

Business is not immune from moral hazard. The more society shields business from risk, the less careful business will be.

## OTHER PROTECTIONS AGAINST BUSINESS RISK

Besides protecting business against future risk, once an unexpected event harms business, the government often steps in to help business recover. Once again, the terrorist attack of September 11, 2001 provided an excellent opportunity. Taking advantage of the resulting hysteria, Congress moved swiftly to approve financial support for the airlines, which were already reeling well before the disaster. Not surprisingly, Congress offered nothing to the workers who lost jobs from the same event, providing further evidence of the asymmetric treatment of business and workers.

Business also frequently wins protection against the risk of regulations even when they are necessary to prevent harm to the environment or human life. I will return to this subject later in my discussion of cost-benefit analysis.

Even speculators enjoy a certain degree of protection against risk. Alan Greenspan, Chairman of the Federal Reserve Board, has explained numerous times how the Fed stands ready to protect business against the risk of a massive crisis:

> With leveraging there will always exist a remote possibility of a chain reaction, a cascading sequence of defaults that will culminate in financial

implosion if it proceeds unchecked. Only a central bank, with its unlimited power to create money, can with a high probability thwart such a process before it becomes destructive. Hence, central banks have of necessity been drawn into becoming lenders of last resort [meaning that the central bank will lend money when no commercial lender would do so]. But implicit in the existence of such a role is that there will be some form of allocation between the public and private sectors of the burden of risk of extreme outcomes. Thus, central banks are led to provide what essentially amounts to catastrophic financial insurance coverage. Such a public subsidy should be reserved for only the rarest of disasters. [Greenspan 1997b: 5]

This particular protection from risk may not draw much attention since the central bank only has to exercise its role as a lender of last resort very infrequently, but the knowledge that the Fed will step in to try to protect the system from disaster makes banks more willing to lend. In effect, then, this protection is equivalent to a free insurance policy.

The Federal Reserve has other ways of shielding speculators against risk. Long-Term Credit Management was a speculative hedge fund. By using layers of credit, the fund was able to leverage a relatively small investment into an enormous gamble. At its peak, the owners had accumulated investments and profits of $7 billion, while its investments in derivatives reached a staggering $1.3 trillion (Blustein 2001: 307 and 315; and Lowenstein 2000: 192–200).

Long-Term Credit Management made a series of disastrous investments, driving it into bankruptcy. Long-Term's inability to repay its enormous debts threatened to set off a panic that could possibly unravel the entire world financial system. Peter K. Fisher, an executive with the New York branch of the Federal Reserve led an effort to corral major Wall Street firms into bailing out the hedge fund. Although these firms lost money in the bailout, their losses would have been far greater if a panic had broken out (Lowenstein 2000: 194–5).

The government could adopt a very different tactic to limit the risks that such speculative ventures pose. Susan Strange, a creative observer of speculative finance, once suggested "a kind of weapon that leading governments like that of the U.S. could use if they wished against the most bizarre and sophisticated derivatives." She noted that governments could "make such contracts not illegal but legally unenforceable [which] would shift the concern back from the market to the risk taker—possibly giving rise to second and more prudent thoughts" (Strange 1998: 190).

Sometimes, the protection that the government gives creditors by enforcing financial contracts threatens to undermine the entire economy. At those times, the government, by necessity, must favor borrowers over creditors. These measures do counteract the "free insurance policy effect" discussed above, but they are far less likely than the Federal Reserve to act as the lender of last resort. In fact, most lenders appear to be totally unaware of this possibility. Finally, if the absence of these measures could lead to a severe depression, creditors as a whole may benefit as well as borrowers from the non-enforcement of financial contracts.

For this reason, on rare occasions, the government imposes moratoria on debt, which are intended to prevent the economy from spiraling out of control during panics. For example, during the Great Depression, many states passed debt moratoria for farm mortgages (Bolton and Rosenthal 2002). A less well-known incident occurred in 1933, when the government abrogated the gold clause, which was common in many financial contracts written after the dramatic Civil War inflation. These clauses protected creditors by allowing them to demand payment in gold or the equivalent dollar value of gold if gold prices were to rise while the contract was in effect.

At the time, the Roosevelt administration wanted to increase the price of gold. Creditors could have demanded business borrowers to pay an estimated $69 billion dollars worth of extra debt (Kroszner 1999). By lifting the weight of the gold clause, the government freed them from that obligation. Coming in the midst of a serious depression, the burden of this additional obligation—since most borrowers were probably unaware of the gold clause in the first place—could have had disastrous consequences. Without government action, an uncontrolled wave of bankruptcies could have spread, engulfing many of the creditors. So, by forgoing their $69 billion, they might have been made better off. Such measures are rare; they arise only when the level of a crisis rises to the point where business is about to suffer large-scale losses.

Finally, by guaranteeing bank deposits, the Federal Deposit Insurance Corporation provides still another protection against risk. Some proponents of free markets vehemently oppose this particular protection because they believe that this insurance encourages banks to lend irresponsibly. Then, again, the fact that the beneficiaries in this case are the depositors may dampen the enthusiasm of free marketeers for this particular protection. For example, I do not recall comparable rebukes regarding the profligate loans to Latin America and other less developed countries by CitiBank and its fellow bankers.

Probably the most important refuge from risk lies in the limited liability protection granted to joint stock companies, mentioned earlier in this chapter. Before governments began chartering corporations, business people risked losing money over and above the amount originally invested in a company since they were also liable for debts that the company had incurred.

At first, governments granted corporate status as a privilege. Only those ventures that promised to provide some specific public good—building bridges or canals or establishing an insurance company—were supposed to obtain corporate charters. Adam Smith expressed the prevailing view that governments should be very restrictive in granting such charters:

> To establish a joint stock company, however, for any undertaking, merely because such a company might be capable of managing it successfully; or to exempt a particular set of dealers from some of the general laws which take place with regard to all their neighbours, merely because they might be capable of thriving if they had such an exemption, would certainly not be reasonable. To render such an establishment perfectly reasonable, with the circumstance of being reducible to strict rule and method, two other circumstances ought to concur. First, it ought to appear with the clearest evidence that the undertaking is of greater and more general utility than the greater part of common trades; and secondly, that it requires a greater capital than can easily be collected into a private copartnery. If a moderate capital were sufficient, the great utility of the undertaking would not be a sufficient reason for establishing a joint stock company; because, in this case, the demand for what it was to produce would readily and easily be supplied by private adventures. [Smith 1776, V.i.e.36: 757]

In the United States, when the government was going out of its way to discourage trade with Britain during the early nineteenth century, New York began a much more generous policy of granting corporate charters to manufacturers to promote domestic industry. Other states felt they had no choice but to follow New York's lead to prevent potential manufacturers from relocating elsewhere (Moss 2002: 55ff). So, despite considerable popular resistance corporate charters soon became more a right than a privilege. As a result, investors enjoy a considerable shield against risk.

The bankruptcy code provides further protection for business, by creating a pecking order for unsecured creditors by limiting what workers may claim. The law allows workers' claims to be capped at $4,650 for wages, salaries, or commissions, including vacation, severance pay, and sick leave pay earned by an individual within 90 days before the date of the filing of the bankruptcy petition or the date of the cessation of the debtor's business, whichever occurs first. Although the bankruptcy code goes to great lengths to defend the claims of bondholders and other high-ranking creditors, it offers little protection to workers who are due pensions. In fact, some businesses have employed a tactic known as strategic bankruptcy—meaning going into bankruptcy to void obligations to workers (Orr 1998). Even in ordinary bankruptcies, workers may have to content themselves with mere pennies on the dollars that corporations owe them, while business creditors face much less risk.

While too poor to pay their obligations to workers, many bankrupt firms can and often do continue to give lavish fees to managers—frequently the very same ones that drove the firm into bankruptcy in the first place. For example, a bankrupt Pacific Gas and Electric Co. and its parent company awarded eleven top executives more than $30 million in salaries, bonuses and deferred compensation in 2001, a year marked by bankruptcy and blackouts (Peyton 2002).

Similarly, Bernard Ebbers, who resigned as bankrupt WorldCom's chief executive in April 2002, was awarded a pension of $1.5 million a year for the rest of his life and was paying only about 2 per cent interest on $408 million in loans he took from the company. Enforcing the cap on payments to workers could have saved WorldCom about $36 million (Young 2002).

Benjamin Barber summed up that anomalous treatment of business risk:

In contrast to [the] depiction of businessmen as altruistic adventurers who take brave risks on behalf of a timid society, modern executives rank among the world's most conservative risk-avoiders. America has not socialized its industries, but it has been a pioneer in what the social scientist Theodore Lowi has dubbed "the socialization of risk." That is, it leaves the profits for the private sector and places all the risks on the public sector, spreading them judiciously across the backs of the taxpayers. What remains of the distinction between the two sectors once this process is completed? What sense can the free marketeer's plea for "freedom from planning" have under these circumstances? [Barber 1984: 256]

Insofar as risk is concerned, the rhetoric is the exact opposite of the reality. Although corporate profits are supposed to be, at least in part, a reward for risk-taking, the government shields the corporations from risk at every turn. At the same time, corporations work overtime to shift the remaining risks to others. Ordinary individuals bear the risks of workplace accidents and diseases, unemployment, environmental degradation, and defective consumer-products.

## THE ABSENCE OF PROTECTIONS FOR ORDINARY PEOPLE

The term "Chapter 11," usually associated with bankruptcy, has a dual meaning for the corporate sector. In its more familiar guise, Chapter 11 of the bankruptcy code provides a sanctuary for the corporations. Under the guidance of a court, the corporation may present a plan to its creditors in which it may agree to sell off some of its assets while the creditors allow the corporation to reduce the value of its debts.

The more modern Chapter 11 is far more ominous. First written into the North American Free Trade Agreement (NAFTA) with virtually no comment in the press, this new Chapter 11 allows foreign corporations to sue in national courts for profits they claim they could have made in the absence of domestic laws and regulations. This chapter also allows companies to appeal to NAFTA tribunals, which can overrule U.S. court rulings, even those coming from the Supreme Court.

The United States government has been going to great lengths to get similar procedures incorporated in all of its trade agreements. The World Trade Organization already provides for a somewhat similar mechanism, except that under a WTO ruling, the state that brings the challenge has the right to impose penalties on the offending state in the form of tariffs.

True, countries do pass laws and regulations intended to protect domestic producers, but they also pass laws and regulations to protect the health and safety of their citizens. For example, under Chapter 11, corporations who export food to the United States have the right to challenge laws designed to restrict the amount of pesticides in food as a restraint on trade. If the challenge is upheld, the states could still enforce the law, but only if they compensate the exporters. Worse yet, these proceedings take place behind closed doors. The public can only learn about the ruling after the fact.

So, while the U.S. government actively works to minimize risk for corporations, it does relatively little to protect human beings.

Instead, the government actively promotes the Chapter 11 of the NAFTA agreement to the world at large. To the extent that the government succeeds, regulations intended to protect citizens from hazardous products or production techniques will become vulnerable to challenges. The United States government has so far only protested one ruling that challenges a domestic regulation—a prohibition of on-line gambling—a law that the World Trade Organization also ruled to be illegal (Richtel 2004). The federal government has acquiesced in all other such rulings.

## KNIGHT ON TURNOVER AND JOB SECURITY

While the state thoughtfully protects corporations from risk, corporations expose the rest of society to significant risks. As mentioned earlier, workers increasingly lack security in their employment, but they enjoy no profit from bearing such risks. In fact, some of the jobs with the greatest risks pay the lowest wages.

Consideration of the risk of unemployment brings us back to Frank Knight's idea that profit is a reward for successful risk-bearing. Knight seems to have had a relatively restrictive idea of risk bearing. His prototypical risk-bearing entrepreneur risks funds by purchasing labor and materials. Workers' stakes are, in some sense, much higher. As I discussed in the sections on workers' safety in Chapter 3, far too many people risk their own physical well-being on the job.

To his credit, Knight briefly alluded to the problem of workers' risks:

> the risk of destruction and total loss is perhaps as great in fact in the case of the laborer as in the case of the property-owner, and where in the latter case the owner loses only productive power the former loses health or bodily members or his life, which means more. The real merits of this situation are also being recognized by society and we see the growth of legislation designed to transfer the hazard of loss of the economic value of the laborer as a productive agent (and this only, so far) to the business and through it to the consumer of the product. [Knight 1921: 355]

Unfortunately, once Knight made this comment, he let the matter drop. No major political figure even raised the possibility of the sort of legislation that Knight hoped might provide some sort of remedy. In fact, companies are now beginning to have their employees sign agreements—either before they can come to work or before they can receive medical treatment after an injury—to waive their right to sue for injury on the job. If only the asbestos industry had thought of that tactic, their balance sheets could have been much healthier.

Workers' risks go well beyond matters of health and safety, but because these risks are not seen as business risks they fall outside of Knight's concerns. Even risks that might seem to be economic risks, such as having to sell and buy homes to relocate for new jobs, do not qualify as business risks because they do not involve a commercial investment.

In terms of risk, workers suffer under numerous disadvantages relative to business interests. Investors, for instance, can easily diversify, minimizing risk by putting their funds in multiple ventures. Investors can raise money either from banks or through financial markets, shifting some of the risk to those who put up the money. Workers generally have more difficulty borrowing money, except from credit card companies, which charge usurious interest rates.

Yet, today workers are bearing more and more risk. Job insecurity is merely one of the increased risks that workers now face. Even where union contracts supposedly shield workers from some risks, an obscure clause known as *force majeure* (meaning cause beyond control) allows business to ignore the contract.

For example in May 2003, the fourth-largest airline in the United States, Northwest Airlines, citing a decline in Asian traffic because of the outbreak of severe acute respiratory syndrome (SARS), invoked the *force majeure* clause to lay off employees without notice. This action was the third time in 18 months that Northwest had invoked this clause. It had previously done so after the September 11, 2001 terrorist attacks and again in March 2003, citing the war in Iraq (Maynard 2003).

Workers also face financial risks when corporations divert funds from their pension plans. Corporations need only show that their investments of the pension funds will earn enough to cover their obligations. The profits in excess of their obligations belong to the corporation. Corporations often divert money from their pension plans, promising that spectacular profits from investment in the remaining of pension funds will be more than adequate to meet future pension obligations. Profits that fall short of these corporate projections can subject employees to the risk that their pensions will not be able to provide the promised benefits.

One economist proposed that Knight's logic should allow workers to claim a share of firms' profits, over and above their wages, on the grounds that workers bore so much risk (Jonsson 1978). In all fairness to Knight, he was not predisposed to seeing the risks associated with job insecurity. To begin with, Knight was profoundly conservative. In addition, the economic thinking of the time was far more concerned with the inverse of job insecurity; namely, an excessive turnover of workers that represented a cost to business.

Indeed, shortly before Knight published his work, many employers were facing extraordinary rates of turnover. The problem at the time was in large part of business' own making. Business was attempting to speed up production beyond the rate that workers found acceptable, and in many cases endurable. In response, workers tended to leave jobs after a very short period.

For example, at Ford's major factory, annual turnover rates in 1913 had soared to an almost unbelievable 370 per cent.. The company had to hire a total of 50,448 men that year just to maintain an average labor force of 13,623. Company surveys at Ford revealed that more than 7,300 workers left in March 1913 alone. Of these, 18 per cent were discharged; 11 per cent formally quit; and 71 per cent were let go because they missed five days in a row without excuse and so were deemed to have quit. On each day, it was necessary to make use of 1,300 or 1,400 replacement workers without any experience (Raff and Summers 1987, S 63–4). One observer remarked, "the Ford Motor Co. had reached the point of owning a great factory without having enough workers to keep it humming" (Sward 1972: 48–9).

Hiring so many new workers, even unskilled workers, and offering them a minimum of training was an expensive proposition. Stephen Meyer estimated that Ford spent $35 to break in each new worker. With 52,000 workers entering the Ford factory in 1913, the company lost $1,820,000 just because of turnover (Meyer 1981).

Ford's situation may have been more drastic than that of other companies, but it was not unique. As a result, the major corporations at the time were concerned with taking measures to increase workers' attachment to their jobs. Given this atmosphere, I am not surprised that Frank Knight never brought out job insecurity as a risk. Instead, turnover must have appeared more like a serious risk for the entrepreneur.

### RISK AND "SOUND SCIENCE"

Unemployment is only one of the many risks that corporations impose on society. They often sell products that harm consumers—

sometimes with lethal effects. They release toxins that put society as a whole at risk. In the process, the corporation can profit handsomely, while those who bear the risk must suffer the consequences.

Ordinary people have only two avenues of protection: They can appeal to the courts to remedy their circumstances or they can trust that government regulation will protect them. Corporations can and do muster enormous resources to ensure that they are free to operate relatively unencumbered by interference from either regulators or the courts. I have already discussed the tort reform movement, which has successfully limited the ability of individuals to turn to the courts. That movement's momentum will undoubtedly constrain such rights even more in the future unless the public gets involved.

Corporations have succeeded in getting government to subject new regulations to cost-benefit analysis as part of a larger movement to reduce regulator oversight of corporate activities. This particular victory did not come without a touch of irony. The government originally developed cost-benefit as "a means of project 'justification' alone (this word is used in the US Government literature) ... ; in American practice (as distinct from theory) it often has served as window dressing for projects whose plans have already been formulated with little if any reference to economic criteria" (Marglin 1967: 18).

Within a decade, aggressive supporters of cost-benefit analysis turned its original purpose on its head. Rather than supporting government programs, the technique was used to eliminate them. This turn of events cannot be terribly surprising to anybody familiar with cost-benefit analysis.

Although the idea of measuring costs and benefits sounds as if it promises a scientific, objective analysis, in practice, cost-benefit analysis is woefully simple to manipulate. Skilled practitioners of this technique can easily obtain whatever results that they desire. So, depending on its preferences, a government agency can just as easily invoke cost-benefit analysis to reject an action as to justify that same action.

According to the requirement of meeting the test of cost-benefit analysis, the government compares estimates of an economic measure of a potential harm that a regulation might prevent with estimates of the economic costs of prevention. Armed with this new cost-benefit mechanism, the corporate sector or government agencies sympathetic to the corporate sector set out to minimize the estimated risks of harm, while inflating the estimates of the costs of regulation.

Manipulating these estimates is very easy. To begin with, all too often the government has no choice but to accept industry's inflated estimates of the cost of regulations. In addition, since many of the costs and benefits do not involve marketed commodities, placing values on them offers another source of latitude for unscrupulous risk-benefit calculations. Finally, the practice of risk assessment often involves confidently placing precise probabilities on what are really uncertainties.

So while risk assessment might seem to be a proper activity for statisticians or actuaries, in reality, risk assessment—or at least what goes by the name of risk assessment—has turned into a highly charged political activity. In short, when practiced by those with vested interests, risk assessment becomes little more than an exercise in public relations with a pseudoscientific gloss (see Heinzerling and Ackerman 2002).

To lend credibility to their analysis, corporations go beyond manufacturing risk-benefit analyses. They launch smear campaigns against researchers who point to corporate responsibility for creating risks. The corporate-friendly anti-regulators use harsh rhetorical terms, such as "junk science," to denounce studies that support the case for regulatory or compensatory actions. Unlike the "junk science," practiced by those whose work supports the need for regulation, researchers funded by corporations purport to use only "sound science"—at least according to the prevailing corporate rhetoric. Peter Huber, whose book *Galileo's Revenge: Junk Science in the Courtroom* set off the movement to counter junk science, once explained that junk science included under this rubric "anything that associated victim harm with toxic exposure or medical negligence" (cited in Alliance for Justice 1993: 54).

For example, in early 2004, the Union of Concerned Scientists issued a report, signed by 48 Nobel laureates detailing a number of instances in which the Bush administration had violated scientific principles. The report charged that the administration ignored or even distorted scientific information when findings disturbed its political agenda and that the administration stacked scientific panels with people with strong industry connections rather than scientific credentials. One particular incident concerned White House interference with an Environmental Policy Administration report on the dangers of global warming (Union of Concerned Scientists 2004). This stance was consistent with the administration's vigorous dismissal of the scientific concerns about the dangers of global warming: the administration preferred instead to rely upon the reassuring insistence from the petroleum industry that global warming does not represent any threat at all.

Interestingly enough, about the same time as the report appeared, *Fortune* magazine reported on a Defense Department project that examined the grave risks that global warming posed for national security (Stipp 2004). For example, the report speculated:

> Canada might keep its hydropower—causing energy problems in the US. North and South Korea may align to create one technically savvy and nuclear-armed entity. Europe may act as a unified block—curbing immigration problems between European nations—and allowing for protection against aggressors. Russia, with its abundant minerals, oil, and natural gas may join Europe. In this world of warring states, nuclear arms proliferation is inevitable. As cooling drives up demand, existing hydrocarbon supplies are stretched thin. With a scarcity of energy supply—and a growing need for access—nuclear energy will become a critical source of power, and this will accelerate nuclear proliferation as countries develop enrichment and reprocessing capabilities to ensure their national security. China, India, Pakistan, Japan, South Korea, Great Britain, France, and Germany will all have nuclear weapons capability, as will Israel, Iran, Egypt, and North Korea. [Schwartz and Randall 2003]

## DOWNPLAYING RISK FOR THE CORPORATIONS

Corporations responsible for creating risks to health and safety naturally take a keen interest in supporting convenient "sound science," which promises to minimize one particular type of risk—the risk to corporate balance sheets. Accordingly, they generously fund institutions, such as the Harvard Center for Risk Analysis, prestigiously located within the university's School of Public Health. This center specializes in producing studies that reassure the world that the potential harm from food contamination, pesticides, or nuclear power do not pose a threat to society. More than one hundred large corporations and trade associations fund the Center, including such known environmental offenders as Dow, 3M, DuPont, Monsanto and Exxon, in addition to the Chlorine Chemistry Council, the American Automobile Manufacturers Association, the American Petroleum Institute, and the Chemical Manufacturers Association, now called the American Chemistry Council. High-ranking corporate officers from Oxford Oil, the National Association of Manufacturers, Eastman

Chemical, Tenneco Inc., CK Witco Corp., and Novartis Corp. sit on the Center's executive board. Its Advisory Council includes executives from DuPont and the Grocery Manufacturers Association, and the chief attorney for environmental affairs at Exxon Chemical Americas (see Public Citizen 2001).

The Center uses a three-pronged attack on regulation. It minimizes the estimated benefits of regulation while maximizing the estimated costs. Then it caps its case by arguing that money spent on regulation would do far more good in other areas, such as vaccinating children. In their eyes, allocating money for regulation rather than spending it on vaccinations or some other worthy purposes is tantamount to "statistical murder" (see Graham 1995).

The anti-regulators' argument would seem more sincere if they were to devote even a small fraction of their energy into lobbying for the more effective social programs that they recommend in lieu of regulation. To my knowledge, they have not expended any efforts in that direction—not even for the vaccinations that the anti-regulators prefer. Instead, Graham and the anti-regulators seem intent on finding justifications for inaction insofar as protecting health and safety are concerned.

Even more hypocritically, Graham had proposed programs to encourage the cessation of smoking as another cost-effective life-saving strategy—preferable to regulation. He neglected to disclose to his readers that shortly prior to publication of his article, as director of the Harvard Center for Risk Analysis, he had successfully solicited funds from Philip Morris in order to help the Center promote a more "balanced way" of thinking about risk (Ackerman and Heinzerling 2004: 128).

The Center has been very effective in communicating its perspective to the media, regulators, and the courts. Emblematic of its success, President George W. Bush appointed John D. Graham, founding director, to be Administrator of the Office of Information and Regulatory Affairs of the Office of Management and Budget. This seemingly obscure office, established by the 1980 Paperwork Reduction Act, has extraordinary powers. Graham's office has the responsibility to scrutinize any significant or controversial regulation before it can be implemented, including the responsibility for comparing the costs and benefits of regulations. The government relies heavily on the findings of this office. If Graham's operation reports that the risk of a problem is low, then so too would be the presumed benefits of regulation. So, by downplaying risks enough, this office can claim that regulations are unwarranted.

The administration could not have expected Graham to be particularly objective regarding regulations, given his work with the Center. After all, Graham announced in a speech to the Heritage Foundation in 1996: "Environmental regulation should be depicted as an incredible intervention in the operation of society" (Seelye 2001).

Graham did not disappoint enemies of regulation. His office has successfully lobbied to have the Environmental Protection Agency use a new estimate of the value of a human life—$3.7 million, and $2.3 million for people over 70 years of age—alongside the $6.1 million that the agency had previously used. Similarly, Graham's office pressured the agency to publish alternative estimates for the benefits of reductions in annual deaths from particulate matter and ozone. The agency estimated 11,900 fewer deaths; Graham's office, 7,200. The more modest numbers dropped the estimated benefits of regulation from $96 billion by 2020 to $11 billion (Skrzycki 2002). Although these lowered estimates are not legally binding, they allow opponents of regulation to cite them as official figures to exaggerate the costs of regulation. Of course, all such estimates of the value of human life necessarily entail a considerable portion of uncertainty.

How does one value human life anyway? The existing EPA calculations leave much to be desired. The numbers the agency provides depend upon the earnings capacity of the affected people, meaning that those harms that afflict poor people weigh less than those that might affect the rich. To make matters worse, both estimates from the Environmental Protection Agency systematically neglect numerous other adverse effects that the regulations might reduce. Graham's efforts would do nothing to correct these deficiencies. They would merely lower the estimated benefits of regulation.

A constant theme of the corporate risk assessment industry is that an irrational fear of the unknown lies at the heart of the support for regulation. In the words of William Greider, a keen observer of political life in the United States:

A favorite put-down of the unreason in public is the accusation that Americans wish to live in a "risk-free" society ... the complaint is usually expressed by business leaders or conservative scholars who do not themselves live next door to a hazardous-waste dump or downwind from a factory spewing dangerous chemicals into the air. Their economic status and political power

protect them from such risks, though they think others ought to be willing
to accept them. [Greider 1992: 54–5]

While the corporate line is that the public at large is "irrational"
about risk, the corporations and their defenders insist that those
people, such as cigarette smokers, whose behavior puts them at risk,
are actually making rational choices, according to Kip Viscusi, one
of Graham's colleagues whom I will discuss in the next chapter.
Consequently, they should accept the full responsibility for their
actions.

Supposedly, according to the corporate-friendly risk analysis
industry, the world would be a better place if people had a more
"realistic" view of risk, where the corporations get to decide what the
"reality" should be. Unfortunately, substantial unknowns contaminate
supposedly scientific analysis, but when corporate-friendly science
becomes the arbiter of risk, the outcome is virtually certain.

## DEVALUING LIFE

One of the most cynical applications of "scientific risk management"
concerns the Environmental Protection Agency's "Aging Initiative"
announced by EPA Administrator Christie Whitman in late October
2002. The ostensible purpose of this initiative was to protect older
persons from environmental health threats.

The stated goal of the initiative seemed reasonable enough. After
all, the population of the United States is aging rapidly. Part of
this initiative, however, was to find a more "realistic" technique
for putting a value on the benefits of saving a human life. Rather
than displaying much serious interest in helping senior citizens, the
Environmental Protection Agency proposed to measure the benefits
of environment protection in terms of years of life saved.

In other words, the value of preserving the life of a senior citizen
should be less than that of a younger person. This approach plays
upon the common human tendency to mourn the death of a child
more than that of a man who has enjoyed a great portion of his
life. Of course, Graham's logic could just as easily be used to call
for an increase in the value of a policy to save a young person's life
rather than decreasing the value of actions to save the life of an
older person.

Or, alternatively, one could lower the value of older lives while
increasing the value of younger lives. Applying that approach to

environmental regulations could logically redistribute the emphasis without reducing the overall effort to protect human health. If, however, the priority is to protect corporate balance sheets, then the tactic of merely reducing environmental protection becomes the primary objective. In that context, merely devaluing the lives of senior citizens makes perfectly good sense.

Unlike most efforts to cut regulation at the time, no amount of public relations was able to make this effort seem to be anything other than what it was: a crude attempt to minimize environmental protection. The proposal ran into a torrent of criticism. Senior citizens groups vehemently denounced it as the "senior death discount." Eventually, the Environmental Protection Agency had to back down, distancing itself from this approach shortly before the administrator of the agency tendered her resignation (Seelye and Tierney 2003).

## THE MADNESS OF RISK ASSESSMENT

Let us return to the allegedly sound science that underlies cost-benefit analysis. One part of the equation concerns risk assessment. In theory, one should look at the data to get a measure of risk, as in the case of flipping a coin. In the case of most risk assessment, the data is not quite as clear cut, which gives investigators ample opportunity to distort the probabilities.

Take the example of the explosion of the Challenger spacecraft on January 28, 1986, a disaster that captured the attention of the American people for weeks. The government formed a task force to investigate the cause of this tragedy. The committee included Richard Feynman, a famous physicist, who is credited with discovering that a defective O-ring was responsible for the explosion.

Writing about his experience in the investigation, Feynman observed that the people in charge of the space program were (willfully?) ignorant of the risks associated with their project. According to Feynman, Louis J. Ullman, the range safety officer at Kennedy Space Center, where the Challenger launch occurred, said that five of 127 previous rockets had failed, representing about 4 per cent of the total flights. Ullman assumed that manned flights would be safer, so he figured a 1 per cent failure rate. The National Aeronautics and Space Administration told Ullman that the probability of failure was one in 100,000. Ullman could never figure how the agency arrived at its estimate (Feynman 1988: 179). Shortly before the explosion, Bryan O'Connor, NASA's Washington-based director of the shuttle program, recalls that he "asked someone what the probability risk assessment was for the loss of a shuttle. I was told it was one in ten thousand" (Rampton and Stauber 2000: 114)—or one-tenth of Ullman's numbers.

So, we have three official estimates of the risk: 1 in 100; 1 in 10,000; and 1 in 100,000, compared with an historical record of about 4 in 100. Such estimates were bandied about without any discussion of the assumptions upon which they rested.

Later, NASA launched the unmanned Cassini mission to explore Saturn. The danger of the Cassini mission was magnified by the 72.3 pounds of plutonium that it carried for fuel. If the Cassini had crashed, that plutonium would have scattered, causing untold fatalities. What were the risks of an accident? Three out of the 26 earlier U.S. nuclear space missions had involved mishaps, yet NASA attempted to calm public fears about the dangers, again estimating an infinitesimal risk and asserting that if a crash were to occur only 50,000 people would die from the resulting cancers. Fortunately, NASA completed the mission without an accident.

The public views NASA as one of the premier scientific agencies associated with the government. It probably has as much credibility with the public as any arm of the government. Coming from NASA, probabilities of catastrophes would seem fairly credible, unless people realize that NASA manufactures such numbers from whole cloth. The agency's risk assessments were meaningless, except as calming gestures to assure the public that it has no need to worry and that it should allow the authorities to continue their programs.

Public confidence in the space program serves a useful purpose for NASA. In fact, had the Cassini mission failed, the public would have been mostly left to fend for itself, because Congress had amended the Price-Anderson Act to provide protection against liability for accidents for both NASA and its corporate contractors, who actually do the majority of its work.

The danger of nuclear accidents in space is ballooning because the U.S. government is intent on dominating space militarily. Many space weapons require massive power sources. For this reason, the government is committed to developing the nuclear component of the space program, including nuclear-based rockets in an effort known as Project Prometheus.

The government assures the public that they need not fear the risk of one of these nuclear-based rockets crashing back to earth. Of course, the Price-Anderson protection from nuclear accidents would have been unnecessary if this program were as safe as the authorities claim that it is.

People in authority are less likely to take risk assessment seriously. The nuclear power industry again offers a classic example. When addressing the public, the industry insists that nuclear power is perfectly safe and that the risk of an accident is negligible. For example, in the early 1970s, the government of the United States had developed a plan to increase the number of nuclear generating plants from 50 to 950 new constructed in the next 25 years.

In support of this plan, the Atomic Energy Commission sponsored a massive 21-volume Reactor Safety Study in 1987, headed up by Dr Norman Rasmussen of the Massachusetts Institute of Technology. The report predicted that a core damage accident in nuclear power reactors in the United States would occur only once in every 20,000 years of operation, with one reactor running for one year counting as a year of operating experience (Wald 2003b).

Critics condemned the report, observing that the methodology was the same that NASA had already rejected as being overly optimistic. Henry Kendall, a physicist, said that the commission's safety claims "are a conceit based far more on their enthusiasm for the nuclear power program than on solid and convincing proof" (Burnham 1974). Indeed, coming from NASA, whose own record for objective risk appraisal leaves much to be desired, the Atomic Energy Commission report still stands as stark testimony to the flimsiness of risk assessment. A mere four years after the report appeared, the Three Mile Island reactor suffered a catastrophic accident only a few miles from Dr Rasmussen's birthplace of Harrisburg, Pennsylvania.

Peter A. Bradford, a member of the Nuclear Regulatory Commission from 1977 to 1982, observed that before the 1979 accident at Three Mile Island, the commission considered such explosions impossible. After the one at Three Mile Island, he said, the commission still considered them impossible, "because now that we had one, we would be too vigilant for another to occur" (Wald 2003a).

The rush of security concerns that followed in the wake of the attacks of September 11, 2001 cast further light on the relationship between risk assessment and nuclear power. At the time, officials used the convenient threat of the risk of terrorism to justify all manner of policies they had previously been unable to carry out. Yet, when the threat of this supposedly pervasive risk tended to work against desired policies, officials cavalierly swept it aside.

Nowhere was this attitude toward risk more blatant than in the licensing of nuclear power plants. In the wake of the attack on the World Trade Center, when protection against terrorist risk was supposed to be a major factor in virtually all public decisions, the Nuclear Regulatory Commission ruled that the licensing decision may not consider the threat of terrorism because the risk is too speculative. The commission also forbade discussion of the issue in an open licensing hearing because it would give too much information to terrorists and might "unduly alarm the public." In its wisdom, the commission ruled that "we have no way to calculate the probability portion of the equation, except in such general terms as to be nearly meaningless" (Wald 2003a).

What would "unduly alarm" mean? The government has been alarming the public in order to rush through all manner of security measures. Nuclear power facilities seem to be especially inviting targets. Just letting water out of the ponds used for the storage of nuclear waste does not seem to present a great technical challenge to an organization that could simultaneously hijack four jet planes. I can think of only one interpretation of "unduly alarm": discussion of terror threats might make the public less hospitable to the siting of nuclear plants near their homes. You can, however rest assured. The government has plans to have states consider distributing potassium iodide pills to people within ten miles of a reactor to use in the event of a disaster.

In sum, risk assessment appears to be little more than a branch of public relations. The government insists on strict risk assessment when the analysis supports a desired result and ignores it when the outcome would be inconvenient.

## THE POLITICS OF RISK

We can divide risk into three categories: inevitable, avoidable, and imaginary. Inevitable risks can include catastrophic events. For example, we know that sooner or later San Francisco will experience a major earthquake and that a huge meteor will eventually strike the earth. Since the probability that such disasters will occur at any time is so small, most people when organizing their lives take no account of the risks associated with such calamities.

I have already discussed the avoidable risks of the exploding gas tanks in vehicles from Ford and General Motors. These risks were acceptable to the executives who made the decision, because the company calculated that the potential liability that the company faced was less than the cost of preventing the deaths and injuries.

Imaginary risks are more difficult to pin down. For example, although the risks of crime are real, politicians and the media make the public imagine that the risk of crime is far greater than it is in reality. Yet, just as corporations, government, or the media can inflate risk, they can just as easily downplay risks when it suits them. Recall, for example, the claims that risks associated with the space program and nuclear power were far less than they really were.

Risk, as I mentioned earlier, is unavoidable. Even measures to avoid risk often create new risks. For example, medicines used to prevent one condition often create the risks of unexpected side effects. Such unintended consequences are commonplace in efforts to control risk, since people generally lack adequate information to take into account all of the ramifications of any particular choice of action.

Once a potential risk becomes a reality, someone must bear the costs. The rules for assigning such costs are vague. The means are cumbersome. Recall how the litigation has continued for more than a decade regarding Exxon Mobil's liability for the vast *Exxon Valdez* oil spill. So, even when a corporation might eventually pay for such damages, court costs might consume much of what plaintiffs hope to win.

In short, risk is like a hot potato, but one that is part real and part imaginary. Nobody wants to be stuck with it. If people do happen to end up with the hot potato, they want to ensure that others will bear some, if not most, of the cost. Everyone naturally prefers to avoid responsibility for compensating those who compensate the victims.

In a chilling address, Peter R. Fisher, then Under Secretary of the Treasury, told a sympathetic audience: "Think of the federal government as a gigantic insurance company (with a side line business in national defense and homeland security)" (Fisher 2002). Fisher made these remarks after the George W. Bush administration had won two massive tax cuts and pursued two costly wars. The combination of these policies was about to push the federal budget deficit to record heights.

Under Secretary Fisher never mentioned the possibility of limiting future military adventures or even curtailing corporate welfare. Nor did he propose to modify the two massive tax cuts passed during the Bush administration. Instead, he warned of catastrophic consequences if the government does not cut back its "insurance coverage" for non-corporate individuals.

Under Secretary Fisher's silence regarding the tax cuts is not terribly surprising. In fact, some of those who framed the tax cuts looked forward to a fiscal train wreck. In part, their objective was to destroy government programs, such as social security and Medicare, which help to shield individuals from risk, to open the field for corporate providers.

Yet, Fisher did not give the slightest hint of recognition that his recommendations would leave the least fortunate in society to bear even more risks on their own. Indeed, cutting back on assisting individuals in order to reduce the taxes paid by the corporate sector and the very wealthy is a perfect example of shifting the hot potato back to those who could least afford the cost in order to reduce the burden of those who could most afford it.

Fisher, of course, was no stranger to bailing out the rich and powerful. Recall that he was the key figure in orchestrating the bailout of Long-Term Credit Management. Investors around the world had reason to be grateful to Fisher and the Fed. Unfortunately, by all appearances Fisher was by no means as concerned about the risks that ordinary people face—risks, which government programs, such as Medicare, moderate.

### THE PRECAUTIONARY PRINCIPLE

The vagueness of the system for assigning liability gives a substantial advantage to those who would impose risks on the rest of society. For example, critics of genetically modified agricultural products suggest that because the genes in these crops can cross over into other species this technology creates the risk of producing superweeds that can do great damage to the ecosystem (see Wilkinson et al. 2003).

Suppose that before embarking on such a technology, the genetically modified agriculture industry would first have to purchase an insurance policy that would indemnify the rest of society just in case the critics were correct. If such a rule were in effect, this technology would have had to wait to begin until scientists had completed much more testing. Instead, as I have shown, the regulators took a cavalier attitude toward the risks associated with genetically engineered crops.

Many scientists propose an approach that they call the precautionary principle. The precautionary principle shifts the burden of proof regarding the safety of any new technology to those who wish to introduce it. In the words of the 1998 Wingspread Conference in Racine, Wisconsin:

> The release and use of toxic substances, the exploitation of resources, and physical alterations of the environment have had substantial unintended consequences affecting human health and the environment. Some of these concerns are high rates of learning deficiencies, asthma, cancer, birth defects and species extinctions; along with global climate change, stratospheric ozone depletion and worldwide contamination with toxic substances and nuclear materials .... When an activity raises threats of harm to human health or the environment, precautionary measures should be taken even if some cause and effect relationships are not fully established scientifically. [http://www.rachel.org/library/getfile.cfm?ID=189]

Former New Jersey Governor, Christine Todd Whitman, publicly endorsed the precautionary principle in a speech delivered only a few months before her appointment to head George W. Bush's Environmental Protection Agency. She told her audience:

> we must 1) acknowledge that uncertainty is inherent in managing natural resources, 2) recognize it is usually easier to prevent environmental damage than to repair it later, and 3) shift the burden of proof away from those advocating protection toward those proposing an action that may be harmful. [Whitman 2000]

Sadly, during her tenure at the Environmental Protection Agency, Ms Whitman's behavior gave no evidence that she had been sincere in her declaration.

The precautionary principle is the inverse of the criminal justice system in which the defendant is assumed to be innocent until proven guilty; however, the application of the criminal justice standard is inappropriate in the sphere of technology. In the case of the criminal justice system, the trial comes only after the damage is done. The burden of proof is then set to minimize the risk of convicting the wrong person, since the harm done by the crime cannot be reversed.

In the case of weighing the costs and benefits of new and unproven technology, society has the opportunity of preventing harm, perhaps even great harm, even though the extent of the harm cannot be known in advance. Critics charge that the precautionary principle is a recipe for technological inaction. Of course, further research, including small scale testing where feasible, could allow technology to evolve once society has sufficient information.

Even if testing ultimately proves technology to be safe, the research would probably make it more effective. For example, the application of the precautionary principle would require considerable interdisciplinary scientific work, which although its initial focus might survey potential risks, it would also be likely to stimulate fruitful research. The corporate sector, however, has no guarantee that it could earn a profit from that research—any more than the public has any guarantee that the technology will be safe.

Let us assume, for the purpose of argument that the precautionary principle does inhibit increases in productivity, the fact remains that the rich already enjoy many of the benefits of the precautionary principle. The economic system denies the poor comparable protections. For example, governments refuse to let toxic waste dumps, power plants, or even freeways for the most part, locate alongside affluent neighborhoods. The prohibition of such unpleasant intrusions increases the value of the homes of the wealthy, while depressing the value of poor neighborhoods, even though the poor may see relatively few benefits from the improved productivity that supposedly occurs in the absence of the precautionary principle.

This partial application of the precautionary principle—the shifting of the burden of proof from the people adversely affected by a risk-creating policy to those who want to profit from such a policy—is equivalent to an enormous transfer of wealth from the poor to the rich.

This transfer shows up in housing values. People pay a premium for homes in wealthy communities where the clout of the population is sufficient to eliminate threats to the quality of life, such as the risk of having to put up with nearby toxic wastes or excessive traffic.

The example of asbestos is very instructive in indicating how the precautionary principle might work in the long run. Cities in the mid-nineteenth century were very vulnerable to fire. Building codes mandated that asbestos be used as a life-saving precaution. The apparent benefits of this material were so great that nobody seemed to pay attention to the risks.

Interestingly enough, for two decades after German science recognized the link between asbestos and cancer, American science continued to focus on the benefits of asbestos. In the words of one study of the early use of asbestos: "Fire was an immediate and visible risk; asbestos was not" (Maines 2003). In the end, the widespread use of asbestos probably cost far more lives than it saved.

Many critics of the precautionary principle turn around and recommend that we continue with the current approach—what might be called the inverse precautionary principle—that no regulation be enforced without absolute proof of its necessity. Given the inverse precautionary principle, corporations only need to find people willing to produce a study to question the need for the regulation—even if the study flies in the face of the preponderance of scientific evidence.

Business has long known how to find convenient "expert opinions." For decades after smoking was known to be carcinogenic, tobacco companies could find a few scientists who were willing to cast doubt on the dangers of smoking. More recently, business still parades a handful of scientists who will testify that human activity does not cause global warming, despite the overwhelming evidence against their position.

Once business raises doubts about the scientific evidence, the corporations insist that the regulation would do great harm—always including job losses for the working people whose interests they have in mind. Finally, they can call for the government to do more studies before rushing headlong into an "unwarranted action"—what critics call "paralysis by analysis." In all of these endeavors, they are usually successful.

Corporations, of course, are not satisfied with merely debating the scientific value of the precautionary principle. Instead, corporations are beginning to mount an intense offensive, pulling out all the stops to discredit people who publicly advocate the precautionary principle. For example, Tim W. Shestek, an American Chemistry Council lobbyist in Sacramento, recommended that his organization hire Nichols-Dezenhall, a Washington-based firm that employs former FBI and CIA agents, to use deceptive tactics, such as a plan to "create an independent PP watchdog group to act as an information clearinghouse and criticize the PP in public and media forums." The memo also recommends:

Define the issues on our terms to stigmatize the PP [precautionary principle], win control of the message war and build awareness of the negative consequences associated with its implementation; [to conduct] selective intelligence gathering ... about the plans, motivations and allies of opposition activists .... Focus on the PP "movement leadership." [http://www.ewg.org/briefings/acc/California%20PP%20Campaign-2.doc]

More principled critics might admit that the precautionary principle may protect the environment, but they would charge that the general application of the precautionary principle would severely limit the extent of technical progress. While the precautionary principle might contribute to the immediate quality of life, over time technical progress also can augment the quality of life. Defenders of the precautionary principle can legitimately respond that the building up of the scientific infrastructure necessary to enforce the precautionary principle could yield even greater dividends in terms of technological advances.

### BROADER CONSIDERATIONS OF RISK AND INDIVIDUALISM

Considerations of risk throw us back to my earlier analysis of individualism. Long before anybody ever conceived of the concept of risk, I imagine that people frequently acted to protect each other against risks. In some cases, the risk would be communal, as when foreign marauders posed a threat to all. In other cases, the risk would be individual. Just as when more modern communities would band together to rebuild a neighbor's barn after a fire, earlier communities would band together to meet community needs. This collective behavior reflects the fact that we are not, as the modern ideologues would have us believe, merely solitary individuals, connected only through the market. Despite what Ms Thatcher said, communities are real.

In fact, real individualism in navigating one's life is all but impossible today. The public reacts with wonder when a person manages to survive on his own out in the wilderness. Even Defoe's Robinson Crusoe had the advantage of a slave and the materials that his ship offered to him. Community is far more real than the imagined individualism of contemporary ideologues.

Instead of tending to the real issues of community, modern capitalist nations are creating a monstrous sort of global corporate community, exclusively dedicated to the realization of profits. Led in this respect by the United States, these new communities provide generous support to the rich and the powerful, while calling upon the less fortunate to fend for themselves in the name of "individualism."

The present treatment of risk fits right in with this form of community. Poor people are told to buck up and accept their fate when they hit a streak of bad luck. Through the lens of this perverted form of community, unemployment insurance or welfare is nothing more than a subsidy to laziness. In contrast, corporate welfare is necessary for the prosperity of the nation. In effect, we see "individualism" (or capitalism) for the poor; socialism for the rich.

## RISK AND THE INDIVIDUAL IN A MARKET SOCIETY

The state has the power to protect private individuals as well as corporations from risk. I will pass over the extent to which the state defends individuals and/or corporations from risk by means of its military or police powers. Instead I want to take a moment to think about how the state can or should moderate economic risks.

Robert Haveman rhetorically once raised the question, "Does the welfare state increase welfare?" His response was a resounding affirmative: "In my view, the primary economic gain from the welfare state is universal *reduction in the uncertainty* faced by individuals. Life in a market economy is a treacherous enterprise" (Haveman 1985: 449).

Not surprisingly, the origins of the welfare state lie in the late nineteenth-century Germany of Chancellor Bismarck. The specter of the rise of a powerful Social Democratic party , which declared its rhetorical allegiance to the vision of Karl Marx, led Bismarck to pioneer various social programs. At the time, the opposition German Social Democratic Party may have been the largest political party in the world. In addition, during the late nineteenth century, German universities were the finest in the world. Many of the leading intellectuals in the United States went to Germany for their training then returned bringing the German vision of social welfare with them.

The German exhibit at the Paris Exhibition of 1900 impressed the world with the new spirit of German social reform. The Germans showed how the effectiveness of their compulsory, state-administered social insurance system worked, providing coverage against industrial accidents, sickness, and old age (see Rodgers 1998: 13–14). In the United States, in contrast, where fears of revolutionary change were far more remote, social democratic programs were relatively late in coming.

The German academics were aware that nation states are particularly well-suited to mitigating risk. In the first place, people who have studied the mathematics of risk have known for centuries that amalgamating large numbers into a pool makes risk more manageable and more affordable. For example, few people have the financial resources to be able to cover the expenses of any conceivable medical problem. But within a properly-structured, large insurance fund, the contributions of the many can cover the infrequent exceptional expenses of the few. In addition, nation states have the legal wherewithal to gather information that can help in formulating policies that can mitigate risk.

Private insurance companies can also pool risk, but their overhead costs, including lavish salaries for their executives, are much higher than public plans. Private companies must price their policies high enough to cover these costs and to allow for substantial profits. Worse yet, with the development of extensive databases, private insurance companies make extra profits by refusing to pool risks for the population as a whole. Instead, insurance companies "cherry pick" their clientele, refusing to insure people whom the companies believe to pose more than average risks; for example, individuals who live in predominately minority neighborhoods or gay men who might have a higher risk of AIDs. While these choices might make sound business sense for the insurance company, they undermine the original rationale for an insurance company by leaving those who are most vulnerable without coverage, unless the state intervenes.

A troubling, new corporate attitude toward jobs amplifies the need for state intervention. Until fairly recently, large corporations provided pensions, health care, and a degree of job security for many workers. Today, job security is in decline and corporations are phasing out defined benefit pensions. At the same time, corporations are making their workers bear a larger burden of their health-care costs, if they offer any help at all. To make matters worse, large corporations frequently contract out many jobs to non-unionized firms that provide few benefits or to foreign contractors who give no benefits whatsoever. In this new environment, workers are left to their own devices where no state support is available.

Michael Mandel, the economics editor for *Business Week*, made a rough estimate of some of the costs of risk. He included $150 billion for the risks created by recessions, $240 billion from job insecurity, $50 billion for the risks associated with retirement funds, and $135 billion from fear of what he called wage shifts, total $575 billion annually (Mandel 1996: 165). He concluded: "The annual cost of $575 billion may well be an underestimate" (Mandel 1996: 165).

Indeed, the absence of a welfare state creates other costs that Mandel neglected to mention. For example, recall our discussion of tort reform. Two avenues for reducing the cost of litigation are possible. We could, as the corporate sector proposes, restrict the right to sue and limit the potential remedies. Alternatively, we could expand the political responsibility for regulation, thereby eliminating many of the grounds for litigation.

Of course, no society can completely abolish risk, but the government can help to shelter people from some of the consequences of a society led by corporations that focus on self-dealing chasing after profits to the exclusion of any other considerations. Mandel cited the conclusion from one study that regarded the costs of economic fluctuations, which estimated that "consumers would roughly trade all growth for the elimination of fluctuations" (Mandel 1996: 159; citing Campbell and Cochrane 1995: 3).

Unfortunately, while the cost of risks has been soaring, the government has abdicated its responsibility for buffering those costs. The position expressed by Peter Fisher above suggests that the goal of the government is to move even further in that direction. The idea that the government should play a role by reducing risk for the general population flies in the face of the current rhetorical fashion that emphasizes the importance of individual responsibility. Recall Senator Santorum's declaration that making people struggle is a good thing.

But if the social welfare state has the potential to shelter people from the uncertainties of the market system and most people are vulnerable to these uncertainties, why is the support for the social welfare state so weak in the United States today? How did the antipathy for government become so strong?

A number of reasons come into play. To begin with, surveys indicate that the belief in individual responsibility is much stronger in the United States than in Western Europe. Maybe the mythology of Horatio Alger or the cowboy on the frontier affects the mentality of people in the United States.

Some researchers suggest that racism might be involved in the unwillingness to give the state more of a role in protecting individuals. For example, within the United States, those states that are more ethnically fragmented spend a smaller fraction of their budget on social services and productive public goods, and more on crime prevention (Alesina, Glaeser, and Sacerdote 2001: 229).

Daniel Levitas, author of an extensive study on extreme right-wing movements, comes to a similar conclusion. He makes the case that the passage of the 1964 Civil Rights Act, the 1965 Voting Rights Act, and federal enforcement of the 1954 *Brown* decision, which declared segregation in public schools unconstitutional, caused a sizeable number of white people to become more antagonistic toward taxes, believing that the financial product of their hard work was being used to support "undeserving" and "parasitic" elements of the population (read: black people) (Levitas 2002: 102–3). He cites one right-wing activist's interpretation: "The exactions demanded from the self-reliant and the largesse given the lazy, the incompetent, and the non-productive, cannot be an accident: all this MUST be the result of carefully constructed policy with long-range objectives" (Levitas 2002: 103; citing Larson 1979, pp. ix–x). Although he does not imply, any more than the Alesina, Glaeser, and Sacerdote paper does, that all anti-statist views are racist in nature, he does suggest that a growing racism helped to tilt public sentiment in that direction.

Regardless of the cause, the prevailing belief in the United States seems to be that a particular person is rich or poor because of his or her individual efforts. Europeans tend to give more weight to luck or social circumstances (Alesina and Angeletos 2002).

In effect, then, the U.S. mindset calls upon the state to emphasize the minimization of one kind of personal risk—namely crime—while preferring it avoid its responsibility to eliminate the sort of risks that Mandel discussed. Ironically the more energetic efforts in creating economic stability happen to be what is probably the most effective policy in reducing crime.

At the same time, many of the very people who oppose policies that shelter individuals from risk call upon the state to offer wildly generous benefits to the corporate sector. I would prefer that the state be no more considerate of corporations than it would be toward a young, immigrant, single mother of color.

# 7
# Food, Fear, and Terrorism

## THE POLITICAL ECONOMY OF FEAR

While corporations fume at the public's irrational fear of risk, these same corporations are more than willing to prey on such fears when hawking their wares. Even more effectively, conservative politicians have long mastered the practice of building up public fears to divert people from recognizing their real self-interest. In particular, the fear of crime has been a staple of conservative political campaigns for decades—even though crime has been plummeting, defying the dire predictions of the early 1990s (Levitt 2004). Even so, by 2002, the United States counted 6,732,400 adults in jail or prison, or on parole or probation (U.S. Department of Justice 2002, Table 6.1).

Although the tragic pain and suffering of victims of crime is real enough, the public is convinced that the risk of crime is much higher than it actually is. For example, in his lecture given up on reception of his Nobel Prize in economics, Daniel Kahneman noted "that the median estimate of the annual number of murders in Detroit is twice as high as the estimate of the number of murders in the Michigan mind" (Kahneman 2003: 1466–7).

The reason for this excessive fear is not hard to find. The media—especially television—fuels this fear of crime. You only need to turn on almost any television news program—the leading story will be some sensational crime. Although deaths from occupational diseases and injuries are three times greater than the total number or murders, the media incessantly repeats the murder stories while the occupational diseases and injuries go unreported.

This fear has swayed many voters to elect politicians who then turn around and undermine their wages, job security, health care, environmental protection, and other benefits. These corporate-friendly policies, which are responsible for countless deaths from food poisoning, workplace injuries, and environmental pollution, pose far more of a risk to the average citizen than the threat of crime.

In fact, the strategy of locking up as many people as possible does little to eliminate crime. Instead, excessive incarceration creates as much crime as any policy in the country. Once convicted, felons, even those who had been incarcerated for non-violent offenses—have difficulty in finding work. Ex-offenders can be denied public housing, welfare benefits, parental rights, the ability to obtain an education, and the mobility necessary to access jobs that require driving (Travis 2002: 18). Given such restrictive conditions, many ex-offenders see little choice but to return to crime. To make matters worse, many people, convicted of harmless crimes, such as the mere possession of a small quantity of marijuana, are likely to learn dangerous criminal skills during their imprisonment.

The collateral damage from imprisonment reinforces the likelihood of destructive criminal behavior in other ways. Incarceration guts families and even entire neighborhoods—often depriving young people of important support networks (Braman 2002). Although some children admittedly are better off separated from the abusive parents, I cannot believe that most of the 1.5 million children of incarcerated parents are positively affected by their absence (Mumola 2000).

In early 2004, Andrew Fastow, chief financial officer of the disgraced Enron Corporation, and his wife, Lea, who was the assistant treasurer, arranged a plea bargain for their crimes. Their agreement provided that both would not serve time simultaneously, so that their child would have a parent at home. I applaud the court for considering the child, but I have never heard of a poor child winning comparable consideration.

Spending on prisons diverts money from education, where it could provide young people with skills that would allow them to follow alternative futures that make crime less attractive. Gary Becker, the conservative, Nobel Prize-winning economist, took notice of the destructive consequences of excessive incarceration in his *Business Week* column:

> Only a slim majority of young black men are not in prison, on parole, bail, or probation, or have not been arrested at least once. There's reason to believe this shortage of desirable male companions discourages black women from marrying or staying married for long. The downward spiral is self-perpetuating. Studies suggest that the decline in the presence of fathers in black families harms sons more than daughters. As a result, the rapid growth in the number of black men in prisons impairs the following generation of black males as well. A longer-run reform would be to improve the schooling of young blacks, since their earnings still trail those of whites, partly because of the growing economic advantage of a good education. That improvement

will not be easy while so many black families are without two parents. [G. Becker 2003]

Becker's observations are rock-solid. Certainly, employers look unfavorably upon young people without higher education, especially those with a criminal record. So, massive incarceration creates a vicious circle, virtually ensuring the creation of a new generation of felons as those released from prison pass on their trade, as well as their anger and despair, to friends and family members, who may also see little opportunity for constructive lives.

In short, the almost indiscriminate imprisonment of poor people imposes heavy economic and social costs. Society loses the potential creativity of a large section of its youth, while footing an enormous bill to incarcerate an excessive number of people. If wealthy people faced imprisonment for drug charges instead of a quick drug rehabilitation course, the public at large might be more sensitive to such costs.

Despite the heavy burden that excessive incarceration imposes on society, as a political strategy it works magnificently. By exacerbating the fear of crime, more pressing public issues fall from view, leaving politicians free to curry favor with their wealthy campaign contributors, including those who benefit from private prisons.

The politics of fear also operates on an international scale. For many decades, a cleverly cultivated fear of communism loomed large in the American psyche, even though the threat to the United States was virtually nonexistent. Again, this atmosphere of fear has served conservative interests quite well. After all, more and more business had come to depend upon the largess from the Pentagon. In addition, money that goes into defense spending is unavailable for government activities, such as regulation, which business might find inconvenient. The clincher is that the "soft on communism" label effectively undermined the careers of politicians who were less likely to be friendly to business interests. Finally, actively creating instability abroad helps to create a broader market for U.S. arms merchants.

Indeed, once the Cold War ended, business had little reason to celebrate. President George H. W. Bush promised a peace dividend, which, not surprisingly, never materialized. Instead, political operatives hurriedly looked for alternative "enemies" to justify continued massive spending on defense, while diverting attention from more important issues that might not favor business. The first Gulf War offered a brief opportunity to ramp up the military, but after the initial euphoria about the easy victory, the military cast about for a new mission.

Colin Powell, then chairman of the Joint Chiefs of Staff of the U.S. armed forces, expressed the exasperation of the politically connected elements of the military in an interview with the *Army Times* in the spring of 1991: "I'm running out of demons. I'm down to Castro and Kim Il Sung" (Anon. 1991). In reality, the military's supposedly new mission had been in the works for quite a while. Only five days after the fall of the Berlin Wall, Colin Powell already had a proposal for a new strategy.

Within a few months of his 1991 statement, General Powell first began to give the public a glimpse of the ongoing plans for a new enlarged mission of the future military (Powell 1992–93). David Armstrong summed up Powell's approach:

> With the Soviets rapidly becoming irrelevant, Powell argued, the United States could no longer assess its military needs on the basis of known threats. Instead, the Pentagon should focus on maintaining the ability to address a wide variety of new and unknown challenges. This shift from a "threat based" assessment of military requirements to a "capability based" assessment would become a key theme of the Plan. The United States would move from countering Soviet attempts at dominance to ensuring its own dominance. Again, this project would not be cheap. [Armstrong 2002]

Powell was not alone in calling for this reorientation. Richard Cheney, then Secretary of Defense, as well as many of the most aggressive military advocates of the second Bush administration, joined in this call for world domination, disguised as a quest for security. The efforts did not go far at the time. George Stephanopoulos, deputy campaign manager for Governor Bill Clinton of Arkansas, said the first reaction to the Pentagon document was that it seemed to be "one more attempt" by defense officials "to find an excuse for big budgets instead of downsizing" (Tyler 1992).

Later, in the wake of the attacks on the World Trade Center and the Pentagon, the government had no trouble whatsoever whipping up public opinion to support a War on Terror that leads people to ignore matters that would otherwise concern them. For example, Kenneth Adelman, a member of the Pentagon's Defense Policy Board, proposed: "We should not try to convince people that things are getting better .... Rather, we should convince people that ours is the age of terrorism" (Milbank and Allen 2003).

While military strategy might seem a far cry from a study of the condition of the individual in a corporate society, in reality the connection is pretty direct. To begin with, military spending, like tax cuts, effectively starves other parts of the government, making the call for privatization of government services more attractive. In addition, military spending channels money to the large defense contractors, further tilting the economy in favor of the rich and the powerful. Finally, assuming responsibility for dominating the world creates incessant confrontations with forces in far off places. Each of these crises serves to create new fears that make the population more compliant and leaves people less likely to defend their welfare.

The glorification of the military and the police might seem to be at odds with the society that claims individualism as one of its highest values. After all, the military and the police ostensibly serve society as a whole, not the individual. Of course, one could argue that security is a prerequisite of the practice of individualism. That claim may be reasonable, but it also suggests that other forms of social action are also necessary for creating a desirable way of life, thereby negating the generally dogmatic antagonism toward almost all government activities.

The attitude toward the military is consistent with the practice of corporate society in one respect: while abstractly glorifying those who provide security or public safety the state actually does pitifully little for those on the front lines who actually bear the risks. Perhaps the most obvious evidence of this hypocrisy is the pitifully poor medical treatment offered to veterans, but veterans' grievances are far broader. For example, during the ongoing hostilities in Iraq and Afghanistan in 2003, the Pentagon first lobbied against offering "imminent danger pay" to soldiers and then urged Congress to exclude the provisions from the 2004 defense appropriations bill. Only under intense pressure did the government relent (Files 2003). Perhaps most outrageously, the Bush administration was charging soldiers injured in Iraq $8 a day for food when they arrived for medical treatment at the Fort Stewart in Georgia. Again, the government eventually backed down under pressure (Lindorff 2003).

The *Army Times* reacted angrily with an article entitled "An Act of 'Betrayal'" after the Bush administration began planning to cut back on commissaries and schools for military families: "The two initiatives are the latest in a string of actions by the Bush administration to cut or hold down growth in pay and benefits, including basic pay, combat pay, health care benefits and the death gratuity paid to survivors of troops who die on active duty" (Jowers 2003).

This antagonistic stance toward veterans is hardly new. The government continues to be unsympathetic toward veterans suffering from Gulf War illness from the first attack in that region. Earlier, the Reagan administration did everything possible to sabotage the case for Agent Orange compensation. Over and above its desire to limit its expenditures, the government feared making corporate suppliers of toxic materials liable in court (Nicosia 2001: 595).

The earlier-mentioned move by the administration of George W. Bush to limit workers' rights to overtime pay included the provision: "Exemption [from overtime pay rights] is also available to employees in such professions who have substantially the same knowledge level as the degreed employees, but who attained such knowledge through a combination of work experience, training in the armed forces, attending a technical school, attending a community college or other intellectual instruction" (Federal Register Vol. 68, No. 61. 541.301. d). This language meant that employers could categorize veterans as professionals on the basis of their prior military training. As a result, this provision actually penalizes workers for having served in the military.

Of course, the government has no particular desire to harm veterans; its goal is to make life comfortable for the large corporations and the wealthy who wield influence in the corridors of power. These powerful groups want a world with low wages, low taxes, and no liability. Government leaders comply with the wishes of their employers, all the while praising the brave young men and women who protect us from evildoers.

## ASBESTOS AND THE WORLD TRADE CENTER DISASTER

On September 11, 2001, terrorists hijacked four airliners and turned them into weapons, killing about 3,000 people. This number is only a partial accounting of the human toll from the attack. Besides the initial burst of fire and smoke, when the planes exploded, they released a lethal mix of toxic materials:

[B]y some accounts the north tower had as much as 300 to 400 tons of asbestos. Also in the two towers were as many as 50,000 personal computers, each of which contained a wide variety of harmful constituents including four pounds of lead, as well as much lesser but still troubling amounts of mercury.

The towers also contained 300 mainframe computers, and powering all these devices were hundreds of miles of wires and cables containing polyvinyl chloride and copper. The thousands of fluorescent lights used in the towers also contained mercury, a toxic metal. In addition, large amounts of fiberglass, used in insulation, were contained in the towers. To this must be added the unknown tons of plastics, which when burned produce harmful dioxins and furans; an unknown amount of painted or stained products and materials, which were one of many sources of volatile organic compounds within the destroyed buildings; and thousands of chairs and other office furniture containing such chemicals as polybrominated diphenyl ethers, which are persistent organic pollutants believed to pose dangers similar to PCBs. Additionally, several storage tanks containing petroleum products and a number of small hazardous-waste-generating entities at the World Trade Center complex, which were destroyed on September 11th, added to the toxic mix. And two Con Edison substations below 7 World Trade Center contained approximately 130,000 gallons of transformer oil contaminated with PCBs. This listing is only illustrative and does not capture the full breadth of the toxic constituents that were dispersed into the environment on September 11th. [Nordgrén, Goldstein, and Izeman 2002]

The level of asbestos contamination in this densely populated area actually exceeded levels found in Libby, Montana, where the now bankrupt company, W. R. Grace originally mined much of the material contaminating New York.

The asbestos that eventually spewed out from the World Trade Center touched on many of the themes addressed in this book, including risk, corporate power, corporate responsibility, working conditions, tort reform, and sound science. More concretely, between Libby, Montana and the toxic air of New York City, the asbestos deposited around the explosion left a trail of deception, corruption, and death.

### AMAZING GRACE

In Libby, the asbestos exposure level was so high that the government designated the community as a toxic superfund site. A *Seattle Post-Intelligencer* investigation found that in this small town with a reported population of 2,626 in 2000 at least 192 people have died from the asbestos in the mine's vermiculite ore, and doctors say the toll could be much higher. Doctors and local families report that at least another 375 people have been diagnosed with fatal diseases caused by asbestos, including a cousin of a former Montana governor, who became the head of the Republican National Committee, in January 2002, only a few months after the September 11 attacks. Dr Alan Whitehouse, a lung specialist from Spokane and an expert in industrial diseases, said another 12 to 15 people from Libby are being diagnosed with the diseases—asbestosis, mesothelioma, and lung cancer—every month (Schneider 1999).

W. R. Grace, the company that operated the local asbestos mine, had a questionable environmental history. The 1999 movie, "A Civil Action," dramatized the company's dark side. Five children and one adult died in Woburn, Mass. of acute lymphocytic leukemia from exposure to chemicals in their drinking water. The chemicals sickened others. After a long and tortuous proceeding, the Environmental Protection Agency finally found Grace to be responsible for dumping toxic chemicals into two of Woburn's wells. Grace paid a fine of $10,000 for lying to the Agency. The company also paid $8 million to eight families in return for their dropping their lawsuits.

The federal slap on the wrist for behavior that put lives of an entire community at risk stands in stark contrast to the punishment for behavior that might cause losses to investors. For example, in 1998, the Securities and Exchange Commission sued Grace for manipulating earnings in one of its divisions. To settle the suit, Grace set up a $1 million financial education fund (see Anon. 1999).

Grace was far from forthcoming about the dangers from asbestos. Only a couple of months before the attack on the World Trade Center, the *New York Times* published an article that detailed how W. R. Grace, fully knowing about the lethal effects of asbestos, became a leader in the fireproofing business by marketing an asbestos-laden product as asbestos free. The report continued:

> When the fledgling Environmental Protection Agency proposed an outright asbestos ban in the early 1970s, Grace successfully lobbied for a threshold just high enough to keep [their widely-used asbestos product] Monokote on the market. When workplace-safety officials proposed limits that Monokote could not meet, Grace's arguments helped delay them for years. Then, Grace used Monokote's legality to justify calling it asbestos-free.
>
> By current rules, Monokote at times would have shed triple the number of asbestos fibers allowed, according to Grace's records. That level, federal researchers estimate, translates into more than 10 deaths for each 1,000 laborers who used the spray daily over their working careers. [Moss and Appel 2001]

Grace's silence increased the dangers of Monokote. Because the product was supposedly safe, workers applied it without any protective gear, putting their lives at risk. As a result, Grace's deception contributed to the bankruptcy of Grace and a host of other companies

W. R. Grace applied much higher standards to the government. The Reagan administration appointed J. Peter Grace to lead the Grace Commission, which launched a ruthless assault on what it perceived as federal waste, perks, and dubious spending. Mr Grace took to his task with gusto, calling for the wholesale elimination of program after program all in the name of efficiency.

Not surprisingly, the Grace Commission recommended the axing of many environmental regulations. Sadly, the choice of Grace and other asbestos vendors to unleash their deadly product, when they knew its ultimate effects, saddled federal and state governments with billions in court costs, health coverage and a host of other expenses (see Bowker 2003: 156–7).

Ironically, waste, perks, and dubious spending became a hallmark of W. R. Grace. Some time later, a *Wall Street Journal* reporter noted the irony: "some say J. Peter Grace's company could use the same advice [that Mr Grace gave to the government]." Apparently, his son, Peter Grace III used about $1.3 million from a Grace subsidiary for working capital without proper authorization. Among the beneficiaries of this corporate generosity, was J. Peter Grace, who continued to enjoy lavish benefits. The elder Grace was getting $165,000 annually for nursing home care, $200,000 for security guards, and $74,000 for a New York apartment for his family's use, as well as a full-time cook from corporate funds. "The very things the Grace Commission said about the government were true within Grace," says Jack Shelton, an ex-employee and head of American Breeders Service, a cattle-breeding business Grace sold last year. "The corporate culture had gotten mired down, lazy and fat" (Miller et al. 1995).

Some of the W. R. Grace asbestos was sprayed on the structural supports for the interior of the World Trade Center building. This asbestos closed a symbolic circle, since the company's founder, William Russell Grace, was the mayor of New York who accepted the Statue of Liberty from the French in 1885.

The company that sprayed the asbestos had a less exalted pedigree. According to the *New York Times*:

The company that applied the wool-like sheathing was run by a reputed Gambino crime family member, Louis DiBono, who in 1990 was gunned down on orders of John Gotti. The manner in which Mr. DiBono obtained the work was then included in a criminal investigation into Port Authority construction contracting. Mr. DiBono was contracted to apply the fireproofing material starting in 1969. The project began with fireproofing containing asbestos but most of the floors were protected with another form of fireproofing. After health concerns arose about the asbestos, he was hired by another firm to oversee removal of the early fireproofing ....

James Verhalen, chairman of United States Mineral Products of Stanhope, N.J., said the steel had been allowed to rust during storage. A competitor whose own cement-like product came to dominate the industry says the material used on the trade center did not stick well and was prone to deterioration .... The consultant, Roger G. Morse [from Verhalen's firm], said years of inspections had revealed that whole sections of the original fireproofing had fallen away and other sections had deteriorated, leaving the steel inadequately protected. Mr. Morse says Mr. DiBono's firm had improperly sprayed the fireproofing onto rusted steel, which would have caused it to slough off. [Glanz and Moss 2001]

## CONTROLLING THE MESSAGE

The level of asbestos around the World Trade Center following the attack was even more dangerous than that of Libby, where the asbestos had originated. Rather than warning the public about the immanent dangers, the administration cynically assured everybody that the scientific evidence showed the site to be safe. In fact, the site was anything but safe.

To begin with, the administration had callously sacrificed scientific analysis for crude public relations. What could have motivated the government to downplay the risks during this crisis? We now know that the leadership of the administration had an overriding concern to create the appearance of normalcy in New York as soon as possible. According to a report of the Inspector General of the Environmental Protection Agency, the administration was especially eager to reopen the New York Stock Exchange, as a symbol of national strength (Office of Inspector General. Environmental Protection Agency 2003).

Unfortunately, this symbolism proved painfully hollow. To begin with, who in their right mind would actually look upon the New York Stock Exchange as a symbol of national strength rather than a venue of financial manipulation? More seriously, the national and local government agencies that vouched for the safety of the site were risking the lives of countless people. Robin Herbert and Stephen Levin, the directors of a federal screening program at Mount Sinai Hospital, told the House Subcommittee on National Security, Emerging Threats and International Relations on October 2003, that of 8,000 Ground Zero workers that the hospital screened, 75 per cent had persistent respiratory problems. Pregnant mothers who were near the disaster area bore children who were about a half pound lighter (see Schneider and McCumber 2004: 338–9).

Was the government's assurance that the site was safe meant to help the administration appear to have the situation under control? That motive makes some sense. While a relatively fearful atmosphere can make the public willing to allow the government more powers, an excess of fear can easily turn to panic.

More shallow economic motives may have also been at play. When Governor Christine Todd Whitman, Environmental Protection Agency Administrator, traveled to address New York City on September 13, 2001, she delivered a reassuring promise from President Bush:

> We're getting in there and testing to make sure things are safe .... Everything will be vacuumed that needs to be, air filters (in area buildings) will be cleaned, we're not going to let anybody into a building that isn't safe. And these buildings will be safe. The president has made it clear that we are to spare no expense on this one, and get this job done. [France and Check 2001]

A thorough cleanup would not have been very expensive considering the number of lives at stake, but the government never followed through with its pledge. If the government could walk away from the responsibility of this extraordinary level of contamination, industry could claim an equal right to avoid its own responsibilities, especially when the damage could be much less severe than those that the government ignored.

Certainly, companies facing massive asbestos liabilities, such as Halliburton, which I discussed earlier, had a strong interest in minimizing the dangers associated with the hazards of this material. In this regard, Cate Jenkins, a courageous, whistleblowing scientist from the Environmental Protection Agency whose efforts have shaped much of my thinking about this event, warned:

> The World Trade Center contamination zone is the asbestos industry's battleground. What happens here shapes future cleanups of other asbestos

sites as well as litigation in the years to come. There is legislation in Congress at this very minute that would prevent anyone exposed to WTC dust from ever collecting any compensation after contracting asbestos induced mesothelioma or lung cancer, because their exposures were not "work place related." [Jenkins 2003]

Indeed, William M. Corcoran, Vice President, W. R. Grace & Co. wrote to Michael Shapiro, Principal Deputy Assistant Administrator, Office of Solid Waste and Emergency Response of the EPA, on February 6, 2002 and then to EPA Administrator Christine Todd Whitman on August 4, 2002, making the case that the lax cleanup at the World Trade Center should serve as a precedent for Grace to reduce its responsibilities in Libby.

To make matters worse, the EPA has begun major initiatives to downgrade its current carcinogenicity rating for chrysotile asbestos. The agency already classifies all fibers smaller than 5 microns as being non-carcinogenic, even though the smaller fibers have more potential to do damage. Now, the EPA proposes to downgrade even larger fibers.

While the Environmental Protection Agency was assuring the public about the safety of the area around the World Trade Center, many inside that agency had serious concerns. In fact, the agency took the trouble to use a far more sensitive test for its own offices than it applied to the surrounding areas.

The intense pressure for delivering a calming message actually came from a far less known government agency, the Council on Environmental Quality, headed by James Connaughton, a well-connected lawyer, who before his appointment by President Bush made a career of representing companies charged with creating toxic pollution. For example, one of his major clients, American Smelting and Refining Co. Inc. and two subsidiaries, as of September 30, 1999, were defendants in 1,377 lawsuits brought by 5,950 primary and 1,036 secondary plaintiffs seeking substantial actual and punitive damages for personal injury or death allegedly caused by exposure to asbestos <http://www.litigationdatasource.com/asarco_inc.txt>.

According to a *Washington Post* portrait of Mr Connaughton: "As a partner in the firm of Sidley Austin Brown & Wood, Connaughton represented General Electric Co. and the mining company Asarco Inc. in battles with the EPA over Superfund cleanup requirements. He also lobbied on behalf of Alcoa Inc., the Chemical Manufacturers Association and other prominent corporate interests with pollution problems." The article cites a senior administration official, who reported "More than any single person, Jim Connaughton is the architect of the administration's environmental policy" (Pianin 2003a).

Relations between Connaughton's operation and the EPA were tense to say the least. According to a *New York Times* reporter who had access to internal documents:

> there were "screaming telephone calls" about the news releases between Tina Kreisher, then an associate administrator, and Sam Thernstrom, then the White House council's communications director. The E.P.A.'s chief of staff, Eileen McGinnis, had to ask the head of the White House council, James L. Connaughton, to urge his staff to "lighten up," according to interviews with the inspector general's office. Ms. Kreisher, who now works as a speechwriter at the Department of the Interior, is quoted as saying she "felt extreme pressure" from Mr. Thernstrom. [Lee 2003]

The ultimate source of this pressure may have come from President Bush himself. According to Michael Catanzaro, Communications Director for the Senate Environment and Public Works Committee, the president himself made the decision to put the Council on Environmental Quality in charge of the multi-agency task force that organized the response effort (Catanzaro 2003).

## THE PRECAUTIONARY PRINCIPLE AGAIN

The cavalier attitude toward the health risks imposed on people in the largest city in the country represents one of the strongest arguments for the precautionary principle. Disregarding its lethal properties, asbestos has a marvelous ability to reduce risks by retarding fire and insulating from heat. Asbestos also proved to be useful in many products ranging from automobile brakes to roofing shingles.

When modern industry first began to use asbestos intensively, the risks were unknown, but so too was the logic behind the precautionary principle. Once industry became engaged in manufacturing asbestos products, it wielded its power to shield itself from government regulation. Success in this regard was not particularly difficult because the public was largely kept ignorant of the growing medical evidence of the dangers associated with asbestos. Industry was not alone in its desire to continue using asbestos. The Navy packed its ships with asbestos to protect its sailors from fire. Unfortunately, in the process, it put the lives of many more ship workers at risk.

In retrospect, the asbestos industry left behind a massive toll of death and disease. The companies most responsible lack the resources to even begin to compensate their victims. As a result, a wave of bankruptcy has been spreading across the economy.

In searching for the way out of the morass of bankruptcy, corporate health counts for much more than human health. For example, Michael Bowker described the outcome of the asbestos-induced Johns Manville bankruptcy:

> In the end, after tens of millions of dollars were spent on legal and experts' fees and the issue had been dragged through the courts for more than a dozen years, the "bottom line" looked like this: While Johns-Manville paid its debts to commercial creditors on a dollar-for-dollar basis and was allowed to do business as usual, future asbestos claimants were paid ten cents for every dollar they had won from the company through the legal system. That lasted until July 2001, when the amount dropped to five cents on the dollar. As a result, most mesothelioma victims, who often face up to a half million dollars in health care costs to help them battle the enormous discomfort of the incurable disease, were regularly paid less than $20,000 by the J-M Trust. [Bowker 2003: 262]

Even the current corporate-friendly bankruptcy laws appear to pose too much risk to corporate health. As a result, as I mentioned earlier, Congress stepped in to try to offer even more protections for the corporations facing asbestos liability at the expense of people whose health was ruined by the material. Lurking in the background is the ever present call for tort reform, which would limit the ability to sue effectively for damages, such as those caused by the asbestos industry.

Why do these issues rarely get the exposure that they deserve? The complex web of corporate ownership links the media with some of the companies troubled by asbestos liabilities. For example, major media companies, such as Viacom and GE, the respective owners of the CBS and NBC television network as well as many other media outlets, are actively lobbying for relief for their own serious asbestos liability exposure (see Murray and Kranhold 2003).

## THE WAR ON TERROR

The main response to the attacks on the World Trade Center and the Pentagon was the declaration of a War on Terror. Over and above the military attacks on Afghanistan and Iraq, this new policy unleashed a torrent of domestic policy changes. I cannot pretend to know how this new political environment following the declaration of a War on Terror will evolve, but one initial impact has been to radically redefine the relative powers of individuals, corporations, and the state. In a larger sense, this new political environment is a manifestation of trends that have been underway for some time. Perhaps, an organized movement will reverse some of these changes, but at the time of this writing, nothing of the sort has happened.

John Poindexter, who first came to public attention as National Security Advisor during the Reagan administration, seemed to be symbolic of the new state of affairs. At the time, the administration attempted to circumvent legislation that prevented it from financing a terroristic revolution against the government of Nicaragua. In this case, the president declared that these terrorists were the moral equivalent of the Founding Fathers. Poindexter was involved in a complex scheme to sell arms to Iran in return for money and hostages, while illegally diverting the proceeds to the Nicaraguan paramilitaries.

The resulting controversy threatened to engulf President Reagan, who successfully feigned ignorance about the whole affair. A number of lesser figures, including Poindexter, could not escape facing consequences for their actions—at least temporarily. A jury found Poindexter guilty of five counts of conspiracy, obstruction of justice, and false statements to Congress, although a court later reversed the convictions on a technicality.

Poindexter then went on to become senior vice president of Syntech, a high technology company that produces communications equipment. Then, under the administration of George W. Bush, Poindexter resurfaced in public life as the head of the Defense Advanced Research Projects Agency's Total Information Awareness Project. The objective of this office was to assemble the extensive information held by private companies together with government information to construct a massive database that would include every resident of the United States. Existing law forbade the government from directly collecting much of this data, but the law lacked any provision to prevent the government from purchasing such information from private companies, such as Syntech, which won a large contract from Poindexter's office. So the same person convicted of destroying and falsifying information that the public needed to be able to understand the depths of the illegal acts of the government, retreats to the corporate sector, and then returns to the government to gather every imaginable sort of information about the public. This government's demands for information know no bounds—including a requirement that librarians divulge the reading habits of their patrons when the government asks them to do so.

Alas, Admiral Poindexter did not pass through this period unscathed. In July 2003, the United States Senate voted to deny funds for its Total Information Awareness program, renamed as Terrorism Information Awareness to deflect the public distaste for this dangerous project. Then in August, in an effort to tap every conceivable source of information, the admiral ran into a firestorm of protest when he unveiled an unusual futures market in which people could speculate on the probabilities of terrorist attacks, assassinations and coups. A few days later, he announced his intention to resign from what the *New York Times* called, "the wacky espionage operation he runs at the Pentagon" (Anon. 2003).

While civil libertarians might take heart that the futures market in terrorism may not see the light of day, they have little else to celebrate. After Congress denied the administration funds for the Information Awareness Office that Poindexter ran, the Pentagon announced the termination of that operation. Undeterred, the Department of Defense reported that some of its egregious projects would merely be shifted to other areas within the Pentagon (Hulse 2003). In addition, "Congress left undisturbed a separate but similar $64 million research program run by a little-known office called the Advanced Research and Development Activity (ARDA) that has used some of the same researchers as Poindexter's program" (Sniffen 2004).

Eventually, the leadership in this area shifted to Homeland Security, which set about contracting with corporations, which were free to collect data in ways in which the government was supposedly not permitted to do. By operating offshore, such companies had even more leeway to combine the information from commercial databases, private businesses, and government (O'Harrow 2004). To give some idea about the massive quantity of available information, Wal-Mart alone apparently has about half as much information as the entire internet (Flint 2004). So, Poindexter's other more ominous projects continue, although with less fanfare and without the admiral's leadership.

At the same time that the government makes such intrusive demands for personal information from the public, it restricts information about its own activities and those of the corporations.

I have already mentioned the report of the Union of Concerned Scientists that discussed efforts to stifle scientific research. Earlier, in 2003, Representative Henry A. Waxman, the ranking Democrat on the House Committee on Government Reform published a 40-page report detailing a number of cases in which the administration "has manipulated the scientific process and distorted or suppressed scientific findings."

Much of this information was absolutely unrelated to terrorism. In one instance, the government denied a microbiologist, James Zahn, permission to publish findings on the dangers of antibiotic-resistant bacteria near hog farms in the Midwest. The report also covered the cases, such as global warming and sex education. Any connection between terrorism and the abuses documented in the report would be far-fetched to say the least (Marquis 2003).

The second Bush administration embarked on a massive purge of available information about government activities. Although the administration justified many of its actions as an effort to withhold information from terrorists, this administration has attempted to curtail public access to all sorts of information that has no possible connection with public safety. Even well before September 11, 2001, the Bush administration had steadfastly refused to make information available to Congress, let alone the public, about its meetings with corporate leaders in fashioning its energy policy (see United States General Accounting Office 2003).

Even though the justification about withholding information to prevent terrorism might sound reasonable to some, the sincerity of the administration's motives are suspect. For example, in the wake of the attack on the World Trade Center, the Environmental Protection Agency had identified 123 chemical plants where a terrorist attack could, in a "worst-case" scenario, kill more than 1 million people. In a 1999 report, published well before the September 11 attacks of 2001, the federal Agency for Toxic Substances and Disease Registry, part of the U.S. Department of Health and Human Services, issued a dire warning: "security at chemical plants ranged from fair to very poor." The report pointed to precedents where industrial chemicals "have been used by terrorists as improvised explosives, incendiaries and poisons in several recent incidents .... [T]hey have rapid, highly visible impacts on health, they are accessible; and they can be dispersed by smoke, gas clouds, or food and medicine distribution networks." In a separate assessment issued in October 2001, Army Surgeon General Lt. Gen. James B. Peake estimated that a terrorist attack launched on a chemical plant located in a densely populated area could cause as many as 2.4 million fatalities or injuries (Common Cause 2003). In short, these chemical plants might be nothing less than prepositioned weapons of mass destruction.

The chemical industry assured the government that it had voluntarily developed guidelines to ensure public safety. A March 2003 General Accounting Office study questioned whether voluntary guidelines were adequate. In addition, Sal DePasquale, a former security official at Georgia-Pacific Co. who had helped draw up the American Chemistry Council's voluntary security plan, wrote that because of cost concerns, the industry has resisted suggestions that it upgrade the training of its security forces to allow guards to carry guns. He warned: "Across the country there are huge storage tanks with highly dangerous materials that are far from adequately secured" (Mintz 2003).

Indeed, these fears might have been well-founded. Mohamed Atta, widely regarded as the September 11 ringleader, reportedly scouted a chemical plant in Tennessee. Given the eagerness with which the government moved to invade individual privacy in order to reduce the threat of terrorism, you might expect that the government would take measures to ensure the security of chemical plants. Indeed, a bill by Senator Corzine from New Jersey passed the Senate Environment and Public Works Committee by a vote of 19–0 to tighten security at chemical plants.

The petrochemical industry went into high gear to shut down this measure. Industry supplied eight senators who were critical of the Corzine bill with more than $850,000. Not surprisingly most Republican senators on the committee subsequently withdrew support (Common Cause 2003). So even though the chemical industry offers inviting targets to terrorists, the political influence of the industry trumped considerations of security.

I don't want to give the impression that the government was completely unmindful about security issues with the chemical industry. Less than a month after the September 11 attack, the government began rushing to pull information from its web sites. Section 112(r) of the Clean Air Act requires that each facility that uses or stores extremely hazardous chemicals file a Risk Management Plan to be made available to the public. The EPA removed from its web site information that includes measures taken by a facility to prevent an accidental release and response plans to protect human health and the environment in the event of a release (Carroll 2001).

Although this information could be useful to terrorists, industry had different reasons for resisting its availability long before terrorism entered into the debate. Congress mandated the release of this information to help citizens protect themselves from the dangers associated with toxic releases. Industry naturally would prefer to avoid citizen complaints or local legislation intended to protect human health. While consumer sovereignty is supposed to be a defining characteristic of modern American society, citizen sovereignty certainly is not.

So, the Environmental Protection Agency may have been sincere in its actions as an attempt to deprive terrorists of potentially dangerous information. I cannot rule out the possibility, however, that the fear of terrorism provided a justification for the government to do a favor for industry. Certainly, such behavior is consistent with the other actions of the Bush administration. We need only recall how the government dismissed the problem of terrorism in regulating the safety of the nuclear power industry. Similarly, the Federal Energy Regulatory Commission has ruled that neither citizens nor even state and local governments have a right to information regarding the risks of planned liquefied natural gas terminals (Kelly 2004).

A Government Accountability Study reported that security at nuclear energy plants was lax (Davidson 2004). Should anyone be surprised that the response of the government was to classify information regarding security without pressuring the industry to improve its defences?

Within the political environment of the War on Terror, we heard nothing of consumer sovereignty. Instead, the administration called upon everybody to make sacrifices in the name of the greater good—everybody, that is except the corporate sector and the wealthy beneficiaries of the Bush Administration's massive tax cuts. This disregard for the welfare of individuals extended even to those individuals whom the state supposedly honors most highly—veterans.

The atmosphere of a War on Terror serves a very useful purpose for both government and the corporations. Presenting government as the people's ultimate protector, transforms any criticism of government actions—and by extension those of the corporations—into an act of treason. John Poindexter, although he is no longer openly engaged in government, is symbolic of the state of affairs, in which the government is free to gather, hide, or distort information—whatever is expedient (or profitable).

The War on Terror has another attractive feature for corporations. The FBI has greatly diminished its efforts to investigate white-collar crime. The Los Angeles office supposedly has reduced the number of agents in this area from 185 to 75. The selective application of policy undermines any credibility of the claim that concern about terrorism is foremost in the minds of policy makers.

The second Bush administration has successfully magnified the danger of terrorism, and then presented itself as the only possible protection against such risks. This behavior is not at all unique to this administration. For example, the government had exaggerated the military threat posed by the Soviet Union, Cuba, and even Nicaragua; however, the extremes to which the government has taken this tactic during the second Bush administration are unprecedented. Charles Tilly has compared this posture with regard to danger to the behavior of a racketeer:

> If protection rackets represent organized crime at its smoothest, then war making and state making—quintessential protection rackets with the advantage of legitimacy—qualify as our largest examples of organized crime. But consider the definition of a racketeer as someone who creates a threat and then charges for its reduction. Governments' provision of this protection, by this standard, often qualifies as racketeering. To the extent that the threats against which a government protects its citizens are imaginary or are consequences of its own activities, the government has organized a protection racket. Since governments themselves often constitute the largest current threats to the livelihoods of their own citizens, many governments operate in essentially the same ways as racketeers. [Tilly 1985: 171]

I disagree with Tilly in one respect. He seems to paint the government as an independent agent. I have been emphasizing that the government typically works at the behest of the rich and the powerful corporations. Otherwise, Tilly has caught much of the spirit of the War on Terror.

### FEAR OF IRRATIONALITY OR IRRATIONALITY OF FEAR

People like John Graham (mentioned in Chapter 6) have fiercely criticized regulation, arguing that the only basis for many regulations is irrational fear. One could just as well argue that many corporations have an irrational fear of regulation. In fact, many regulations have saved corporations considerable amounts of money (see Porter and van der Linde 1995). For example, companies facing high costs of disposing of a toxic waste learn how to reuse the materials, saving the cost of repurchase.

Corporate fear of regulation seems to border on the irrational. A business columnist in the *New York Times* reported:

> A survey of global chief executives released by PricewaterhouseCoopers at the World Economic Forum found that 59 percent viewed overregulation as a significant risk or, worse, one of the biggest threats to the growth of their companies—far more than viewed global terrorism .... What has alarmed many is Section 404 of the Sarbanes-Oxley Act, which requires chief executives and chief financial officers to certify the adequacy of their internal controls. Then outside auditors must attest to that opinion. [Norris 2004]

In other words, the executives are terrified that they might have to take responsibility for what goes on in their corporations, preventing them from pleading ignorance in court. As a class, these same corporate leaders have been using their immense influence to promote a political agenda that demands that everybody else be accountable for their actions.

Recall how the corporate sector has been effective in requiring government agencies to use cost-benefit analysis to justify regulations. Ironically, nobody—not even John Graham—seems to have applied the same tough-minded risk analysis to the military budget, which is the dominant source of government spending, or to the War on Terror.

Because politicians closely represent corporate interests, this selective application of risk analysis to inconvenient regulations leaves the same political leaders who oppose regulation on the grounds that it foolishly protects people against unlikely risks, turning around and supporting bloated defense budgets that are hugely disproportional to any threat posed by poor, underdeveloped nations.

### THE WAR ON TERROR AND STATISTICAL MURDER

To his credit, John Graham did issue a call for experts to attempt to quantify the indirect costs of inconvenience and loss of privacy associated with tighter domestic security. In Graham's words, "People are willing to accept some burdens, some intrusion on their privacy and some inconvenience" (Andrews 2003). Apparently, he merely wanted to learn how much people were willing to sacrifice rather than to evaluate the costs and benefits of the domestic security regulations.

Two of Graham's colleagues from Harvard, Kip Viscusi and Richard Zeckhauser, seem to have done the sort of study that he had in mind—at least the *New York Times* article that drew attention to Graham's call for a study of the costs and benefits of policies to prevent terrorism seemed to suggest as much (Andrews 2003).

This linkage between Graham and the researchers made eminent sense. The first of these two authors, Kip Viscusi, has a long career of advocacy for tort reform. Between 1987 and 2002, he had earned over $600,000 as an expert witness in liability cases for the tobacco industry. He had estimated that the states actually enjoyed a budgetary windfall from tobacco sales because people died more quickly as a result of smoking (Glenn 2002). Viscusi and his co-author, Richard Zeckhauser, were both important figures in developing the "Aging Initiative." To his credit, Zeckhauser was one of the authors of the earlier-discussed 1975 report that indicated that employers faced the equivalent of a risk of only 52 cents for violating safety and health regulations.

How did Viscusi and Zeckhauser go about applying cost-benefit analysis to the War on Terror? They asked some typical Americans—students enrolled at Harvard Law School—if they would support racial profiling at airports if that practice would prevent a 60-minute delay for all other air passengers, assuming that they themselves would not be singled out as suspicious travelers. They found that 73.9 per cent favored profiling others to save 60 minutes so long as they would not be singled out for profiling. The number fell to 56.3 per cent if the students could be singled out—a less than likely experience for most Harvard law students (Viscusi and Zeckhauser 2003).

This study calls out for two comments. First, just imagine how industry would howl if the Environmental Protection Agency were to consider the results of a survey that asked individuals who believed themselves to be affected by dangerous pollutants from a corporate chemical plant, if they would accept an exhaustive government regulatory audit of the management of all properties in the neighborhood that seriously affected human health. Just as these law students would not mind racial profiling of others, the people near the chemical plant would probably not mind the audit of the management of properties owned by fictitious corporate individuals.

Second, this study made no effort to measure the potential benefits of racial profiling; instead, the study implicitly assumed that racial profiling would be an effective measure to prevent terrorism. Interestingly enough a little more than a decade earlier, Viscusi and Zeckhauser had written:

> Often too much weight is placed on risks of low probability but high salience (such as those posed by trace carcinogens or terrorist action); risks of commission rather than omission; and risks, such as those associated with frontier technologies, whose magnitude is difficult to estimate. Too little effort is spent ameliorating voluntary risks, such as those involving automobiles and diet. [Viscusi and Zeckhauser 1990: 559]

In this earlier study, Viscusi and Zeckhauser brought together several threads of the statistics of risk: (1) People have difficulty evaluating risks; (2) they will tend to be susceptible to overreacting to the fears of terrorism; (3) the blame for many of the problems associated with risk lies with individual behavior rather than corporate malfeasance. Their first point is indisputable. Their third point reveals their own corporate-leaning bias. Their second point anticipated just how effective the war on terrorism would be in distracting people from their real interests.

So, sadly, neither John Graham nor his colleagues have the slightest interest in pursuing a take-no-hostages cost-benefit approach to domestic security measures comparable to the skeptical stance Graham and his coterie advocate for regulations that inconvenience business. As the *New York Times* article noted: "Mr. Graham, a passionate champion of cost-benefit analysis who taught at Harvard before joining the administration, stopped short of saying that government officials might somehow assign a price for costs like lost privacy or convenience" (Andrews 2003).

Indeed, when Graham's office presented its annual report to Congress about the costs and benefits of government regulations, one of the four chapters related to 69 regulations associated with homeland security. The agency did not bother to assign benefits to any of these regulations. Its efforts to estimate costs were modest, to say the least, offering only crude estimates for a mere 13 of these regulations (Office of Management and Budget. Office of Information and Regulatory Affairs 2003). In the 2004 draft report, the agency restricted its discussion of the costs of homeland security regulations to rules imposed by the Coast Guard. This approach reduced the estimated cost of homeland security rules to one-tenth of 1 per cent of all regulatory costs (Office of Management and Budget. Office of Information and Regulatory Affairs 2004a).

To my knowledge, nobody has applied a Graham-like methodology to evaluate government efforts to protect the public against the potential risks posed by enemies of this nation. The closest example that I have seen came in a brief mention of a calculation by the famous artificial intelligence expert, Marvin Minsky, that the probable cost per life saved from increased airline security was $100 million and that other uses for the money could save far more lives (Begley 2002).

Similarly, Jeffrey Reiman observed that in 1973, the federal government employed 1,500 marshals to guard airliners against hijackers, compared to 500 inspectors for the Occupational Safety and Health Administration (Reiman 1996: 70). As mentioned earlier, OSHA inspectors are fairly effective; the problem is that they are understaffed and enforcement, once they uncover safety violations, is inadequate to say the least. Considering that almost 70,000 people per year die from occupational injuries and diseases, increasing the number of OSHA inspectors makes good sense. Nobody to date—certainly not John Graham—has accused the government of statistical murder on this account.

One government program, associated with the war on terrorism threatens to create statistical murders far less hypothetical than those identified by the John Graham school of cost-benefit analysis. In mid-2003, the Bush administration proposed to divert $145 million from infectious disease funding in order to develop an anthrax vaccine (Friedman 2003). The Centers for Disease Control report that as of December 2001, 42 million people are estimated to be living with just one infectious disease—HIV/AIDS. In contrast, five people died from the anthrax attacks. Similarly, the government has embarked on an ambitious program to inoculate the American public against smallpox, a disease that currently affects nobody, with a vaccine that itself poses serious health risks.

While protection against smallpox and anthrax might deter a potential terrorist from launching an improbable attack with such weapons, programs to defend against these diseases would not be particularly effective in eliminating terrorism. The most likely response to such a strategy would be to cause any would-be bio-terrorist simply to shift to an alternative method. Certainly, anthrax and smallpox do not exhaust the lethal possibilities of bio-warfare. At the same time, restoring our deplorably underfunded public health system to a reasonable level would do far more to protect the public from present threats from infectious diseases, besides shoring up society against bioterrorism.

## FOOD, TERRORISM, AND THE INDIVIDUAL'S RIGHT TO KNOW

The food industry offers another excellent example of the diminished rights of the individual relative to the corporate sector within the context of the War on Terror. Even in the absence of any intentional terrorist acts, both industries presently create serious health risks to the public. I have already discussed the widespread deaths and illnesses from food-borne illnesses.

The potential for terrorists to use the food supply to harm the public is fairly obvious. For example, a single 4-ounce ground beef patty may contain flesh from more than a thousand different carcasses (Smith et al. 2000). As a result, a single carcass could infect a wide range of people across the country. Protecting against such a low-tech attack would be challenging, not to mention costly.

Just as the food industry has been quite successful in preventing the government from using its regulatory powers to protect the public from food-borne contamination, it is proving equally effective in minimizing government efforts to protect the food supply against terrorism (Sparshott 2003). In fact, the Department of Agriculture began a new inspection system in Fall 2002, which reduced the percentage of meat crossing the border that is inspected to 6 per cent from 17 per cent (E. Becker 2003b).

Terrorism does represent a potential threat, but far more people routinely die each year from food-borne illnesses than died in the worst terrorist attack in United States history. I suspect that the annual death toll from the chemical industry would also greatly exceed that of the terrorist attack of September 11. Again, the government refuses to apply the same risk analysis to its anti-terrorism actions that it demands for other kinds of regulatory mandates.

At the same time, the urgency of the War on Terror supposedly demands that the government have the right to intrude into virtually every aspect of individual behavior—all the while remaining extremely circumspect about what it requires from the corporate sector.

The administration has even gone so far as to help corporations to avoid their responsibility to inform the public about their activities in the name of Homeland Security. In other words, information, like accountability, becomes a one way street.

How, then, does the idea of democracy and consumer sovereignty square with this new regime in which corporations and the government have massive databases about individuals while individuals are kept in the dark about what government and corporations do? After all, individuals' ability to choose their representatives and to purchase products that serve their best interests depends on their having access to adequate information.

# 8
# Individuals as Citizens

## MESMERIZING SOCIETY

Perhaps the history of the errors of mankind, all things considered, is more valuable and interesting than that of their discoveries. Truth is uniform and narrow; it constantly exists, and does not seem to require so much an active energy, as a passive aptitude of soul in order to encounter it. But error is endlessly diversified; it has no reality, but is the pure and simple creation of the mind that invents it. In this field the soul has room enough to expand herself, to display all her beautiful and interesting extravagances and absurdities. [Franklin et al. 1785: xvii–xviii]

Benjamin Franklin was one of a distinguished panel of commissioners that the King of France appointed in 1784 to investigate Anton Mesmer—part charlatan, part visionary, Mesmer's work in animal magnetism presaged modern hypnotism and later influenced psychologists, such as Sigmund Freud. Mesmer won a passionate following in France. The French government, at the suggestion of Marie Antoinette, offered Mesmer a life pension and enough money to set up a clinic. Mesmer created a controversy by refusing to allow the government representatives to supervise the clinic. Displeased by Mesmer's refusal, the King appointed the commission, which also included such renowned scholars as Jean Sylvain Bailly, a leading French astronomer, Antoine Laurent Lavoisier, the great chemist, and Joseph Ignace Guillotine, physician and inventor of the famous execution instrument that bore his name.

The commission's conclusions were similar to those that I have found in analyzing corporate society: "endlessly diversified" error, replete with "beautiful and interesting extravagances and absurdities."

Franklin and his fellow commissioners recognized that Mesmer's work had some connection to the truth, despite the errors that he was propounding. After all, for error to be effective, it must be more than a boldface lie. Effective error requires some small particles of truth in order to make believers more comfortable.

The phalanx of error that I have been analyzing is not the product of a single individual. For more than a century, some of the best minds in society have worked tirelessly to construct this error. Some did so consciously; others just became carried away with the spirit of the times. The overarching error surrounds each of us, affecting us as individuals when we shop, vote, or go to work. In the process, the corporate world has largely succeeded in mesmerizing society.

This book represents my attempt to break through these errors to help to develop a more rational view of society. The cult of individualism that mesmerizes is rooted in two errors. Each raises a different question. First, does individualism succeed in producing a better standard of living measured by the goods and service consumed by people—not just an average standard of living in which the wealth of a few individuals may conceal the poverty of large numbers of less fortunate individuals—but the standard of living enjoyed by the poorest levels of society?

Second, even if the poor can consume a high quantity of goods and services, does the market actually ensure a high quality of life? Do larger hot tubs or more powerful cars compensate for the lack of affordable health care, poor quality public schools, a profit-minded media that aims for the lowest common denominator, and an individualistic ethic which tends to numb feelings of empathy?

## A FULLY INFORMED PUBLIC

In the popular vision of a laissez-faire economy, the democratic rights of the individual represent one of the most treasured virtues of a market economy. By this logic, those who want to interfere with the market are fundamentally undemocratic. Instead of government "commanding" the people, individuals are free to make their own economic choices, while the government must heed the will of the public—well, anyway at least in theory—and let the market proceed unhindered.

In order for this system to work as imagined, several preconditions are essential. First and foremost, the public must be fully informed. Sadly, good information is not easy to come by for several reasons, none of which bode well for the individual.

To begin with, the basic conduits of information remain within the corporate sector. This problem becomes more severe with every passing day because of the precipitous pace of corporate consolidations. Mergers of every conceivable form of media are occurring with breakneck speed. The Bush administration attached so much importance to the corporate interest in fostering these mergers that it threatened to veto a massive $375 billion omnibus spending bill because of the inclusion of two congressional mandates that both houses of Congress had approved—one to prohibit the government from carrying through on its proposal to make millions of workers ineligible for overtime pay and another preventing the Federal Communication Commission from following through on a ruling to lift the caps on media mergers.

A small congressional conference committee buckled under pressure from the White House, stripping both provisions from the bill without public debate behind closed doors, even though both houses of Congress had passed both provisions in open debate. The corporations that control the media know that if they pass on critical information to the public, the government will be less inclined to bestow such favors on them, including tax breaks and subsidies.

Even if the corporate media wished to function as public-spirited information sources, they mostly remain dependent on their advertising revenues. The casual audience member knows that the proportion of broadcast time devoted to advertising has been rapidly increasing. Even the supposedly non-commercial Public Broadcasting System now relies on "enhanced underwriter acknowledgments," which to the untrained eye are indistinguishable from commercials. As a result, the media cannot risk offending their customers—the corporations that place the vast majority of the advertisements that flood the airways and consume the majority of space in newspapers and magazines. In this respect, the advertising business is one area of economic activity in which consumer sovereignty is largely a reality—except that the corporate advertisers are the sovereign consumers.

The situation becomes even more complicated because the owners of the great corporate media rarely confine themselves to a single industry. All too often, they are part of an entertainment conglomerate, or even worse, an entertainment conglomerate which exists as a part of a much larger business.

Because of their interests in other sectors of the economy, the corporate media are even less likely to publicize information that may be inconvenient for their other holdings than they are to offend their advertisers. Can you imagine the NBC network, owned by General Electric, being overly critical of nuclear power plants when General Electric is a major player in that industry? The media's silence regarding deaths in the workplace is relevant in this respect.

Besides, even if such information would make for good journalism, it would make for poor entertainment. What David Chase, creator and executive producer of the hit television show *The Sopranos*, said about television drama probably holds for the entire gamut of American media. He explained to the *New York Times*, "The function of an hour drama is to reassure the American people that it's O.K. to go out and buy stuff. It's all about flattering the audience, making them feel as if all the authority figures have our best interests at heart" (Heffernan 2004).

If that bias were not enough, we can mention the obvious fact that the owners and managers of the corporate media are themselves very rich. These people are not likely to push forward ideas that are not in the interest of the rich and powerful. Not surprisingly, when the public does hear about the activities of their political representatives from the media, the subject is more likely to concern the politicians' activities in the bedroom than what they did for the boardrooms of corporate America.

Finally, the primary objective of the corporate media is the maximization of their profits. The corporate media seek out methods of cutting costs whenever they can without harming their bottom-line. Since the corporate media feel no moral obligation to inform the public, they replace journalism with tawdry entertainment, often replete with product placement to encourage the appropriate levels of consumption.

## KEEPING THE PUBLIC IN THE DARK

Investigative journalism—the kind of reporting that helps people to make informed decisions about society—makes a particularly inviting target for economizing. To begin with, investigative journalism is very expensive. After all, serious journalism requires considerable time and resources. In addition, serious journalism may reach conclusions that run counter to the corporation's interests. Besides, the media has conditioned much of the public to be satisfied with stories about celebrities or tabloid crimes. Given this environment, increasingly the corporate media lazily passes on public relations feeds from other corporations or from government agencies, without any critical comment.

Or else, journalists simply turn to corporate-subsidized think tanks to give their "expert" opinions. Recall the statement in the earlier-discussed Manhattan Institute's fund-raising brochure for its tort reform movement: "Journalists need copy, and it's an established fact that over time they'll 'bend' in the direction in which it flows."

No organization has been more successful in influencing the media than the Heritage Foundation. According to the foundation's Annual Report:

> During 2002, the ideas, proposals, scholarship and views of Heritage's analysts and executives were featured in more than 600 national and international television broadcasts, more than 1,000 national and "major market" radio broadcasts, and some 8,000 newspaper and magazine articles and editorials. In short, when Washington listens, it frequently hears the voice of The Heritage Foundation. [Heritage Foundation 2003: 33]

The Heritage Foundation wins further influence over the news media by doing the work of overworked and understaffed newsrooms, although the foundation represents this activity as just helping "reporters better understand the facts." According to the Annual Report:

> No single initiative has been more effective in this regard than the Center for Media and Public Policy's Computer-Assisted Research and Reporting (CARR) program .... [T]he CARR program offers journalists training in a cutting-edge discipline: data analysis .... During 2002, [Heritage] provided training and assistance to dozens of reporters and news researchers—becoming "part of the newsroom team" on a variety of high-impact stories.
>
> As The Washington Post noted in an April 19, 2002 feature on the CARR program, "All Washington think tanks are in the business of supplying journalists—as well as legislators and other decision-makers—with their take on policies and issues, most often in the form of briefings, papers or books. But Heritage is taking this relationship to a new level by providing reporters with raw data and showing them how to analyze it, essentially offering to serve as a news-room's own research department." [Heritage Foundation 2003: 31; see also Deane 2002]

Even when the corporate media does investigative journalism on its own, they are selective about their targets. In the words of Seymour Hersh, one of the rare masters of investigative journalism, who worked for years at the *New York Times*: "The *Times* wasn't nearly as happy when we went after business wrongdoing as when we were kicking around some slob in government" (Gouldon 1988: 297).

Similarly, the corporate media frames public debates in ways that obscure important issues. For example, an inheritance tax that falls upon a tiny minority of the population suddenly becomes a "death tax." Since everybody dies sooner or later, a large portion of the public gets the impression that such a death tax may affect them. The actual rare incidence of the inheritance tax may occasionally be mentioned deep in the story, but the media never makes the underlying issues clear, let alone informs people about how the policy will affect them.

As a result of the woeful performance of the corporate media, we have a public that is extremely knowledgeable about celebrities, scandals, and sports. All too often, media pundits smugly deplore this ignorance, without finding any blame closer to home. Instead, they act as if the people themselves are incapable or unwilling to handle complex information.

This arrogant attitude toward the public is unwarranted. In fact, the widespread knowledge of sports belies the convenient excuse of a supposed general incapacity for understanding complex information. Most sports fans are extraordinarily knowledgeable. The typical fan can draw upon detailed statistical information, understand complex strategies, and even comprehend various psychological influences on performance. If the public had a comparable understanding of public affairs, society would be far more democratic; the economy, more efficient; and life, in general, more rewarding.

This frightening chasm between the depth of knowledge of sports and an appalling ignorance about public affairs has a number of causes. First, most young people have experience in sports; but few people of any age get a chance to participate in public affairs in any meaningful way.

Second, sports writers typically present their information in clear and compelling language that draws in their audience. By contrast, much of the writing about public affairs is a mixture of oblique references to "sources say," together with simplistic, partial, misleading, and prejudicial reporting. Most troubling, much of the corporate media incorporates corporate or governmental misinformation presented with propagandistic prose, as when the inheritance tax mutates into a "death tax." In general, this part of the news feed is far less interesting than the sports section. No wonder the public seems so ignorant!

To add insult to injury, despite the corporate sector's overwhelming influence, the right wing has repeated the charge that the media suffers from a liberal bias so many times that much of the public accepts this claim. To the extent that this disinformation campaign convinces people, the public will have even greater difficulty in filtering through the corporate bias to understand complex political questions.

To make matters worse, although one of the chief purposes of the media is to provide a check on government, the government itself exercises excessive control over the flow of information, both directly and indirectly. Certainly, public officials go out of their way to withhold information from the public, even while they invade citizens' privacy, attempting to amass more and more information about the people they supposedly represent. In one of the more outrageous incidents, the Bush administration met in secret with corporate leaders to frame the energy policy that it issued in May 2001. According to a report from the General Accounting Office:

> the Secretary of Energy discussed national energy policy with chief executive officers of petroleum, electricity, nuclear, coal, chemical, and natural gas companies, among others. The Secretary of Energy also reportedly asked nonfederal parties for their recommendations for short- and long-term responses to petroleum product price and supply constraints. Several corporations and associations, including Chevron, the National Mining Association, and the National Petrochemical & Refiners Association, provided the Secretary of Energy with detailed energy policy recommendations. [United States General Accounting Office 2003]

Unfortunately, the Office of the Vice President has so far refused to divulge anything significant about the meetings, including the people with whom he met, even though these corporate officials helped to draft the legislation—a hypocritical stance for an administration intent on accumulating every conceivable sort of information about the public.

### KEEPING THE CONGRESS IN THE DARK

Often Congress is kept almost as much in the dark as the public at large. Debates regarding complex legislation that may contain more than 1,000 pages rarely go beyond the superficial. At best, only a handful of people will have read the entire text of major pieces of legislation, much of which comes at the behest of corporate lobbyists. In the case of the far-reaching PATRIOT Act of 2001, Congress voted on the legislation without even giving the legislators the opportunity to read the text. Only later, after bills pass, do most legislators find out exactly what they voted into law.

In some cases, the government has gone so far as to coerce people who might otherwise provide Congress with the information necessary to make intelligent decisions. For example, in 2003 the Bush administration desperately wanted to pass a terribly flawed bill to provide prescription-drug benefits to seniors. The administration succeeded, but only after strong-arming a number of congressional representatives. The $400 billion cost was a major sticking point for a number of the balking conservatives.

Medicare's chief actuary had calculated that the real cost was going to be $500 billion to $600 billion, a large enough discrepancy to have doomed the legislation. The administration threatened to fire the actuary if he dared to let Congress know the facts (Rogers 2004).

The indirect techniques for controlling the flow of information are even more ominous. The broadcast media depends upon the government for licenses. Not infrequently, corporations hold these licenses in violation of various laws. Even when licenses are not an issue, the media depends upon the government for access. In effect, the government feeds breaking stories to corporations whose media favors government policies. Finally, because the corporate media often have interests far outside of their media empires, they depend on the government for contracts and other favors.

Writing about the implicit pact between Rupert Murdoch's media empire and the U.S. government, Alexander Cockburn wrote that in return for favorable treatment, the media mogul offers "a privatized version of a state propaganda service" (Cockburn 2003: 2). This verdict may be a bit overstated for some of the media, but certainly the media mostly reports in a manner extremely favorable to the government. Beginning at least as early as the Alien and Sedition Acts of 1798, those exceptional reporters who failed to understand the limits of their designated role faced retribution from the government. Seeing what happened to the few brave souls who acted independently, the rest were careful not to make the same mistake.

Given the subservient attitude of journalists, much of the news often amounts to little more than an unpaid advertisement for the government. Government officials seem to acknowledge this relationship, comparing the news to an advertising campaign. For example, in 2002 when the Bush administration began to "sell" the public on its plan to invade Iraq, the initial reaction was not supportive at all. Andrew H. Card Jr., the White House chief of staff who was coordinating the effort, explained: "From a marketing point of view ... you don't introduce new products in August" (Bumiller

2002). Within a few months, a credulous press had repeated the administration's false claims to the point that that the advertising campaign eventually succeeded and the invasion began with a good deal of public support.

Finally, and most ominously, the government increasingly exercises enormous power in determining the flow of information coming out of academia, funding what it likes while taking stern measures against those whose results are not welcome. Although academia represents only a small part of the system of information production and independent voices make up only a tiny part of academia, losing this minuscule beachhead would be a serious loss.

Given all of these impediments to a free flow of information, we should be somewhat forgiving in dealing with the ignorance of the public regarding difficult issues.

## ELECTIONS

What political involvement exists for individuals largely involves periodic elections. But even here, public participation is pitifully small. Above all, money, not people, determines elections. Take the word of Ari Fleischer, President George W. Bush's Press Secretary. On 17 June 2003, he explained to reporters during a press briefing, "I think that the amount of money that candidates raise in our democracy is a reflection of the amount of support they have around the country." As if to prove his point, not long afterward, his boss, the president, left on a whirlwind political fund-raising tour. Although this money is supposed to be for a primary race in which the president faced no challengers, this trip was expected to bring his campaign contributions for the three-month period up to around $30 million dollars. The sort of support that the president enjoyed on the tour was relatively limited, excluding, for the most part, everybody but the rich and powerful—or in his own words, "the haves and the have mores."

Within this perverse system virtually nobody can make a significant run for public office without the support of the rich and powerful. No wonder that one commentator could say without undue exaggeration: "Politicians see corporations as constituents and industries as clients" (Draffan 2003: 19). We might well count this arrangement as another victory for consumer sovereignty—but again these consumers are the corporations that can afford to buy the politicians.

Even in small town elections, where people used to know the candidates personally, expensive television advertising campaigns have typically become the major factor in deciding elections. The situation is far worse in state and national elections. By providing only embarrassingly superficial information, television stations leave candidates little choice but to purchase advertising to get their message across. The public then chooses which politician to select just as people decide whether to buy Coke or Pepsi.

As elections approach, candidates compete with each other to buy air time, allowing the media to raise their advertising rates, making the politicians even more dependent upon corporate funds—a brilliant business strategy, but one that has lethal consequences for the democratic process.

Given this environment, politics is fast merging with entertainment. After all, celebrities already have far-reaching name recognition. Their exposure allows them to merely exude an image rather than address issues. So far, California has led the way, electing two actors to the Senate and an equal number as governor, one of whom became president.

Besides running celebrities, negative advertising campaigns are the most cost effective political strategy. Negative advertising can take the most reasonable proposal of an opponent and distort it into an unrecognizable form, smothering any possibility of serious debates about pressing issues.

Moreover, political leaders flood the public with disinformation while withholding vital information about their activities. The Bush administration may have gone further than others in fighting against the public's right to know, but to my knowledge no modern administration has been enthusiastic about releasing information.

Disgusted by the process, less than half of all eligible voters even trouble themselves to cast a ballot. Poor people are far less likely to vote than the better off part of society, reinforcing the political system's bias in favor of those with money. The obvious unfairness of the system discourages the poor even more. To make matters worse, cynical political advisors intentionally devise strategies to make people even more disgusted with the electoral process so that an even smaller minority of voters can effectively determine the outcome. For example, Ed Rollins, who served as political director for the Reagan White House, actually paid Black clergymen to encourage their congregation not to vote (see Ganz 1994).

Of those people who do bother to vote, many, if not most, rely heavily on information from the appalling coverage on television, more often than not making the election of the most qualified candidates unlikely, if not impossible. The political performance of the elected officials almost inevitably validates this lack of confidence in the system. In order to have a chance to win re-election, public officials must devote most of their attention to raising money for the next election cycle. Typically, candidates' best strategy for fund-raising is to vote in the interest of wealthy corporate interests, hoping that another round of misleading television advertisements will make their behavior appear to be in the public interest.

## A HINT OF A GOOD SOCIETY

Throughout this book, I have been critical of corporate society, by which I mean a society dominated by immense, profit-seeking corporations. An economy dominated by business is bad enough, but when control falls to a small number of corporations, the result can be horrendous. The mythology of capitalism pretends that these large corporations earn their profits by virtue of their ability to create new value. Theoretically, a corporation can harness a new idea to an innovative product, providing society with something that had previously been unavailable.

Three problems undermine this pleasant fiction. First, corporations actually develop relatively few innovative ideas; instead, innovative ideas generally evolve out of a complex pattern of science and technology that originates in the public sphere, specifically government or university financed research and development (see Perelman 2002).

Second, much of this supposed creation of value is nothing more than the exercise of uncompetitive market power to extract the larger costs from customers. Think of the Nike shoes that only cost a few dollars to manufacture, probably selling for fifty times as much to the retail customer.

Finally, more often than not, firms' profits owe more to the shifting of costs onto others rather than to the creation of value. When corporations disperse pollutants in the environment, others, often society as a whole, must bear the costs. When corporations fail to provide an adequate standard of living for their workers, their actions put further burdens on society. For example, paying workers poverty-level wages makes both education and health care more expensive, creating greater costs for society as a whole. Poverty wages also create welfare costs and higher rates of incarceration. While creating costs for the rest of society, corporations and their rich owners clamor for tax cuts. I might also add that despite the claim of consumer sovereignty, corporations often profit by scrimping on the quality or quantity of products that they deliver to unsuspecting consumers.

Yes, corporations still market many of the commodities that people need and enjoy, but corporations do not actually make these products—people do. True, for some activities, large organizations are more efficient than smaller ones, but large organizations do not have to be corporations. No law of nature requires that people can only be productive and creative within the confines of a corporation.

Elsewhere, I have addressed the possibility of alternative forms of organization (Perelman 2000b). In this work, I limited myself to exploring how corporate power affects people within the existing system, in particular within the contemporary United States. Even so, I urge you to consider the possibility of going beyond superficial reforms that might make corporate society "nicer."

# Concluding Remark

This book has made the case that individualism represents a dead-end in a corporate society. Although corporate interests proclaim a sincere belief in individualism, those fictitious individuals—corporations—are unwilling to accept the responsibilities of individuals. Corporate leaders know full well that individualism is a dead end. They join together in powerful interest groups to win even more power for themselves.

Despite the imposing powers of the corporations, in the long run, corporate power will be self-defeating, even for the corporations themselves. Focused on maximizing their next quarterly profit report, corporations ignore the two key bases of economic activity: human creativity and the environment. The all-powerful profit motive, which guides business behavior, gives corporations no reason to treat the environment with care; nor does it give the corporations any reason to ensure that human creativity be nurtured, except when it serves their narrow purposes. Instead, the corporations push to get their labor and resources at the cheapest possible price, leaving the rest of society to absorb the costs of corporate irresponsibility.

Without thorough attention to the human and environmental basis of production, sooner or later, the economy is certain to come to grief. While some might be tempted to cheer the end of corporate power, the costs of such a breakdown will impose an enormous toll—mostly on the poor. Better that we take matters into our own hands before it is too late.

Unfortunately, as long as corporations can muster so much power and influence, people, acting alone, will inevitably be reduced to being mere spectators in society. Only when people find the means to organize into powerful blocs to challenge corporate power will they be able to control their destiny. Otherwise, the blocs of corporate interests will only intensify their dominance over the rest of society. As a result, health, education, the environment, and social life in general will remain peripheral considerations to the overriding corporate quest for profit.

Obviously, such organization cannot sprout up overnight. People will have to show patience, contenting themselves for a while with only modest successes or even successful failures, which point the way to more effective organization.

Can we win this battle? Yes. Certainly with enough determination, we can. In fact, the odds are in our favor. Consider the opinion of Adam Smith's close friend, David Hume:

> Nothing appears more surprising to those, who consider human affairs with a philosophical eye, than the easiness with which the many are governed by the few .... [A]s FORCE is always on the side of the governed, the governors have nothing to support them but opinion. [Hume 1752: 32]

The opinion to which Hume referred was the opinion of the masses. Once people understand the nature of corporate society they will realize, in the words of Benjamin Barber:

> It [The corporation] is an enemy of democracy in all its forms .... If the corporation is not to defeat democracy then democracy must defeat the corporation—which is to say that the curbing of monopoly and the transformation of corporatism is a political, not economic, task. Democracy proclaims the priority of the political over the economic; the modern corporation rebuts that claim by its very existence. [Barber 1984: 257]

# References

Ackerman, Frank and Lisa Heinzerling. 2004. *Priceless: On Knowing the Price of Everything and the Value of Nothing* (New York: New Press).

Agrawal, Anup, Jeffrey F. Jaffe, and Jonathan M. Karpoff. 1999. "Management Turnover and Corporate Governance Changes Following the Revelation of Fraud." *Journal of Law and Economics*, Vol. 32, No. 1 (Part 2) (April): pp. 309–42.

Aizcorbe, Ana M., Arthur B. Kennickell, and Kevin B. Moore. 2003. "Recent Changes in U.S. Family Finances: Evidence from the 1998 and 2001 Survey of Consumer Finances." *Federal Reserve Bulletin* (January): pp. 1–32.

Alchian, Armen A. and Harold Demsetz. 1972. "Production, Information Costs, and Economic Organization." *American Economic Review*, Vol. 62, No. 5 (December): pp. 777–96.

Alesina, A., E. Glaeser, and B. Sacerdote. 2001. "Why Doesn't the US Have a European-Style Welfare State?" *Brookings Papers on Economic Activity*, No. 2, pp. 167–277.

Alesina, Alberto F. and George-Marios Angeletos. 2002. "Fairness and Redistribution: US versus Europe." Department of Economics, Massachusetts Institute of Technology Working Paper No. 02-37 (October).

Allen, Arthur. 2002. "The Not-So-Crackpot Autism Theory." *New York Times Magazine* (November 10).

Allen, James. 1937. *Reconstruction: The Battle for Democracy* (New York: International Publishers).

Allen, Mike. 2003. "Cheney's Ties to Halliburton Deferred Compensation Package Counts, Report Indicates." *Washington Post* (September 26): p. A 7.

Alliance for Justice. 1993. *Justice for Sale: Shortchange the Public Interest for Private Gain.* <http://www.allianceforjustice.org/research_publications/publications/collection/Justice_for_Sale.html>

Amick, Benjamin C., Peggy McDonough, Hong Chang, William H. Rogers, Carl F. Pieper, and Greg Duncan. 2002. "Relationship Between All-Cause Mortality and Cumulative Working Life Course Psychosocial and Physical Exposures in the United States Labor Market From 1968 to 1992." *Psychosomatic Medicine*, Vol. 64, No. 2 (May/June): pp. 370–81.

Anderson, Sarah and John Cavanagh. 2000. *The Top 200: The Rise of Global Corporate Power* (Washington, D.C.: Institute for Policy Studies).

Andrews, Edmund L. 1996. "Don't Go Away Mad, Just Go Away; Can AT&T Be the Nice Guy As It Cuts 40,000 Jobs?" *New York Times* (February 13): p. D1.

——. 2003. "Measuring Lost Freedom vs. Security in Dollars." *New York Times* (March 11).

Anon. 1938. "The Used Car." *Fortune*, Vol. 17 (June).

——. 1991. "Overheard." *Newsweek* (April 22): p. 19.

——. 1999. "Conflict in Commands Cited in Mars Orbiter Expiration." *Wall Street Journal* (April 22): p. 19.

——. 2003. "Poindexter's Follies" [editorial]. *New York Times* (July 30).

——. 2004. "Where Your Food Comes From." *New York Times* (January 23).

Appelbaum, Eileen. 2002. "Flexibility Pays." *Houston Sunday Chronicle* (May 12).

Armstrong, David. 2002. "Dick Cheney's Song of America: Drafting a Plan for Global Dominance." *Harpers* (October): pp. 76–83.

Babiak, P. 1995. "When Psychopaths Go to Work." *International Journal of Applied Psychology*, Vol. 44, No. 12: pp. 171–88.

Bak, Per. 1997. *How Nature Works: The Science of Self-Organized Criticality* (Springer).

Bakan, Joel. 2004. *The Corporation: The Pathological Pursuit of Profit and Power* (New York: Free Press).

Baker, John S., Jr. 2002. "Corporations Aren't Criminals." *Wall Street Journal* (April 22): p. A 18.

Barber, Benjamin R. 1984. *Strong Democracy: Participatory Politics* (Berkeley: University of California Press).

Barboza, David. 2003. "Monsanto Sues Dairy in Maine Over Label's Remarks on Hormones." *New York Times* (July 11).

Barstow, David. 2003a. "Deaths on the Job, Slaps on the Wrist." *New York Times* (January 10).

——. 2003b. "Officials at Foundry Face Health and Safety Charges." *New York Times* (December 16).

Barstow, David and Lowell Bergman. 2003a. "At a Texas Foundry, an Indifference to Life." *New York Times* (January 8).

——. 2003b. "Family's Profits, Wrung From Blood and Sweat." *New York Times* (January 9).

——. 2003c. "Deaths on the Job, Slaps on the Wrist." *New York Times* (January 10).

Basso, Pietro. 2003. *Modern Times, Ancient Hours: Working Lives in the Twenty-First Century* (London: Verso).

Baum, Dan. 1996. *Smoke and Mirrors: The War on Drugs and the Politics of Failure* (Boston: Little, Brown).

Beard, Charles and Mary. 1933. *The Rise of American Civilization* 2 vols. in one (New York: Macmillan).

Becker, Elizabeth. 2002. "Critics Take Aim at Guidelines on Standards for Food Safety." *New York Times* (November 2).

——. 2003a. "Government in Showdown in Bid to Shut Beef Processor." *New York Times* (January 23).

——. 2003b. "Meat Inspections Declining, Impact of Policy Is Contested." *New York Times* (July 9).

Becker, Gary S. 1968. "Crime and Punishment: An Economic Approach." *Journal of Political Economy*, Vol. 76, No. 2 (March–April): pp. 169–217.

——. 2003. "How to Level the Playing Field for Young Black Men." *Business Week* (August 4): p. 24.

Begley, Sharon. 2002. "Dear W: Scientists Offer President Advice on Policy." *Wall Street Journal* (January 27).

Bierce, Ambrose. 1958. *The Devil's Dictionary* (New York: Dover Publications); first published in 1906 as *The Cynic's Word Book*.

Blaszczyk, Regina Lee. 2000. *Imagining Consumers: Design and Innovation from Wedgwood to Corning* (Baltimore: Johns Hopkins University Press).

Bleiberg, Robert. 1981. "Nuclear Threat: Three Mile Island May Yet Claim Further Victims." *Barrons* (March 23): p. 7.

Blustein, Paul. 2001. *The Chastening: The Crisis that Rocked the Global Financial System and Humbled the IMF* (Cambridge: Perseus Books Group).

Bolton, Patrick and Howard Rosenthal. 2002. "Political Intervention in Debt Contracts." *Journal of Political Economy*, Vol. 110, No. 5 (October): pp. 1103–34.

Booth, Alison L., Marco Francesconi, and Jeff Frank. 2002. "Temporary Jobs: Stepping Stones of Dead Ends?" *Economic Journal*, Vol. 112, No. 480 (June): pp. F189–F213.

Boskin, Michael J., Ellen R. Dulberger, Robert J. Gordon, Zvi Griliches, and Dale W. Jorgenson. 1998. "Consumer Prices, the Consumer Price Index, and the Cost of Living." *Journal of Economic Perspectives*, Vol. 12, No. 1 (Winter): pp. 3–26.

Boushey, Heather. 2003. "Who Cares? The Child Care Choices of Working Mothers." Center for Economic and Policy Research. Data Brief No. 1 (May 6). <http://www.cepr.net/Data_Brief_Child_Care.htm>

Bowker, Michael. 2003. *Fatal Deception: The Untold Story of Asbestos: Why It Is Still Legal and Still Killing Us* (Emmaus, PA: Rodale).

Bradsher, Keith. 2004. *High and Mighty* (NY: PublicAffairs).

Braman, Donald. 2002. "Families and Incarceration." in Marc Mauer and Meda Chesney-Lind, eds. *Invisible Punishment: The Collateral Consequences of Mass Imprisonment* (New York: New Press): pp. 117–35.

Brenner, Meyer Harvey. 1976. *Estimating the Social Costs of National Economic Policy: Implications for Mental and Physical Health and Clinical Aggression, Report to the Joint Economic Committee* (Washington, D.C.: U.S. Government Printing Office).

Bridges, William. 1994a. *Job Shift: How to Prosper in a Workplace Without Jobs* (New York: Addison-Wesley).

——. 1994b. "The End of the Job." *Fortune* (September 19): pp. 62–74.

Britt, Bill. 2004. "Automakers Tap Minds of Consumers." *Automotive News* (February 2).

Brooks, Rick. 2002. "Big Incentives Won Alabama a Piece of the Auto Industry." *Wall Street Journal* (April 3): p. A1.

Bumiller, Elisabeth. 2002. "Bush Aides Set Strategy to Sell Policy on Iraq." *New York Times* (September 7).

——. 2003. "Cheney Returns Fire in Battle on Tax Cuts." *New York Times* (January 11).

Burke, Thomas Frederick. 2002. *Lawyers, Lawsuits, and Legal Rights: The Battle over Litigation in American Society* (Berkeley: University of California Press).

Burnham, David. 1974. "Union of Concerned Scientists and Sierra Club Release Report Highly Critical of AEC's Reactor Safety Study." *New York Times* (November 24): p. 57.

Burrough, Bryan and John Helyar. 1990. *Barbarians at the Gate: The Fall of RJR Nabisco* (New York: Harper and Row).

Burtless, Gary. 1999. "Squeezed for Time: American Inequality and the Shortage of Leisure." *Brookings Review*, Vol. 17, No. 4 (Fall): pp. 18–22.

Bush, George W. 2004. "Remarks at a Bush–Cheney Reception in Atlanta, Georgia (15 January)." *19 January Weekly Compilation of Presidential Documents*, Volume 40; Issue 3.

Caballero, María Jose. 2003. "The Prestige Disaster. One Year On." <http://www.greenpeaceusa.org/images/user/2/i806.pdf>

Campbell, John Y. and John H. Cochrane. 1995. "By Force of Habit: A Consumption-Based Explanation of Aggregate Stock Market Behavior." National Bureau of Economic Research Working Paper No. 4995.

Campbell-Kelly, Martin and William Aspray. 1996. *Computer: A History of the Information Machine* (New York: Basic Books).

Carroll, Jill. 2001. "Government Agencies Pull Sensitive Details on Chemical Plants, Oil Pipes From Sites." *Wall Street Journal* (October 3): p. A 10.

Catanzaro, Michael. 2003. "Setting the Record Straight: The White House, 9/11, and Air Quality." *Human Events Online* (October 2). <http://www.humaneventsonline.com/article.php?id=1986>

Centers for Disease Control. 2002. "Workers' Memorial Day (April 28, 2002)." *Mortality and Morbidity Weekly Report* (April 26). <http://www.cdc.gov/mmwr/preview/mmwrhtml/mm5116a1.htm>

Cheung, Steven N. S. 1983. "The Contractual Nature of the Firm." *Journal of Law and Economics*, Vol. 26, No. 1 (April): pp. 1–22.

Clark, Gregory. 1994. "Factory Discipline." *Journal of Economic History*, Vol. 54, No. 1 (March): pp. 128–63.

Cockburn, Alexander. 2003. "'I am Thy Father's Ghost': A Journey into Rupert Murdoch's Soul." *Counterpunch*, Vol. 10, No. 19 (November 1–15): pp. 1–3, 5–6.

Cohen, Mark A. 1989. "Corporate Crime and Punishment: A Study of Social Foreign and Sentencing Practice in the Federal Courts, 1984–1987." *American Criminal Law Review*, Vol. 26, No. 3 (Winter): pp. 605–60.

Coke, Sir Edward. 1612. "The Case of Sutton's Hospital", 10 *English Reports*, Vol. 77 (Edinburgh: William Green & Sons): pp. 937–76.

Common Cause. 2003. "Despite Terrorism Threat, Chemical Industry Succeeds in Blocking Federal Security Regulations" (January 27). <http://www.commoncause.org/publications/jan03/012703_2.htm>

Conlin, Roxanne Barton. 1991. "Litigation Explosion Disputed: Studies Refute the Critics." *National Law Journal* (July 29).

Costa, Dora L. and Matthew E. Kahn. 2000. "Power Couples: Changes in the Locational Choice of the College Educated, 1940–1990." *Quarterly Journal of Economics*, Vol. 115, No. 4 (November): pp. 1287–315.

Court, Jamie. 2003. *Corporateering: How Corporate Power Steals Your Personal Freedom … And What You Can Do About It* (New York: J. P. Tarcher).

——. 2004. "Supremes Limit Punitive Damages." *Dollars and Sense*, No. 252 (March/April): pp. 13–14.

Crepinsek, Mary Kay, Nancy R. Burstein, and Linda M. Ghelfi. 2004. *Maternal Employment and Children's Nutrition*, 2 vols. (Washington, DC: U.S. Department of Agriculture Economic Research Service) (EFAN04006-1 and EFAN04006-2) <http://www.ers.usda.gov/publications/efan04006/efan04006-1/> and <http://www.ers.usda.gov/publications/efan04006/efan04006-2/>

Cross, Gary. 1989. *A Quest for Time: The Reduction of Work in Britain and France, 1840–1940* (Berkeley: University of California Press).

Cutler, David M. and Lawrence H. Summers. 1988. "The Costs of Conflict Resolution and Financial Distress: Evidence from the Texaco-Penzoil Litigation." *Rand Journal of Economics*, Vol. 19, No. 2 (Summer): pp. 157–72.

Darity, William Jr. and Bobbie L. Horn. 1988. *The Loan Pushers: the Role of Commercial Banks in the International Debt Crisis* (Cambridge, MA: Ballinger).

Davidson, Keay. 2004. "Security Faulted at Nuclear Reactors; Plants Vulnerable to Terrorist Attacks, GAO Report Finds." *San Francisco Chronicle* (September 15).

Dawson, Michael. 2003. *The Consumer Trap: Big Business Marketing in American Life* (Urbana: University of Illinois Press).

Deane, Claudia. 2002. "Computer-Assisted Influence? Think Tank Seeks Payoff Aiding Press With Data." *Washington Post* (April 19).

Department of Trade and Industry. United Kingdom. 2002. *More People Want Flexible Hours Than Cash, Company Car Or Gym* (December 30).

Dickens, Edwin. 1995. "The Great Inflation and U.S. Monetary Policy in the Late 1960s: A Political Economy Approach." *Social Concept*, Vol. 9, No. 1 (July): pp. 49–82.

——. 1997. "The Federal Reserve's Tight Monetary Policy During the 1973–75 Recession: A Survey of Possible Interpretations." *The Review of Radical Political Economics*, Vol. 29, No. 3 (Summer): pp. 79–91.

Dixon, K. A. and Carl E. Van Horn. 2003. "The Disposable Worker: Living in a Job-Loss Economy." *Work Trends* (John J. Heldrich Center for Workforce Development, Rutgers University), Vol. 6, No. 2 (July). <http://www.heldrich.rutgers.edu/Resources/Publication/99/WorkTrendsXIVTheDisposableWorkerFinalReportPDFVersionJuly03.pdf>

Dowie, Mark. 1977. "How Ford Put Two Million Firetraps on Wheels." *Business and Society Review* (Fall): pp. 46–55.

Draffan, George. 2003. *The Elite Consensus: When Corporations Wield the Constitution* (New York: Apex Press).

Drucker, Peter F. 1976. *The Unseen Revolution: How Pension Fund Socialism Came to America* (New York: Harper and Row).

Dubin, Jeffrey and Geoffrey Rothwell. 1990. "Subsidy to Nuclear Power Through Price-Anderson Liability Limit." *Contemporary Policy Issues*, Vol. 8 (July): pp. 73–79.

Duca, John V. and Jason Saving. 2001. "The Political Economy of the Mutual Fund Revolution: How Falling Mutual Fund Costs Have Affected Congressional Elections." Federal Reserve Bank of Dallas, unpub. (June).

Easterbrook, Frank H. and Daniel R. Fischel. 1982. "Antitrust Suits by Targets of Tender Offers." *Michigan Law Review*, Vol. 80, No. 6 (May): pp. 1155–78.

Easterlin, Richard A. 1995. "Will Raising the Incomes of All Increase the Happiness of All?" *Journal of Economic Behavior and Organization*, Vol. 27, No. 1 (June): pp. 1–34.

Estes, Ralph W. 1995. *Tyranny of the Bottom Line: Why Corporations Make Good People Do Bad Things* (San Francisco: Berrett-Koehler).

Etzioni, Amitai. 1988. *The Moral Dimension: Toward a New Economics* (NY: The Free Press).

Fairman, Charles. ed. 1987. *Reconstruction and Reunion 1864–88*, Vol. VII, Part 2 of *Oliver Wendell Holmes Devise History of the Supreme Court of the United States* (New York: Macmillan).

Federal Trade Commission. 2003. *Slotting Allowances in the Retail Grocery Industry: Selected Case Studies in Five Product Categories.* <http://www.ftc.gov/os/2003/11/slottingallowancerpt031114.pdf>

Feynman, Richard Phillips. 1988. *What Do YOU Care What Other People Think?* (New York: Norton).

Fields, Barbara Jeanne. 1990. "Slavery, Race and Ideology in the United States of America." *New Left Review*, No. 181 (May/June): pp. 95–118.

Files, John. 2003. "White House Backs Retaining Pay Raises for Troops Abroad." *New York Times* (16 August).

Firestone, David. 2003. "Pentagon Seeking to Deploy Missiles Before Full Testing." *New York Times* (February 27).

Fisher, Franklin M., Zvi Griliches, and Carl Kaysen. 1962. "The Costs of Automobile Changes Since 1949." *Journal of Political Economy*, Vol. 70, No. 5 (October): pp. 433–51.

Fisher, Peter R. 2002. "Beyond Borrowing: Meeting the Government's Financial Challenges in the 21st Century: Remarks to the Columbus Council on World Affairs Columbus, Ohio" (November 14). <http://www.treas.gov/press/releases/po3622.htm>

Flint, Robert. 2004. "How Wal-Mart Treads Heavily in Foreign-Exchange Forest." *Wall Street Journal* (November 17).

Ford, H. and S. Crowther. 1930 "The Fear of Overproduction." *Saturday Evening Post*, Vol. 203 (July 12).

France, David and Erika Check. 2001. "Asbestos Alert." *Newsweek* (September 14). <http://msnbc.com/news/629268.asp?0sp=w12b2&cp1=1>

Frank, Robert H. 1985. *Choosing the Right Pond: Human Behavior and the Quest for Status* (New York: Oxford University Press).

Franklin, Benjamin, et al. 1785. *Report of Dr. Benjamin Franklin and Other Commissioners, Charged by the King of France, with the Examination of the Animal Magnetism, as Now Practised at Paris,* Translated from the French with a historical introduction [by William Godwin] (London: J. Johnson).

Frey, Bruno S. and Alois Stutzer. 2002. *Happiness and Economics: How the Economy and Institutions Affect Well-Being* (Princeton: Princeton University Press).

Friedman, Lisa. 2003. "Waxman Blasts Bush Funding for Anthrax Study Calls Diversion 'Mistake'." *Los Angeles Daily News* (July 12).

Friedman, M. 1962. "Monopoly and the Social Responsibility of Business and Labor." in *Capitalism and Freedom* (Chicago: University of Chicago Press): pp. 119–36.

Frontline. 2003. "A Dangerous Business: Toothless in Washington." <http://www.pbs.org/wgbh/pages/frontline/shows/workplace/osha/>

Fuentes, Annette. 2003. "Autism in a Needle? The Toxic Tale of Vaccinations and Mercury Poisoning." *In These Times* (December 8): pp. 14–17, 28.

Galanter, Marc. 1992. "Pick a Number, Any Number." *American Lawyer* (April).

Ganz, Marshall. 1994. "Voters in the Crosshairs." *The American Prospect*, Vol. 5, No. 16 (December 1). <http://www.prospect.org/print-friendly/print/V5/16/ganz-m.html>

Gersema, Emily. 2003. "Bush Won't Sign Bill to Release Stores Involved in Meat Recalls." *Boston Globe* (March 13): p. A 2.

Glaeser, Edward L. 1998. "Are Cities Dying?" *Journal of Economic Perspectives*, Vol. 12, No. 2 (Spring): pp. 139–60.

Glantz, Stanton A., Karen W. Kacirk, and Charles McCulloch. 2004. "Back to the Future: Smoking in Movies in 2002 Compared with 1950 Levels." *American Journal of Public Health*, Vol. 94, No. 2 (February): pp. 261–3.

Glenn, David. 2002. "Calculated Risks: Harvard Professor Says Smokers Know Exactly What They're Doing." *Chronicle of Higher Education* (May 31): p. 14.

Golden, Lonnie and Helene Jorgensen. 2002. *Time After Time: Mandatory Overtime in the U.S. Economy*. Economic Policy Institute. <http://www.epinet.org/briefingpapers/120/bp120.pdf>

Gordon, Colin. 1994. *New Deals: Business, Labor, and Politics in America* (Cambridge: Cambridge University Press).

Gordon, Greg. 2003. "Asbestos Victims Get Relief in Senate Judiciary Vote." *Minneapolis Star Tribune* (June 27).

Gorelick, Steven. 1998. "Hiding Damaging Information from the Public." *The Ecologist*, Vol. 28, No. 5 (September 1).

Gould, Stephen J. 1980. *The Panda's Thumb* (New York: W. W. Norton).

Goulden, Joseph C. 1988. *Fit To Print: A. M. Rosenthal and his Times* (Secaucus, NJ: L. Stuart).

Graham, Howard Jay. 1938. "The 'Conspiracy Theory' of the Fourteenth Amendment." *Yale Law Journal*, Vol. 47; reprinted in Kenneth M. Stammp and and Leon F. Litwack, eds. *Reconstruction: An Anthology of Revisionist Writing* (Louisiana State University Press, 1969): pp. 107–31.

——. 1968. *Everyman's Constitution: Historical Essays on The Fourteenth Amendment* (Madison: State Historical Society of Wisconsin).

Graham, John D. 1995. *Comparing Opportunities To Reduce Health Risks: Toxin Control, Medicine and Injury Prevention* (Dallas: National Center For Policy Analysis). <http://www.ncpa.org/studies/s192/s192.html>

Grant, James. 1996. *The Trouble With Prosperity: The Loss of Fear, the Rise of Speculation, and the Risk to American Savings* (New York: Times Books).

Gray, Wayne B. and John T. Scholz. 1991. "Do OSHA Inspections Reduce Injuries: A Panel Analysis." National Bureau of Economic Research Working Paper No. 3774 (July).

Greenhouse, Linda. 2003. "Free Speech for Companies on Justices' Agenda." *New York Times* (April 20).

Greenspan, Alan. 1997a. "Performance of the U.S. Economy." Testimony before the Committee on the Budget, United States Senate (January 21). <http://www.federalreserve.gov/boarddocs/testimony/1997/19970121.htm>

——. 1997b. "Introduction." in *Maintaining Financial Stability in a Global Economy: A Symposium Sponsored by the Federal Reserve Bank of Kansas City, Jackson Hole, Wyoming* (August 28–30): pp. 1–6.

——. 1997c. "Statement Before the Committee on Banking, Housing, and Urban Affairs, U.S. Senate (26 February)." *Federal Reserve Bulletin*, Vol. 83, No. 4 (April): pp. 254–9.

Greider, William. 1992. *Who Will Tell the People: The Betrayal of American Democracy* (New York: Simon & Schuster).

Grimaldi, James V. 2002. "Cheney's 'Win-Win' Acquisition as Firm's CEO Became Liability: Halliburton's Purchase of Dresser Put It at Risk Over Asbestos Claims." *Washington Post* (August 11): p. A 4.

Gross, Daniel. 2003. "The Cheney Curse: The Veep Hasn't Helped Halliburton." *Slate* (October 14). <http://slate.msn.com/id/2089811/>

Gumbel, Andrew. 2004. "Betrayed by an Oil Giant, 15 years after the Exxon Valdez Disaster, the Coast Remains Polluted and Compensation is Unpaid." *Independent* (London) (March 25).

Gutierrez, Hector. 2003. "Frontier Mechanic Believed Plane Was Unsafe, Affidavit Says." *Rocky Mountain News* (January 3).

Hacker, Louis, M. 1940. *The Triumph of American Capitalism: The Development of Forces in American History to the End of the Nineteenth Century* (New York: Simon and Schuster).

Halberstam, David. 1986. *The Reckoning* (New York: William Morrow).

Hallinan, Joseph T. 2004. "Suit Wrinkle: In Malpractice Trials, Juries Rarely Have the Last Word Large Awards Grab Attention, But Often Aren't Paid Out." *Wall Street Journal* (November 30): p. A 1.

Hartmann, Thom. 2002. *Unequal Protection: The Rise of Corporate Dominance and the Theft of Human Rights* (Emmaus, PA: Rodale Press).

Haveman, Robert. 1985. "Does the Welfare State Increase Welfare? Reflections on Hidden Negatives and Observed Positives." *De Economist*, Vol. 133, No. 4: pp. 445–66.

Hays, Constance L. 2004. "What Wal-Mart Knows About Customers' Habits." *New York Times* (November 14).

Heffernan, Virginia. 2004. "The Real Boss of 'The Sopranos'." *New York Times* (February 29).

Heinzerling, Lisa and Frank Ackerman. 2002. "Pricing the Priceless: Cost-Benefit Analysis of Environmental Protection." *University Pennsylvania Law Review*, Vol. 150 (May): pp. 1553–84.

Helliwell, John F. 2002. *Globalization and Well-Being* (Vancouver: UBC Press).

Henwood, Doug. 2003. *After the New Economy* (New York: New Press).

Heritage Foundation. 2003. *Annual Report*. <2004http://www.heritage.org/About/loader.cfm?url=/commonspot/security/getfile.cfm&PageID=39932>

Herling, John. 1962. *The Great Price Conspiracy* (Washington, D.C.: R. B. Luce).

Hirsch, Fred. 1976. *Social Limits to Growth* (London: Routledge and Kegan Paul).

Hirschman, Albert O. 1982. *Shifting Involvements: Private Interest and Public Action* (Princeton: Princeton University Press).

Huber. Peter. 1988. *Liability: The Legal Revolution and its Consequences* (New York: Basic Books).

——. 1991. *Galileo's Revenge: Junk Science in the Courtroom* (New York: Basic Books).

Hulse, Carl. 2003. "Congress Shuts Pentagon Unit Over Privacy." *New York Times* (September 26).

Hume, David. 1752. "On the First Principles of Government." in *Essays: Moral, Political, and Literary*, edited by Eugene F. Miller (Liberty Press: Indianapolis, 1985): pp. 32–6.

Hunnicut, Benjamin Kline. 1988. *Work Without End: Abandoning Shorter Hours for the Right to Work* (Philadelphia: Temple University Press).

Iyengar, Sheena S. and Mark R. Lepper. 2000. "When Choice is Demotivating: Can One Desire Too Much of a Good Thing?" *Journal of Personality and Social Psychology*, Vol. 79, No. 6 (December): pp. 995–1006.

Jenkins, Cate. 2003. "Comments on the EPA Office of Inspector General's Interim Report Titled: 'EPA's Response to the World Trade Center Towers Collapse:' A Documentary Basis for Litigation, July 4, 2003." United States Environmental Protection Agency.

Jenkins, Holman W., Jr. 1998. "The Rise and Stumble of Nike." *Wall Street Journal* (June 3): p. A19.

Jonsson, Ernst. 1978. "Labour as Risk-Bearer." *Cambridge Journal of Economics*, Vol. 4, No. 2 (December): pp. 373–80.

Jowers, Karen. 2003. "An Act of 'Betrayal': In the Midst of War, Key Family Benefits Face Cuts." *Army Times* (November 11).

Kahneman, Daniel. 2003. "Maps of Bounded Rationality: Psychology for Behavioral Economics." *American Economic Review*, Vol. 93, No. 5 (December): pp. 1449–75.

Kane, Thomas J. and Douglas O. Staiger. 2002. "The Promise and Pitfalls of Using Imprecise School Accountability Measures." *Journal of Economic Perspectives*, Vol. 16, No. 4 (Fall): pp. 91–114.

Kang, Stephanie. 2003. "Naming the Baby: Parents Brand Tots With What's Hot." *Wall Street Journal* (December 26).

Kanigel, Robert. 1997. *The One Best Way: Frederick Winslow Taylor and the Enigma of Efficiency* (New York: Viking).

Kaplan, George A. et al. 1996. "Inequality in Income and Mortality in the United States: Analysis of Mortality and Potential Pathways." *British Medical Journal*, Vol. 312 (April 20): pp. 999–1003.

Karamzin, N. M. 1957. *Letters of a Russian Traveller, 1789–1790* (NY: Columbia University Press).

Karpoff, Jonathan M., D. Scott Lee, and Valaria P. Vendrzyk. 1999. "Defense Procurement Fraud, Penalties, and Contractor Influence." *Journal of Political Economy*, Vol. 107, No. 4 (August): pp. 809–42.

Katz, Jane. 1997. "The Joy of Consumption." *Regional Review of the Federal Reserve Bank of Boston* (Winter): pp. 12–17.

Kaufman, Jonathan. 1998. "Striking it Richer: Amid Economic Boom, Many of the 'Haves' Envy the 'Have-Mores'—They Know They're Well Off, But Can't Help Coveting." *Wall Street Journal* (August 3): p. A 1.

Kautsky, Karl. 1899. *The Agrarian Question*, translated by Pete Burgess (London: Zwan, 1988).

Keller, Edmund R. 1977. "The Trouble with Oligopoly is the Price." *Antitrust Law and Economics Review*, Vol. 9, No. 2: pp. 73–91.

Kelley, Governor Edward W., Jr. 1995. "Federal Open Market Committee Meeting Transcripts." (August 22). <http://www.federalreserve.gov/FOMC/transcripts/1995/950822Meeting.pdf>

Kelly, William J. 2004. "Patriot Act Restricts Access to LNG Safety Studies." *California Energy Circuit* (March 19). <http://www.californiaenergycircuit.net/displaystory.php?task=show&sid=331&un=&ut=&pd=&seid=10798 49433>

Kenney, Charles. 1999. "Does Growth Cause Happiness, or Does Happiness Cause Growth?" *Kyklos*, Vol. 52, No. 1: pp. 3–26.

Kettering, Charles F. 1929. "Keep the Consumer Dissatisfied." *Nation's Business* (January): pp. 30–1, 79.

Keynes, John Maynard. 1930. "Economic Possibilities for Our Grandchildren." *Nation and Athenaeum* (October 11 and 18); reprinted in *Essays in Persuasion*. vol. 9. *The Collected Works of John Maynard Keynes*, Donald Moggridge, ed. (London: Macmillan, 1972): pp. 321–31.

Kiester, Edwin, Jr. 1994. "The GI Bill May Be the Best Deal Ever Made by Uncle Sam." *Smithsonian Magazine*, Vol. 25, No. 4 (November): pp. 129–32.

Klein, Naomi. 2000. *No Space, No Choice, No Jobs, No Logo: Taking Aim at the Brand Bullies* (New York: Picador USA).

Knight, Frank. 1921. *Risk, Uncertainty, and Profit* (Chicago: University of Chicago Press).

Kolko, Gabriel. 1965. *Railroads and Regulation, 1877–1916* (Princeton: Princeton University Press).

Kramer, Staci D. 2002. "Content's King: Jamie Kellner Controls Turner's Programming Riches." *Cableworld* (April 29).

Kremer, Michael. 1993. "The O-Ring Theory of Economic Development." *Quarterly Journal of Economics*, Vol. 58, No. 3 (August): pp. 551–76.

Kronholz, June. 2003. "Education Firms See Money In Bush's School-Boost Law." *Wall Street Journal* (24 December): p. B 1.

Kroszner, Randall S. 1999. "Is It Better to Forgive than to Receive? Repudiation of the Gold Indexation Clause in Long-Term Debt during the Great Depression." Manuscript. Chicago: University of Chicago, Graduate School of Business. <http://gsbwww.uchicago.edu/fac/randall.kroszner/research/>

Krugman, Paul. 2001. "Nation in a Jam." *New York Times* (May 13).

Kyrk, Hazel. 1923. *A Theory of Consumption* (Boston: Houghton Mifflin).

Landrigan, Philip J. 1992. "Commentary: Environmental Disease— A Preventable Epidemic." *American Journal of Public Health*, Vol. 82, No. 7 (July): pp. 941–3.

Lane, Robert Edwards. 2000. *The Loss of Happiness in Market Democracies* (New Haven, CT: Yale University Press).

Larson, Martin A. 1979. *The Continuing Tax Rebellion: What Millions of Americans Are Doing to Restore Constitutional Government* (Old Greenwich, CT: The Devin-Adair Company).

Lasch, Christopher. 1979. *The Culture of Narcissism* (New York: Warner Books).

Layard, Richard. 2002–03. "Happiness: Has Social Science a Clue?" Lionel Robbins Memorial Lectures 2002/3. Lecture 1. "What is happiness? Are

We Getting Happier?" <www.lse.ac.uk/Press/currentPressReleases/Lionel_ Robbins_Layard_happiness.htm>

Lee, Jennifer. 2003. "Details Emerge on Post-9/11 Clash Between White House and E.P.A." *New York Times* (October 10).

Lefebvre, Henri. 1971. *Everyday Life in the Modern World*, Sacha Rabinovitch, trans. (New York: Harper & Row).

Leigh, J. Paul, Steven B. Markowitz, Marianne Fahs, Chonggah Shin, and Philip J. Landrigan. 1997. "Occupational Injury and Illness in the United States: Estimates of Costs, Morbidity and Mortality." *Archives of Internal Medicine*, Vol. 167 (July): pp. 1557–68.

Leigh, J. Paul, Steven Markowitz, Marianne Fahs, and Philip Landrigan. 2000. *Costs of Occupational Injuries and Illnesses* (Ann Arbor: University of Michigan Press).

Lemieux, Thomas and David Card. 1998. "Education, Earnings, and the 'Canadian G.I. Bill'." National Bureau of Economic Research Working Paper No. w6718 (September).

LeRoy, Greg. 1994. *No More Candy Store: States and Cities Making Job Subsidies Acountable* (Chicago and Washington D.C.: Federation for Industrial Retention and Renewal).

Levitas, Daniel. 2002. *The Terrorist Next Door: The Militia Movement and the Radical Right* (New York: St Martin's Press).

Levitt, Steven D. 2004. "Understanding Why Crime Fell in the 1990s: Four Factors that Explain the Decline and Six that Do Not." *Journal of Economic Perspectives*, Vol. 18, No. 1 (Winter): pp. 163–90.

Linder. Marc. 1994. *Labor Statistics and Class Struggle* (New York: International Publishers).

Linder, Marc and Ingrid Nygaard. 1998. *Void Where Prohibited: Rest Breaks and the Right to Urinate on Company Time* (Ithaca, NY: ILR Press).

Lindorff, Dave. 2003. "Dishonorable Discharge: Bush Administration Slashes Veteran's Benefits." *In These Times* (November 26).

Lippmann, Walter. 1914. *Drift and Mastery: An Attempt to Diagnose the Current Unrest* (New York: Mitchel Kennerley; Englewood Cliffs, NJ: Prentice Hall, 1961).

Lowenstein, Roger. 2000. *When Genius Failed: The Rise and Fall of Long-Term Capital Management* (New York: Random House).

Lucchetti, Aaron. 1996. "An Auto Worker Earns More Than $100,000, But at a Personal Cost." *Wall Street Journal* (August 1): p. A 1.

Luce, Henry R. 1950. "The Reformation of the World's Economies." *Fortune* (February): p. 62; cited in Dawson 2003, p. 8.

McCurdy, Charles. 1975. "Justice Field and the Jurisprudence of Government-Business Relations: Some Parameters of Laissez Faire Constitutionalism, 1863–1897." *Journal of American History*, Vol. 61 (March): pp. 970–1005.

McDonough, William. 1995. "International Economic Cooperation: Roy Ridge Memorial Lecture." in *Federal Reserve Bank of New York 1994 Annual Report*: pp. 1–15.

McKendrick, Neil. 1982. "Commercialization of Potteries." in Neil McKendrick, John Brewer, and J.H. Plumb, eds. *The Birth of a Consumer Society: The Commercialization of Eighteenth-Century England* (London: Hutchinson): pp. 100–45.

Mckinnon, John D. 2003. "Warning of Pension-Plan Shortfall Raises Pressure for Financial Fix." *Wall Street Journal* (September 5): p. A 1.

McQueen, Humphrey. 2003. *The Essence of Capitalism: The Origins of Our Future* (Montreal: Black Rose Books).

Madrick, Jeff. 1998. "Computers: Waiting for the Revolution." *New York Review of Books*, Vol. 45, No. 4 (March 26): pp. 29–33.

Magee, Stephen, William Brock, and Leslie Young. 1989. *Black Hole Tariffs and the Endogenous Policy Theory* (Cambridge: Cambridge University Press).

Maines, Rachel. 2003. "Asbestos and Fire: Technological Tradeoffs and the Body at Risk, 1870–1990." The Center for the History of Business, Technology, and Society, Research Seminar Paper No. 102, Hagley Museum and Library (December 11).

Mandel, Michael J. 1996. *The High Risk Society: Peril and Promise in the New Economy* (New York: Random House).

Marchand, Roland. 1991. "The Corporation Nobody Knew: Bruce Barton, Alfred Sloan, and the Founding of the General Motors 'Family'." *Business History Review*, Vol. 65, No. 4 (Winter): pp. 825–75.

Marglin, Stephen. 1967. *Public Investment Criteria: Benefit-Cost Analysis for Planned Economic Growth* (Cambridge, MA: MIT Press).

Marling, Karal Ann. 1994. *As Seen on TV: The Visual Culture of Everyday Life in the 1950s* (Cambridge: Harvard University Press).

Marquis, Christopher. 2003. "House Committee Charges Bush Administration with Persistently Misusing Scientific Data to Serve its Ideology and Corporate Friends." *New York Times* (August 8).

Marx, Karl. 1849. "Wage Labor and Capital." in Karl Marx and Frederick Engels, *Selected Works in Three Volumes* (NY: International Publishers, 1972): i, pp. 142–74.

——. 1857–58. *Grundrisse* (New York: Vintage, 1973).

——. 1977. *Capital*. Vol. 1 (New York: Vintage).

Mathewson, Stanley. 1939. *Restriction of Output Among Unorganized Workers* (Carbondale: Southern Illinois University Press, 1969).

Maynard, Micheline. 2003. "Citing SARS, Northwest Invokes Clause to Allow Layoffs." *New York Times* (May 9).

Mead, P. S. et al. 1999. "Food-Related Illness and Death in the United States." *Emerging Infectious Diseases*, Vol. 5 (September–October): pp. 607–25.

Meyer Stephen. 1981. *The Five Dollar Day: Labor Management and Social Control in the Ford Motor Company, 1908–1921* (Albany: State University of New York Press).

Milbank, Dana and Mike Allen. 2003. "Security May Not Be Safe Issue for Bush in '04." *Washington Post* (August 22): p. A 1.

Miller, James P. et al. 1995. "Bad Chemistry: W. R. Grace is Roiled By Flap Over Spending and What to Disclose." *Wall Street Journal* (March 10): pp. A 1 and A 16.

Miner, Barbara. 2004. "Why the Right Hates Public Education." *The Progressive* (January): pp. 22–4.

Mintz, John. 2003. "Bush Seeks Voluntary Chemical Plant Security Steps; Criticized as Vulnerable to Terrorism, Industry Fighting Democratic Proposal for Mandatory Measures." *Washington Post* (April 8): p. A 10.

Mishel, Lawrence, Jared Bernstein, and Heather Boushey. 2003. *The State of Working America, 2002* (Ithaca: Cornell University Press).

Mokhiber, Russell. 1988. *Corporate Crime and Violence: Big Business Power and the Abuse of the Public Trust* (San Francisco: Sierra Club Books).

Mokhiber, Russell and Robert Weissman. 2003. "Hide and Seek." (January 30). <http://lists.essential.org/pipermail/corp-focus/2003/000143.html>

Moore, Barrington. 1966. *Social Origins of Dictatorship and Democracy* (Boston: Beacon Press).

Moore, David W. 2003. "Half of Young People Expect to Strike it Rich but Expectations Fall Rapidly with Age." *Gallup News Service* (March 11). <http://www.gallup.com/poll/releases/pr030311.asp>

Moss, David A. 2002. *When All Else Fails: Government as the Ultimate Risk Manager* (Cambridge: Harvard University Press).

Moss, Michael and Adrianne Appel. 2001. "Protecting the Product: Company's Silence Countered Safety Fears About Asbestos." *New York Times* (July 9).

Mumola, Cristopher J. 2000. *Incarcerated Parents and Their Children* (Washington, DC: Department of Justice: Bureau of Justice Statistics).

Murray, Alan. 2004. "Business Elite Vows to Take on Kerry if he Taps Edwards." *Wall Street Journal* (July 6): p. A 4.

Murray, Shailagh and Kathryn Kranhold. 2003. "Asbestos Factions Struggle to Settle Their 30-Year War." *Wall Street Journal* (October 15): p. A 1.

Myers, David G. and Ed Diener. 1996. "The Pursuit of Happiness." *Scientific American*, Vol. 274, No. 5 (May): pp. 70–2.

Nader, Ralph. 1995. "Nader's Raid on Corporate Reports: If Tort Liability is Such a Crippler to American Industry, Why do Companies Downplay That Effect in Their SEC Reports." *Recorder* (May 10): p. 8.

Nagin, Daniel S., James B. Rebitzer, Seth Sanders, and Lowell J. Taylor. 2002. "Monitoring, Motivation, and Management: The Determinants of Opportunistic Behavior in a Field Experiment." *American Economic Review*, Vol. 92, No. 4 (December): pp. 850–73.

Nakazawa, Tetsuya, Yasushi Okubo, Yasushi Suwazono, Etsuko Kobayashi, Shingo Komine, Norihisa Kato, Koji Nogawa. 2002. "Association Between Duration of Daily VDT Use and Subjective Symptoms." *American Journal of Industrial Medicine*, 42: 5 (November): pp. 421–6.

Nardinelli, Clark. 1982. "Corporal Punishment and Children's Wages in 19th Century Britain." *Explorations in Economic History*, Vol. 19, No. 3 (July): pp. 283–95.

National Research Council. 2004. *Biological Confinement of Genetically Engineered Organisms* (Washington DC: National Academies Press).

Nestle, Marion. 2003. *Safe Food: Bacteria, Biotechnology, and Bioterrorism* (California Studies in Food and Culture) (Berkeley: University of California Press).

Neumann, Peter. 1995. *Computer Related Risks* (Reading, MA: Addison-Wesley).

Nicosia, Gerald. 2001. *Home To War: A History of the Vietnam Veterans' Movement* (New York: Crown Publishers).

Nordgrén, Megan D., Eric A. Goldstein, and Mark A. Izeman. 2002. *The Environmental Impacts of the World Trade Center Attacks: A Preliminary*

*Assessment* (National Resource Defense Fund) (February). <http://www.nrdc.org/cities/wtc/wtc.pdf>

Norris, Floyd. 2004. "Too Much Regulation? Corporate Bosses Sing the Sarbanes-Oxley Blues." *New York Times* (January 23).

Norwood, Stephen H. 2002. *Strikebreaking and Intimidation: Mercenaries and Masculinity in the Twentieth-Century America* (Chapel Hill: University of North Carolina Press).

Office of Inspector General. Environmental Protection Agency. 2003. *EPA's Response to the World Trade Center Collapse: Challenges, Successes, and Areas for Improvement.* Report No. 2003-P-00012 (August 21). <http://www.epa.gov/oig/ereading_room/WTC_report_20030821.pdf>

Office of Management and Budget. Office of Information and Regulatory Affairs. 2003. *Informing Regulatory Decisions: 2003 Report to Congress on Costs and Benefits of Federal Regulations and Unfunded Mandates on State, Local, and Tribal Entities* <http://www.whitehouse.gov/omb/inforeg/2003_cost-ben_final_rpt.pdf>

——. 2004a. *Informing Regulatory Decisions: 2004 Report to Congress on Costs and Benefits of Federal Regulations and Unfunded Mandates on State, Local, and Tribal Entities: Draft.* <http://www.whitehouse.gov/omb/inforeg/draft_2004_cbreport.pdf>

——. 2004b. *Fiscal Year 2004 Budget* (Washington, D.C.: U.S. Government Printing Office): Table 12.

O'Harrow, Robert, Jr. 2004. "Bahamas Firm Screens Personal Data to Assess Risk Operation Avoids U.S. Privacy Rules." *Washington Post* (October 16): p. A 1.

Ordonez, Jennifer. 2000. "An Efficiency Drive: Fast-Food Lanes, Equipped With Timers, Get Even Faster." *Wall Street Journal* (May 18).

Orr, Douglas V. 1998. "Strategic Bankruptcy and Private Pension Default." *Journal of Economic Issues*, Vol. 32, No. 3 (September): pp. 669–87.

Orren, Karen. 1991. *Belated Feudalism: Labor, The Law, and Liberal Development in the United States* (Cambridge: Cambridge University Press).

Patterson, Orlando. 1982. *Slavery and Social Death: A Comparative Study* (Cambridge: Harvard University Press).

Pension Benefit Guaranty Corporation. 2004. "PBGC Releases Fiscal Year 2003 Financial Results" (January 15). <http://www.pbgc.gov/news/press_releases/2004/pr04_20.htm>

Perelman, Michael. 1999. *The Natural Instability of Markets: Expectations, Increasing Returns and the Collapse of Markets* (New York: St Martin's Press).

——. 2000a. *The Invention of Capitalism: The Secret History of Primitive Accumulation* (Durham: Duke University Press).

——. 2000b. *Transcending the Economy: On the Potential of Passionate Labor and the Wastes of the Market* (New York: St Martin's Press).

——. 2002. *Steal this Idea: Intellectual Property Rights and the Corporate Confiscation of Creativity* (New York: Palgrave Macmillan).

Peyton, Carrie. 2002. "PG&E, Parent's Bonuses Unveiled $30 Million Paid to 11 Execs in a Year of Blackouts, Fiscal Woe." *Sacramento Bee* (March 14).

Pianin, Eric. 2003a. "In Pollution Debates, Bush's Man Seeks Harmony Amid the Storm." *Washington Post* (August 5): p. A 13.

——. 2003b. "Farm Dioxins Won't be Monitored: Fertilizer Posed Little Risk in Studies, EPA Says." *Washington Post* (October 18): p. A 10.

Pigou, Arthur Cecil. 1920. *The Economics of Welfare* (London: Macmillan).

Porter, Michael E. and Claas van der Linde. 1995. "Green and Competitive: Ending the Stalemate." *Harvard Business Review*, Vol. 73, No. 5 (September–October): pp. 120–34.

Portnoy, Frank. 2003. *Infectious Greed: How Deceit and Risk Corrupted the Financial Markets* (New York: Times Books).

Posner, Richard A. 1986. *Economic Analysis of Law* (Boston: Little, Brown, & Co.).

Poterba, James M., Steven F. Venti, and David A. Wise. 2001. "The Transition to Personal Accounts and Increasing Retirement Wealth: Macro and Micro Evidence." <http://econ-www.mit.edu/faculty/poterba/files/PVW-Trans1.pdf>

Powell, Colin L. 1992–93. "U.S. Forces: Challenges Ahead." *Foreign Affairs*, Vol. 71, No. 5 (Winter): pp. 32–46.

Prendergast, Canice. 2002. "The Tenuous Trade-Off Between Risk and Incentives." *Journal of Political Economy*, Vol. 110, No. 5 (October): pp. 1071–1102.

President of the United States. 2002. *Economic Report of the President* (Washington, D.C.: U.S. Government Printing Office).

——. 2003. *Economic Report of the President* (Washington, D.C.: U.S. Government Printing Office).

Presser, Harriet B. 1999. "Toward a 24-Hour Economy." *Science* (June 11): pp. 1778–9.

——. 2000. "Nonstandard Work Schedules and Marital Instability," *Journal of Marriage and the Family*, Vol. 62, No. 1 (February): pp. 93–110.

Productscan. 2003. "Build a Better Mousetrap." 2003 New Product Innovations of the Year." (December 27). <http://www.productscan.com/news/news_mouse03.pdf>

Public Citizen. 1998. The Facts About Product Liability Lawsuits. <http://www.citizen.org/congress/civjus/tort/articles.cfm?ID=568>

——. 2001. *Safeguards at Risk: John Graham and Corporate America's Back Door to the Bush White House.* <http://www.citizen.org/documents/grahamrpt.pdf>

Public Citizen. Critical Mass and Energy Project. 2001. "Price Anderson Act: The Billion Dollar Taxpayer Subsidy for Nuclear Power." <http://www.citizen.org/cmep/energy_enviro_nuclear/electricity/P_Anderson/articles.cfm?ID=4912>

Public Citizen. Government Accountability Project. 2002. Press Release: "USDA Tells Inspectors to Give Deference to Meat Companies, Stop Production Lines Only in Certain Circumstances" (October 31). <http://www.citizen.org/pressroom/release.cfm?ID=1260>

Raff, Daniel M. G. and Lawrence H. Summers. 1987. "Did Henry Ford Pay Efficiency Wages?" *Journal of Labor Economics*, Vol. 5, No. 4 (Part 2) (October): pp. S57–S86.

Rampton, Sheldon and John Stauber. 2000. *Trust Us, We're Experts: How Industry Manipulates Science and Gambles With Your Future* (New York: J. P. Tarcher).

Reiman, Jeffrey H. 1996. *And the Poor Get Prison: Economic Bias in American Criminal Justice* (Boston: Allyn and Bacon).

Richtel, Matt. 2004. "U.S. Online Gambling Policy Violates Law, W.T.O. Rules." *New York Times* (March 26).

Robertson, David Brian. 2000. *Capital, Labor, and State: The Battle for American Labor Markets from the Civil War to the New Deal* (Lanham, MD: Rowman & Littlefield Publishers).

Rodgers, Daniel T. 1998. *Atlantic Crossings: Social Politics in a Progressive Age* (Cambridge: Belknap Press).

Rogers, David. 2004. "Medicare Actuary Warned Bush Overhaul Would Exceed Budget." *Wall Street Journal* (March 25).

Ross, Nancy A., Michael C. Wolfson, Jean-Marie Berthelot, George A. Kaplan, and John W. Lynch. 2000. "Relation between Income Inequality and Mortality in Canada and in the United States: Cross Sectional Assessment Using Census Data and Vital Statistics." *British Medical Journal*, Vol. 320 (April 1): pp. 898–902. <http://www.bmj.com/cgi/content/full/320/7239/898>

Ruhm, Christopher J. 2000. "Are Recessions Good For Your Health?" *Quarterly Journal of Economics*, Vol. 115, No. 2 (May): pp. 617–50.

Rustad, Michael. 1998. "Unraveling Punitive Damages: Current Data and Further Inquiry." *Wisconsin Law Review*, No. 1 (Spring): pp. 15–69.

Sapolsky, Robert M. 1994. *Why Zebras Don't Get Ulcers: A Guide to Stress, Stress-Related Diseases, and Coping* (New York: W. H. Freeman and Company).

Scheiber, Harry N. 1988. "Original Intent, History, and Doctrine: The Constitution and Economic Liberty." *American Economic Review*, Vol. 78, No. 2 (May): pp. 140–4.

Scheve, Kenneth F. and Matthew J. Slaughter. 2001. *Globalization and the Perceptions of American Workers* (Washington, D.C.: Institute for International Economics).

Schlosser, Eric. 2001a. *Fast Food Nation: The Dark Side of the All-American Meal* (Boston: Houghton Mifflin).

——. 2001b. "The Chain Never Stops." *Mother Jones* (July/August).

Schneider, Andrew. 1999. "A Town Left To Die." *Seattle Post Intelligencer* (November 18). <http://seattlepi.nwsource.com/uncivilaction/lib18.shtml>

Schneider, Andrew and David McCumber. 2004. *An Air That Kills: How the Asbestos Poisoning of Libby, Montana Uncovered a National Scandal* (New York: G. P. Putnam's Sons).

Schneider, Andrew and Lise Olsen. 2000. "Cheney's Firm Backed Asbestos Legislation: Halliburton Financed Sponsors of Measure to Limit Liability in Lawsuits." *Seattle Post-Intelligencer* (August 4): p. A 1.

Schor, Juliet. 1998. *The Overspent American: Upscaling, Downshifting, and the New Consumer* (New York: Basic Books).

Schultz, Ellen E. 1999. "Companies Reap a Gain off Fat Pension Plans." *Wall Street Journal* (June 15).

——. 2003. "Firms Had a Hand in Pension Plight." *Wall Street Journal* (July 10): p. A 1.

——. 2004. "Companies Sue Union Retirees to Cut Promised Health Benefits: Firms Claim Right to Change Coverage." *Wall Street Journal* (November 10): p. A 1.

Schwartz, Peter and Doug Randall. 2003. *An Abrupt Climate Change Scenario and Its Implications for United States National Security* (October). <www.ems.org/climate/pentagon-climate-change.pdf>

Scitovsky, Tibor. 1976. *The Joyless Economy: An Inquiry into Human Satisfaction* (New York: Oxford University Press).

——. 2003. "Firms Had a Hand in Pension Plight." *Wall Street Journal* (July 10): p. A 1.

Seelye, Katharine Q. 2001. "Bush is Choosing Industry Insiders to Fill Several Environmental Positions." *New York Times* (May 12): p. A 10.

Seelye, Katharine Q. and John Tierney. 2003. "E.P.A. Drops Age-Based Cost Studies." *New York Times* (May 7).

Sharipo, M. and D. Ahlburg. 1983. "Suicide: The Ultimate Cost of Unemployment." *Journal of Post Keynesian Economics*, Vol. 5, No. 2 (Winter): pp. 276–80.

Shnayerson, Michael and Mark J. Plotkin. 2002. *The Killers Within* (Boston: Little Brown).

Shogren, Elizabeth. 2003. "Tighter Rules Likely for Welfare Families: A Senate Panel Approves a Bill That Would Force More Recipients to Find Jobs, Work Longer Hours." *Los Angeles Times* (September 11).

Shorrock, Tim. 2003. "Labor's Cold War: Freshly Unearthed Documents May Force the AFL-CIO to Face Up to Past Betrayals." *The Nation* (May 19).

Simon, Stephanie. 2001. "Biotech Soybeans Plant Seed of Risky Revolution." *Los Angeles Times* (July 1).

Skrzycki, Cindy. 2002. "The Wrong Price on a Life Lost?" *Washington Post* (December 10): p. E 1.

Slichter, Sumner H. 1919. *The Turnover of Factory Labor* (New York: D. Appleton).

Sloan, Alfred P. 1963. *My Years With General Motors, Inc.* (Garden City: Anchor Books).

Smith, Adam. 1759. *The Theory of Moral Sentiments*, D. D. Raphael and A. L. Macfie, eds. (Oxford: Clarendon Press, 1976).

——. 1776. *An Inquiry into the Nature and Causes of the Wealth of Nations*, 2 vols. R. H. Campbell and A. S. Skinner, eds. (New York: Oxford University Press, 1976).

——. 1978. *Lectures on Jurisprudence*, R. L. Meek, D. D. Raphael, and P. G. Stein, eds. (Oxford: Clarendon University Press).

Smith, G. C., K. E. Belk, J. A. Scanga, J. N. Sofos and J. D Tatum. [Colorado State University] 2000. "Traceback, Traceability and Source Verification in the U.S. Beef Industry." Presented at the XXI World Buiatrics Congress, on December 5, 2000 in Punta del Este, Uruguay.

Smith, Richard Alan. 1961. "The Incredible Electrical Conspiracy." *Fortune* (April): p. 178.

Sniffen, Michael J. 2004. "Privacy Fears Haven't Killed Data-Mining: Other Agencies Pursue Anti-Terrorism Project Halted at Pentagon." *Seattle Times* (February 23).

Soh, Byung Hee. 1986. Political Business Cycles in Industrialized Democratic Countries." *Kyklos*, Vol. 39, No. 1, pp. 31–46.

Sparshott, Jeffrey. 2003. "Food Importers Seek Easing of Rules: Bioterror Protection Will Be Costly." *Washington Times* (April 21).

Stefancic, Jean and Richard Delgado. 1996. *No Mercy: How Conservative Think Tanks and Foundations Changed America's Social Agenda* (Philadelphia: Temple University Press).

Stipp, David. 2004. "The Pentagon's Weather Nightmare." *Fortune*, Vol. 149, No. 3 (February 9).

Strange, Susan. 1998. *Mad Money: When Markets Outgrow Governments* (Ann Arbor: University of Michigan Press).

Strope, Leigh. 2004. "Government Tells Employers How to Avoid Paying OT." *Associated Press* (January 6).

Stutzer, Alois. 2004. "The Role of Income Aspirations in Individual Happiness." *Journal of Economic Behavior and Organization*, Vol. 54, No. 1 (May): pp. 89–109.

Sward, Keith. 1972. *The Legend of Henry Ford* (New York: Atheneum).

Taylor, Frederick Winslow. 1911. *The Principles of Scientific Management* (New York: W. W. Norton & Co., 1967).

Tejada, Carlos. 2002. "Frequenting Facilities: How Often Can Workers Take Nature Calls?" *Wall Street Journal* (August 28): p. B 3.

Thatcher, Margaret. 1987. *Woman's Own* (London) (October 31).

Thomas, Keith. 1964. "Work and Leisure." *Past and Present, No. 29* (December): pp. 50–66.

Thompson, E. P. 1963. *The Making of the English Working Class* (New York: Vintage).

Tillinghast-Towers Perrin. 1995. *Tort Cost Trends: An International Perspective* (New York).

Tilly, Charles. 1985. "War Making and State Making as Organized Crime." in Peter Evans, Dietrich Rueschemeyer, and Theda Skocpol, eds. *Bringing the State Back* (Cambridge: Cambridge University Press): pp. 169–91.

Tobias, Andrew. 1976. *Fire and Ice: The Story of Charlse Revson—The Man Who Built the Revlon Empire* (New York: William Morrow).

Tomsho, Robert. 1995. "Growing Pains." *Wall Street Journal* (April 11): p. A1.

Townsend, Joseph. 1786. *A Dissertation on the Poor Laws by a Well Wisher to Mankind*. Reprinted in John R. McCulloch, ed. *A Select Collection of Scarce and Valuable Economic Tracts* (New York: Augustus M. Kelley, 1966): pp. 395–450.

Travis, Jeremy. 2002. "Invisible Punishment: An Instrument of Social Exclusion." in Marc Mauer and Meda Chesney-Lind, eds. *Invisible Punishment: The Collateral Consequences of Mass Imprisonment* (New York: New Press): pp. 15–36.

Tucker, P., S. Folkard, and I. Macdonald. 2003. "Rest Breaks and Accident Risk." *The Lancet*, Vol. 361, No. 9358 (April 12): p. 680.

Tyler, Patrick E. 1992. "Lone Superpower Plan: Ammunition for Critics." *New York Times* (March 10).

Tyrrell, Emmett, Jr. 1995. "The Continuing Crisis." *American Spectator* (April).

Union of Concerned Scientists. 2004. *Scientific Integrity in Policymaking: An Investigation into the Bush Administration's Misuse of Science* (February). <http://www.ucsusa.org/global_environment/rsi/report.html>

United States Congress. Joint Economic Committee. 1996. *Improving the American Legal System: The Economic Benefits of Tort Reform* (Washington, D.C.: U.S. Government Printing Office).

United States Department of Justice. 2002. *Sourcebook of Criminal Justice Statistics Online.* <http://www.albany.edu/sourcebook/2002/pdf/t3133. pdf>

United States Food and Drug Administration. Center for Food Safety and Applied Nutrition. 1995. FDA's Policy for Foods Developed by Biotechnology. <http://www.cfsan.fda.gov/~lrd/biopolcy.html>

United States General Accounting Office. 2003. *Energy Task Force Process Used to Develop the National Energy Policy.* GAO-03-894 (August). <http://www. gao.gov/new.items/d03894.pdf>

Veblen, Thorstein. 1899. *The Theory of the Leisure Class: An Economic Study of Institutions* (New York: Mentor Books, 1953).

Viscusi, W. Kip. 2004. "The Blockbuster Punitive Damages Award." John M. Olin Center for Law, Economics, and Business, Discussion Paper No. 473.

Viscusi, W. Kip. and Richard J. Zeckhauser. 2003. "Sacrificing Civil Liberties to Reduce Terrorism Risks." *Journal of Risk and Uncertainty*, Vol. 26, Nos. 2–3 (March–May): pp. 99–120.

Volcker, Paul A. 1982. "Testimony before the Statement Joint Economic Committee, 26 January 1982." *Federal Reserve Bulletin*, Vol. 68, No. 2 (February): pp. 88–90.

Wald, Matthew L. 2003a. "N.R.C. Excludes Terrorism as Licensing Consideration." *New York Times* (January 7): p. A 11.

——. 2003b. "Dr. Norman C. Rasmussen, 75, Expert on Nuclear Power Risk, Dies." *New York Times* (July 28).

Warhol, Andy. 1975. *The Philosophy of Andy Warhol: from A to B and Back Again* (New York: Harcourt Brace Jovanovich).

Weidlich, Thom. 2002. "Who Says Unions Must Dislike the Chief?" *New York Times* (December 15).

Welch, David. 2003. "How Nissan Laps Detroit." *Business Week* (December 22): pp. 58–60.

White, Michelle J. 2004. "Asbestos and the Future of Mass Torts." *Journal of Economic Perspectives*, Vol. 18, No. 2 (Spring): pp. 183–204.

Whitman, Christine Todd. 2000. "Effective Policy Making: The Role of Good Science." Symposium on Nutrient Over-Enrichment of Coastal Waters (Washington, D.C., October 13). <http://gos.sbc.edu/w/whitman2.html>

Wilensky, H. 1961. "The Uneven Distribution of Leisure: The Impact of Economic Growth on 'Free Time'." *Social Problems*, Vol. 9, pp. 35–56.

Wilkinson, Mike J., Luisa J. Elliott, Joël Allainguillaume, Michael W. Shaw, Carol Norris, Ruth Welters, Matthew Alexander, Jeremy Sweet, and David C. Mason. 2003. "Hybridization Between Brassica napus and B. rapa on a National Scale in the United Kingdom." *Science*, Vol. 302, No. 5643 (October 10).

Wilkinson, Richard G. 1997. *Unhealthy Societies: The Afflictions of Inequality* (London: Routledge).

Willmore, Ian. 2002. "Slick Business?" *Observer Online* (November 24). <http:// observer.guardian.co.uk/comment/story/0,6903,846684,00.htm>

Wilson, Duff. 2001. *Fateful Harvest: The True Story of a Small Town* (New York: HarperCollins).

Woodward, Bob. 1994. *The Agenda: Inside the Clinton White House* (New York: Simon & Schuster).

——. 2000. *Maestro: Greenspan's Fed and the American Boom* (New York: Simon & Schuster).

Wriston, Walter B. 1982. "Banking Against Disaster." *New York Times* (September 14).

——. 1986. *Risk and Other Four-Letter Words* (New York: Harper & Row).

——. 1992. *The Twilight of Sovereignty: How the Information Revolution Is Transforming Our World* (New York: Scribner).

Young, Shawn. 2002. "Getting Laid Off Hurts Worse When Employer Is Bankrupt." *Wall Street Journal* (September 30): p. A 1.

Zachary, G. Pascal. 1995. "Study Predicts Rising Global Joblessness." *Wall Street Journal* (February 22): p. A2.

——. 1996. "Manpower to Offer Physicists as Temps." *Wall Street Journal* (November 27): pp. A 2 and A 14.

Zachary, G. Pascal and Bob Ortega. 1993. "Down the Up Escalator: Why Some Workers are Falling Behind." *Wall Street Journal* (March 10): p. A 1.

Zeckhauser, Richard and Albert Nichols. 1978. "The Occupational Safety and Health Administration: An Overview." in *Study on Federal Regulation*, Appendix to vol. 6: *Framework for Regulation*, U.S. Senate Committee on Governmental Affairs, 95th Cong., 2d Sess. (Washington, D.C.: U.S. Government Printing Office): pp. 163–248.

Zeckhauser, Richard and W. Kip Viscusi. 1990. "Risk Within Reason." *Science*, Vol. 248, No. 4955 (May 4): pp. 559–64.

Zweig, Phillip L. 1995. *Wriston: Walter Wriston, Citibank, and the Rise and Fall of American Financial Supremacy* (New York: Crown Publishers).

# Index